AMERICA'S
BANQUET OF CULTURES

Harnessing Ethnicity, Race, and Immigration
in the Twenty-First Century

RONALD FERNANDEZ

Westport, Connecticut
London

E
184
,A1
F474
2000

Library of Congress Cataloging-in-Publication Data

Fernandez, Ronald.
    America's banquet of cultures : harnessing ethnicity, race, and immigration in the twenty-first century / Ronald Fernandez.
      p. cm.
    Includes bibliographical references and index.
    ISBN 0–275–95871–X (alk. paper)
    1. United States—Ethnic relations. 2. United States—Race relations. 3. United States—Emigration and immigration. 4. Minorities—United States—Social conditions. 5. Immigrants—United States—Social conditions. 6. United States—Ethnic relations—Forecasting. 7. United States—Race relations—Forecasting. 8. United States—Emigration and immigration—Forecasting. I. Title.
E184.A1F474   2000
305.8'00973—dc21   99–088491

British Library Cataloguing in Publication Data is available.

Copyright © 2000 by Ronald Fernandez

Library of Congress Catalog Card Number: 99–088491
ISBN: 0–275–95871–X

First published in 2000

Praeger Publishers, 88 Post Road West, Westport, CT 06881
An imprint of Greenwood Publishing Group, Inc.
www.praeger.com

Printed in the United States of America

The paper used in this book complies with the Permanent Paper Standard issued by the National Information Standards Organization (Z39.48–1984).

10 9 8 7 6 5 4 3 2 1

To Chuck Harrison,

We loved you, we miss you.

"What concerns is the fact that the strands are here.
We must have a policy and an ideal for an actual situation.
Our question is, What Shall We Do with Our America?"

—Randolph Bourne, *Trans-National America*, 1916

Contents

Preface: Four All-Americans

DIVERSITY INCARNATE[1]

His great grandmother was a proud member of a tribe that "never enslaved" the Africans who escaped plantation life. Family historians say that Edward's grandmother, half-African, half-Seminole, also had a very special skill: She spoke Chinese, an ability acquired after twenty years of work in a Florida laundry.

When the federal government forcibly exiled the Seminoles to Oklahoma, some refused to go. Using everything from canoes to rafts, these Seminoles paddled into the Caribbean or stowed away on trading ships bound for the neighboring islands. Thus, Edward's great grandfather was Bahamian and a subject of the king of England; others relatives were Cuban and subjects of the king of Spain. Somehow they all settled in Florida, where some of Edward's kin spoke Spanish, some did not, and all called themselves colored on a good day and "niggers" when the white crackers snapped their whiplike tongues.

Color always trumped ethnicity when Edward was a child. Like the eraser on a giant pencil, the one-drop (of African blood) rule simultaneously expunged Edward's Seminole, Bahamian, and Cuban roots. They corralled our people into neighborhoods marked "colored," and the only time Edward saw a white person was in the background threats of his mom. Just before she spanked him for an offense, the angry, tired woman would loudly proclaim, "I'll kill you before I'll let them kill you." "Them" meant white people, the "almost nonexistent" force that nevertheless dominated every moment of the boy's segregated existence. "You hope someone made a mistake"; you believe or convince yourself that if you "touch all the bases," you can play the game.

It's not you as an individual; it's a system designed by someone who hated kids.

As a ten year old, Edward wanted a hamburger, the kind they served at the Royal Castle Restaurant. So, he skipped lunch for two days, put the eighty cents in his pocket, and "pumped, then coasted" on his bike until he arrived "at the Castle." Elvis crooned, "Don't be cruel," as the eager boy bopped his way to the counter; Edward waited his turn, ordered his burgers, and sat down.

"They ate my ass alive." With Elvis's lyrics still in his ear, Edward heard the cooks scream, "What the hell you doing, nigger; you know coloreds don't sit in this place." Edward didn't know. This was white turf, never a part of his stomping grounds. He got on his bike, pumped—no coasting—all the way home, and still has no answer to his childhood question. "Why didn't the other customers help?" He could understand the need for poorly paid cooks to beat up on a kid, but why didn't the other customers help? "They just sat there."

In retaliation Edward and his brother would go to other Castles, order a pile of burgers, sit down, listen to the abuse, and know, as they left with a smile, that the burgers would go to waste. It was a "moral victory."

The Marines helped Edward. Once they figured out that "I could read" (i.e., that Edward had a brain), he received the discipline he wanted, the opportunities he needed, and the promise of the money he never had. Edward meant to make use of the GI Bill if he could somehow survive not only Vietnam but also a "Cinderella liberty" (back by midnight) in the Philippines.

R&R (rest and relaxation) seemed an odd way to define the shipboard experience of Marines crowded onto ships. Yet Edward and his friends happily obeyed orders when, with the huge troop boats moored in the ocean, small crafts took the Marines to shore. They walked over a bridge spanning the waste-filled "Shit River," down an avenue housing the bars used by the white soldiers, and up to a "T" where, on either side, black soldiers tried to find solace from the war and a form of "self-imposed" segregation.

Just before they turned into pumpkins, the black Marines walked down the avenue and over the bridge leading to the beach. Here, many soldiers threw coins into the river as brown-skinned Filipino children eagerly dived from the bridge to compete for the soldiers' spare change. But, when some white soldiers threw bricks instead of coins, the black soldiers saw red. Edward explained that the Philippines was the best place for black Marines on liberty; "the Filipinos treated us like Filipinos. We were part of their family."

Watching the whites unload a salvo of bricks, many black soldiers instantly reexperienced their unique version of childhood humiliation(s). But this time, instead of children in shock, battle-scarred men watched helpless Filipinos scurry to avoid the barrage of bricks. The result was a "race riot" on the beach that led to more war in Vietnam. While Edward stayed on the sidelines, he watched as a fellow Marine would occasionally indicate, "This (white) guy is ok. Don't fuck with him." Yet other than that, the black-on-white fighting continued until the Cinderella boys returned to a conflict with no light at the end of the tunnel—not for Lyndon Johnson, and not for the whites and blacks who fought at work and at play in Florida, Vietnam, and the Philippines.

Edward got a degree. So many people found he could read that he graduated with a 3.85 average and a religious commitment that now defines his life. Edward Charles Harrison IV became Rasheed Hamza, a devout member of the Muslim faith. As a follower of Allah, Rasheed found both private peace and public pride. However mysteriously, God ruled the universe, and Rasheed Hamza took a name that he wanted, not the counterfeit title (Edward the Fourth) inherited at birth.

When asked if he ever felt attracted to the "Black Muslims," Rasheed says, "No." He doesn't relate to the prejudice against anybody, but he nevertheless has the greatest respect for "their success with the black man." They turned around a lot of drug addicts, and you have to give them credit where credit is due.

Rasheed went all the way. He got a Ph.D. in education, and he did it for himself, for his family, and for his people. He sees no bigger opportunity than that offered by any university in the country. "I mean how can you do better than this?" Kids walk in, Rasheed gets the chance to help them enter the mainstream, and he never wastes time complaining about the environment.

At 52, Rasheed agrees with many of his African-American colleagues; the university is a "plantation," and his everyday life is indeed dominated by the rules of "wwb," (working while black). Thus, at student registration, he now accepts that many youngsters will ask a white clerk for information before they ask the tall, well-dressed black man who helps supervise the mostly white workforce. Why? "Maybe they think I'm an affirmative action hire and don't know anything? Maybe they just can't ask a black guy for help? Who knows?"

Rasheed doesn't. But, in the middle of middle age, he refuses to waste any time bitching about "plantation life." "I've heard all that for years. Let the others talk, but I'm going to spend what time I have left helping these kids. All of them."

Watching Rasheed with the students is a joy. The man loves his work. But he is bothered by life on the "plantation," so much so that he rarely drops his guard and never stops thinking. It would be "irresponsible" to do that.

If someone complains about his work, is it because Rasheed screwed up or because he's black? Did someone disregard one of his ideas because his

suggestions lacked merit, because the colleague was preoccupied with personal problems, or because the white colleague could never take even great
advice from a black man?

Most bothersome of all are the well-meaning whites who want to help but
destroy their own good work with a sure sense of superiority. When push
comes to shove, "They know everything; I'm just the black guy at the table."

As in Edward's childhood, we are all still fenced in by walls of suspicion,
hate, and misunderstanding; whites built the barriers, but today they are just
as penned in as blacks. Everybody is uptight and, as a so-called privileged
class of blacks complains about whites, whites moan, "What more do these
people want? There's no satisfying them. Jesus, look at what we have done
already."

A WHOOP, WHOOP INDIAN

Shashi Singh is a Hindu, an Indian, a woman, and a possible American.
Born in 1979 in the western state of Gujarat, Shashi, her brother, and her
parents came to the United States in 1992. Well off, but not well educated,
her parents linked the family to a human chain that started with her grandmother's brother. As Shashi tells it, relatives would return to Gujarat, spout-
ing stories of great wealth and untold opportunities in the United States.
"It's like a perfect place," especially if you want a fine education for your
only son.

With a look of concern bordering on shame, Shashi expresses guilt about
the thinly veiled criticism of her parents and her Indian roots. "Would I
have said such a thing six years ago? My accepted fate then included an
arranged marriage." Today Shashi thinks that women are men's equals, and
she resents the paternalism of the Indian culture she simultaneously loves.
In fact, while it's still hard to swallow, she now believes that the family
moved so her brother would have a better future. She can also go to school
but only if, like a traditional Indian woman, she stays within the limits set
by thousand-year-old norms. Thus, when she offered her dad sound financial
advice based on a college course, he whisked her off with a look of surprise
and, presumably, a few second thoughts of his own. "Would a daughter have
said such a thing in India?"

Shashi's family arrived in the United States with money, business experience, and a settled group of relatives who, rotating capital among themselves, helped the Singhs finance the purchase of two local businesses.
Within months the family settled in an upscale Connecticut suburb and
eventually adopted a series of American nicknames. One uncle is John, her
father is Frank, and her own mistaken identity is "S.S." Shashi, a young
woman who flawlessly speaks three languages, expresses both exasperation
and anger when she explains her reaction to the reactions of Americans.

"They don't even try to pronounce our names." After a while, "you just give up. They are wrapped up in a little ball and you can't penetrate it."

Shashi wants to know what happened to the "melting pot." If that's the American ideal, one element mixes with the other and the new creation is something different and better than its predecessor. But, in Shashi's experience, the American dish is already prepared; nobody wants additional ingredients. Virtually none of her everyday encounters allows any room for the spices of one of the most developed and appetizing cultures on earth, that of the Indian subcontinent.

In high school Shashi brought friends to her home, anxious to show them the Hindi pantheon: Brahma (the Creator), Shiva (the Destroyer), Vishnu (the preserver), and most intriguing of all, Ganesh, the elephantine god who sits on a rat. Her "friends," instead of wanting to learn, only turned their noses to the sky. "Why do you have so many gods?" When Shashi tried to explain, she only got one reaction: "How strange!" Shashi angrily asks this question: "I learned from your culture, why can't you learn from mine?"

Shashi discovered that women could avoid endless subjugation. She appreciates her new freedom but shies away from other lessons also learned in high school. Some kids were white, others black, and, even though she fit into neither category, Shashi Singh was nevertheless a minority, one of roughly ten in a school containing a thousand students. Shashi explains that in India skin color is also a variable in assessing the worth of other people. But, it's always far less important than religion, caste, or money. "Money outweighs everything."

But not in Connecticut. Shashi, a woman of privilege, identified with the African Americans. In one instance she got caught in the middle of a school controversy. While she was standing with an another student in the hallway, he told her to "look at that nigger" when one of Shashi's African-American friends appeared. Shashi instantly saw red, which moved the young man to say, "You are no better than she."

Complaints to school administrators produced a meeting with roughly fifty students. Shashi and the other "minority" youngsters explained their feelings and experiences. One teacher said, "Maybe you all took it in the wrong way," while the assistant principal added insult to injury when, seemingly bored, he made this remark as he left the room: "You guys just talk. You don't do anything."

The minority kids decided he was right. They charged into the hallway, screaming and kicking lockers with all their might. Teachers appeared from the classrooms and discovered what happened; the next day the assistant principal, near tears, apologized to the student body. Shashi's reaction: "I just wanted to get out of there. I couldn't stand it anymore."

Shashi's "best" experience occurred when her college orientation program repeated a lesson already learned in high school. Without her saying a word, students came up to Shashi and, moving one hand toward and away from their lips, they asked if she was "a whoop, whoop type of Indian."

When, during our interviews, Shashi related this story, we both burst into laughter. It seemed so utterly inconceivable, so incredibly far-fetched. But, "you won't believe how many students have come up to me, moving their hands over their lips in an imitation 'Indian' war chant."

Like the weather, Shashi now accepts the ignorance and ethnocentrism of too many Americans. But, as a 1.5 Indian, as a woman born there but partially raised here, she can never escape the dilemma of being neither this nor that, neither Indian nor American.

Shashi met a young man and, as if in the American Dream, they fell in love. He is an Indian born in the United States, who is also a Jain. Trouble is, according to India's Hindi culture, Jains are "so cheap and selfish they even keep close accounts on family members." Shashi believes none of this, but her parents refuse to allow the young man into their home. As in India or the United States, religion is more important than his other attributes, as her mother emphasizes, "he will never enter this house."

That's bad enough. But, for all his wonderful traits, Shekhar and his family are too Americanized! Watching them from a distance, Shashi can't understand how or why they lost their values. Thus, when Shashi's sister married an African American, Shashi silently exclaimed, "How could you do that?" How could you marry someone who was not an Indian, someone who was not faithful to the family and other values that make us such a distinctive people?

Speaking in Gujarti, Shashi says she is caught—probably forever—between a rock and hard place. She loves the young man, but he is far too Americanized. And her parents? "You have to understand how Indian families are bound." For example, two brothers and their wives could live together, experience a significant degree of everyday conflict, and never change their living arrangements. If one brother tells the other to leave, he will be blamed for the rupture, and, in the ensuing war of whispered words, he will know that the rest of the family believes the gossip being spread by his "oh so innocent brother."

Indian families are bound. And so is Shashi, to her beloved parents, to India, and, for all its unexpected faults, to the United States. "I could never return now. I don't know how I would fit in. I'm so different."

SUM OF THE PARTS

Cindy Clough is a delightful person. Warm, generous, empathetic, witty, and as bright as they come. She has everything, except an ethnic identity. Cindy is nothing. Or, more accurately, she is so many things that even though the European parts add up to a whole, the whole seems empty, devoid of a total that confers ethnic authenticity in her eyes.

Asked about being an American, Cindy hesitates. Of course she is an American. "But American is what you are second." First is an ethnic heritage, and Cindy's is divided up into so many parts that she needs a calculator to compute the percentages. She is one-eighth English, one-eighth Welsh, one-fourth Italian, and one-half Irish. She also believes there is a Scottish component to her background but, since no one will confirm this fact, she leaves it out of her complicated calculations.

"Now don't get me wrong. I don't sit up nights thinking about this." But it is nevertheless a personal void that Cindy can never fill.

She grew up in Connecticut. Like so many of her third- and fourth-generation contemporaries, she first encountered her ethnic heritage in elementary school. A lesson on America as a Nation of Immigrants produced the need for a family tree. When Cindy drew hers, frustration set in. "I was disappointed I was so many things. I wanted to be just one."

At home her Italian-speaking father and her 100 percent Irish mother never emphasized their ethnic origins. Her mom did prepare corned beef and cabbage on St. Patrick's Day—"we still do that now"—but Cindy needs to search her memory for specific examples of "ethnic pride." Interestingly, the Irish side of the family supports an active ancestor association. Cindy even has a book published by the group, but it's more a coffee-table decoration than a thumbed and worn part of Cindy's life.

She does remember that her Irish grandparents hung a shillelagh on their wall. However, she only recently learned what a shillelagh is, and she is not at all certain that her Italian father's explanation bears any relationship to the truth. For example, he calls the English/Welsh side of his heritage a group of "Connecticut Swamp Yankees," without explaining the "swamp" side of the label. Cindy heard that Swamp Yankees have a reputation for cheapness but thinks it is just as likely that "they all lived in a swampy part of Connecticut."

Cindy is also white, yet that label means about as much as the Welsh part of her ancestry. She is remarkably free of the prejudices America contains, to the point that she recently married a member of one of Connecticut's most controversial ethnic groups.

Juan Sierra is a Puerto Rican. He and Cindy met in city hall—Juan manages an office—and after performing his professional duties, Juan asked if he could give Cindy a call. She said, "Sure," but he had to find her number on his own. Juan got the number and a wife as well.

At first Cindy lied to her parents. As she clearly grasped the deep prejudices against Puerto Ricans, when explaining that she had met someone special, she first said he was "Spanish." Her father wanted to know what kind of Spanish. Cindy said, "Puerto Rican," and without another word, her father got up from the table and walked away.

Cindy thinks her father would now deny he ever did that. "Juan is the son he never had," and the two men today share a lasting affection for one another. It took time for Cindy's dad to disregard his prejudices, and even more time for members of Juan's family to disregard theirs.

Cindy was a "white woman" trying to enter Puerto Rican social space. As if penalized for an offense she never committed, a person who only wanted a single ethnicity was being judged by the color of her skin. Even years later, Cindy is still amazed—not by the color prejudice, but by any prejudice at all. "You would think people exposed to as much ugliness as Puerto Ricans would never be prejudiced. But . . ."

While some members of the family even went so far as to suggest that Juan "settle down and marry a nice Spanish girl," others slowly accepted Cindy. She understands their initial apprehensions but not their expressed concern about "darker" members of the family. Apparently one light-skinned relative married a dark-skinned Puerto Rican, and family gossip columnists said that "unfortunately" for the children, they came out dark.

To Cindy this was both awful and amazing. "Juan's relatives think that they (the darker-skinned kids) are a lower class, that they are bad."

Cindy never saw the prejudices coming. She now accepts that "racism" is a part of Puerto Rican culture but, as compensation, she "soaks up" other sides of Juan's ethnicity with as much delight as the disappointment she experienced in the third grade.

Cindy tells a story about New Year's Eve and Juan's genuine concern for her mom and dad's apparent lack of love. In the United States and in the Caribbean, Puerto Rican culture is so centered in the family that New Year's without close relatives is like Puerto Rico without the sun. So, when (years ago) Cindy's parents went to a New Year's Eve party, leaving her without family, Juan interpreted an American custom through Puerto Rican eyes. Cindy explained her family's norm, Juan empathized, and Cindy now often enjoys New Year's Eve in the convivial atmosphere of a Puerto Rican extended family.

Cindy and Juan also attend a Spanish-language Catholic church, and she even cheers Juan on when he plays softball in the "Salsa League." As if a stepdaughter, she now has at least part of an ethnic center, but as she well knows, it is hers by marriage, not by birth. She still has nothing to put before "American" and wonders what she and Juan will do if they ever have children.

Juan has often been the object of hateful remarks. Cindy says, "I appreciate it more now. Prejudice hits home in a different way." Her children would carry the burden of being 50 percent Puerto Rican, plus one-sixteenth English, one-eighth Italian. . . . It's too complicated to imagine, especially for a person who is both baffled and disappointed that people exposed to prejudice could still act that way toward a "white woman" from Connecticut and "darker" members of their own family.

ETHNIC DESPITE HIMSELF

His maternal grandfather was forty-four, his maternal grandmother seventeen. Family legend says, "She was a quite a beauty," but Joseph Gonzalez only remembers painful pinches on the cheek—"¡que guapo!" (How handsome)—from a huge woman who refused to explain why his mother had two fathers.

Ernestina (the alleged beauty) fled Spain with Manuel in 1900. They left his first wife and four children in Europe, yet somehow managed to escape with enough money to buy a boarding house in Lorain, Ohio. Never married, Ernestina and Jose soon produced three children (Joseph's mother among them) in six years. Meanwhile, everybody in the boarding house spoke wonderful Spanish, especially the young man who fell in love with the now twenty-three-year-old Ernestina.

She fled again, never married again, produced another three children with Jorge (the boarder turned lover), and left Joseph's mother Isabel with her natural father. For the fifty years that followed, mother and daughter managed a dangerously uneasy truce because, like the itching from a bad case of poison ivy, Isabel tortured herself about the past that might have been. Occasionally Joseph pressed his mother about the prominently displayed photograph of the well-dressed, mustached man. Isabel never offered any satisfactory explanation. She had two fathers; the rest was history.

Also Spanish, Joseph's father Pepe came to the United States in 1916. He worked in the glass factories of West Virginia—there's still a small Spanish community in Clarksburg—but moved near the Mexican community in Ohio when his own father returned to Spain. Like many immigrants, Joseph's grandfather missed the "old country"; his son, however, remained in the New World, a lonely adolescent who, like Joseph's mother Isabel, never recovered from the unexpected departure of a parent.

Isabel and Pepe set up house in Manhattan. She had brains and ambition; he was illiterate in two languages. She therefore dominated a house where everyone used Spanish as the everyday means of communication. Unfortunately, when Joseph's brother Roberto entered school none of his teachers understood a word of Spanish. For two years Roberto thought of school as an exercise in futility; he eventually finished even high school but always felt unsure of his intelligence and his possibilities.

Joseph was a "mistake" who appeared sixteen years after his brother. Isabel actually considered an abortion—it was 1946—but decided instead to rewrite history with her new son. The family moved to a Queens neighborhood full of Italians and Irish. At home both parents continued to speak Spanish, but not to Joseph. He grew up watching *The Lone Ranger*, *I Love Lucy*, and Willie Mays basket-catching fly balls for the New York Giants.

Joseph's English was perfect, his problems in the classroom nonexistent.

The schoolyard, however, was another matter altogether. With the best of intentions, Isabel wanted to raise an all-American boy, but the move to Queens made Joseph's ethnic roots as conspicuous as Jackie Robinson in a Dodger uniform. *Nobody* in Joseph's Queens neighborhood had a name like Gonzalez, and nobody lived in an apartment with a large red satin picture of a bullfighter. Kids ridiculed Joseph's parents, they nicknamed him "Chico" (the Spanish word for boy), and soon after the influx of Puerto Ricans to New York, Joseph also turned into a "spic."

Joseph tried to hide. Ashamed of his obvious roots, he distanced himself from his parents and from the Puerto Ricans who, speaking Spanish, did not speak to Joseph. Good grades proved to be both an escape and a pathway to college. While his name still stuck out, he moved to Westchester with his older brother and tried to fade into a community that rarely accentuated any ethnic roots.

Joseph managed to hide for almost fifteen years. But, once the federal government started keeping tabs on certain groups in the mid 1970s, Washington arbitrarily made Joseph's ethnicity as positive an attribute as his childhood "friends" made it a negative. At the office Joseph became a valued statistic; the name Gonzalez quickly translated into a Hispanic on the payroll. However, if Joseph satisfied his bosses' need for numbers, he felt cheapened as a person. Joseph Gonzalez was a fraud who capitalized on his name while real Hispanics washed dishes in Manhattan or picked grapes in California.

One day in the early 1980s Joseph read an interoffice memo informing him of yet another two new identities: Joseph Gonzalez was now, officially, a "minority employee" and, because of his Spanish ancestry, also a "Hispanic other." As such, he was appointed to a corporate committee charged with recruiting more people just like him. On the job, Joseph did as he was asked. At home he ridiculed himself, joking to his Norwegian wife that he was an "HHH," a Happy Hispanic Headhunter.

Over time, the recruiting work made this very successful executive reassess his ethnic origins. Joseph finally made peace with his learned sense of ethnic embarrassment and even made sincere efforts to learn Spanish. Trouble was, he spoke with such a pronounced New York accent that real Hispanics asked about his ancestry. When he related his Spanish roots, Joseph suddenly discovered that, especially with some Chicanos, he once again had cause for embarrassment. They blamed Spain for centuries of barbarity in Mexico and placed Joseph's relatives in the same category as other "Eurocentric racists."

In general Joseph's sincerity compensated for his heritage; most Hispanics accepted that he genuinely wanted to help, yet Joseph himself gradually grasped that, despite his Washington-induced desire, Joseph Gonzalez could never be the real thing—not Cuban or Puerto Rican, Mexican or El Salvadoran, Nicaraguan or Guatemalan.

Joseph finally settled on "Latino." Today he proudly identifies with the struggles of people with whom he has almost nothing in common, except liberal politics and a similar last name. As Joseph also realizes that tomorrow may bring yet more new identities, he is fully prepared to ride the mental roller coaster for the foreseeable future. It has now become exciting to have others redefine him, one decade after another.

But, Joseph is also an American. He relishes the nation's rhythms, and he carries in his heart a profound respect for the U.S. Constitution and the rights it continually guarantees. For all its faults, Joseph loves what he now knows to be his true country of origin. Unfortunately, as Joseph also sees firsthand the problems encountered by authentic Latinos, he wants someone to answer the biggest question of all: What's an American? "How," he asks, "can we possibly achieve a sense of national unity when, if my life is at all typical, we continue to define ourselves only on the basis of what divides us."

WHAT SHALL WE DO WITH OUR AMERICA?[2]

This book has one overriding goal: to provide the outlines of a new answer to an old question, "What Shall We Do with Our America?"

Shashi Singh, for example, represents one of more than twenty-three million immigrants who came to the United States since 1965. Moreover, her arrival in 1992 came during a decade of unprecedented migration to the United States. The Immigration and Naturalization Service estimates that the total number of immigrants during the decade 1990–2000 will be 10 million people. This exceeds the previous high of 8.8 million immigrants between 1901 and 1910.[3]

As Randolph Bourne noted, "What concerns is the fact that the strands are here. We must have a policy and an ideal for an actual situation."[4] That situation also includes, as with Rasheed Hamsa, a society in which race continually subsumes ethnic, class, and other identities. Meanwhile, millions of Americans like Cindy Clough lack any meaningful ethnic attachments as they are simultaneously at odds with the conventional wisdom about race and the significance of color. Finally, a man like Joseph Gonzalez struggles with the issues raised by our contemporary efforts to achiever greater degrees of social justice. He wants to be an American but both intimates and acquaintances often refuse to see him as anything other than a Hispanic, who is simultaneously a minority.

What Shall We Do with Our America? Before any attempt at an answer, Part One furnishes an overview of how and why documented and undocumented immigrants came to the United States. Based on an analysis of presidential library and other federal government documents, Part One tries to assign primary responsibility for the present ethnic composition of the

United States of America. My argument is that immigrants should not be blamed for an America that now includes a million newcomers a year.

Part Two offers an analysis of the racial, ethnic, and class factors that so profoundly divide us. My aim is to make room for change, to suggest a possible way out of the black-and-white thinking that produces pain and confusion for so many new and old Americans.

Part Three begins by placing our dilemmas in a global perspective. What can we learn from the experiences of England, Israel, and India? The final chapter offers my answer to Bourne's crucial question, What Shall We Do with Our America?

NOTES

1. None of the names used in these pages is the actual name of a person interviewed. In all instances the men and women interviewed have read my analysis and agreed that my presentation is accurate in relation to their lives and the issues raised by their interviews.

2. See Randolph Bourne "Transnational America," *Atlantic Monthly* 117 (July 1916): 86–97; see, too, Randolph Bourne, *War and the Intellectuals*, edited by Carl Resek (New York: Harper, 1964).

3. *Migration News* 6, no. 2 (February 1999): 3. Philip Martin is the editor of this superb source of information.

4. Bourne, *War and the Intellectuals*, p. 121.

Acknowledgments

My first debt is to some of the most dedicated people in the United States: the archivists at the U.S. Presidential libraries. Especially at the Kennedy and Johnson libraries, all archivists were as open and helpful as any scholar could possibly wish. The Presidential libraries are truly arsenals of democracy.

Burt Baldwin read and reread this manuscript. He is a superb critic and, for more than twenty-five years, a great friend. His criticisms, insights, and suggestions helped this book a great deal.

Hakim Salahu-Din, Monica Johnson, Sadu Sadanand, Serafín Méndez Méndez, Susan Pease, Warren Perry, Evelyn Phillips, Nancy Weissmann, and George Eisen also read parts of the manuscript. I am grateful to each of them, although none bears any responsibility for the final results of our joint efforts.

At Praeger, Jim Sabin is an understanding and supportive editor. Both the title and subtitle are Jim's ideas. He was also especially helpful during what we both agreed were some "interesting moments."

Carrie, Benjamin and, especially, Adam Fernandez generously gave their father time, suggestions, insights, and criticisms.

Brenda Harrison was my associate at many of the library searches and all the community investigations. She read, listened, suggested, criticized, and always supported both this book and me. This book would not exist without her love, intelligence, and wit.

This book is dedicated, with all our love, to Chuck Harrison.

PART ONE

IMMIGRANTS, SERFS, AND REFUGEES: WHO ARE THEY? WHERE DID THEY COME FROM?

1

Old Blood, New Blood, Weak Blood: The Nature of U.S. Immigration Laws

"The national origins system contradicts our basic national philosophy and basic values . . . it judges men and women not on the basis of their worth but on their place of birth . . . this system is a standing affront to many Americans and to many countries."
—Attorney General Robert Kennedy, July 22, 1964[1]

WHO'S RESPONSIBLE?

In December 1997 the U.S. Government Accounting Office (GAO), issued a report that read like an advertisement for Ripley's "Believe It or Not." Rural America, home to an army of patriotic militia groups,[2] also hosted roughly 600,000 illegal agricultural workers. The foreign-born men, women, and children picked crops like strawberries in California, beans in Texas, and tomatoes in Florida. Meanwhile, the Agriculture Department reluctantly agreed that growers "depended" on these illegal workers. It would of course be better for all concerned if domestic help stooped to pick the nation's vegetables; but, in the absence of a homemade supply, the Agriculture Department seconded the growers: America needed, besides the illegal labor, a ready supply of temporary agricultural "guest" workers.[3]

In English that meant more Mexicans, many of whom might overstay their guest privileges. This too was a problem, but not as great as the one faced by growers; their nightmare was an Immigration and Naturalization Service that enforced the law. Suppose, reasoned the farmers, the INS went so far as to raid the farms when the crops were ready to harvest? The tomatoes would rot, the strawberries seep their juices into the fields.[4]

To protect themselves against the possibility of law enforcement, the growers wanted a ready reserve of guest workers. In essence, any day of the week an ugly incident with an immigrant in Los Angeles or Chicago could trigger a political need to enforce the law; and where would that leave the growers and consumers who depended on fruits and vegetables for, respectively, their economic and physical well-being?

In its role as objective analyst, the GAO asked the INS for its response to agribusiness. Were the growers correct? Answer: No way! Agribusiness neglected these facts. First, the INS had spent (1994–1997) over $2 billion on border control[5]; it focused so heavily on keeping the Mexicans out that less than 20 percent of the agency's resources went to officers who identified and apprehended illegal immigrants once they actually entered the United States. Second, enforcement at factories and other work sites "consumed less than 4 percent of INS enforcement activities in fiscal year 1996." (In 1998 the INS devoted 2 percent of its enforcement resources to worksite enforcement. Its investigations only included 3 percent of the nation's employers. Moreover, even though the INS does target specific industries as a result of historical experience, fully 43 percent of its investigations were in industries not targeted by the INS.) Finally, current enforcement on the farms was only a tiny proportion of the agency's already small enforcement activities. End result: All concerned agreed that 37 percent of the agricultural workforce was illegal, but, since the INS had no intention of seriously enforcing the law—"conducting enforcement operations in agriculture is particularly resource-intensive"—farmers had no need for guest workers. They would, apparently, have to make do with the dramatically increasing supply of illegal immigrants—3.9 million in 1992, 5 million in 1996.[6]

How many people read the report? My guess is, not many. But the one certainty is the lovely assessment attributed to baseball icon Yogi Berra: It's déjà vu all over again. The widespread thirst for Mexicans in general and for illegal immigrants in particular is a twentieth-century constant; listen, for example, to Mr. John H. Davis, of Laredo, Texas, pleading for the "temporary admission of illiterate Mexican laborers" in 1920. As Mr. Davis put it to the U.S. House of Representatives, "The Mexican labor has been with us always, as the Negro has been in the South . . . we are wholly dependent upon the Mexican, just as we are dependent on our wives at home. There is nothing done in that country worthwhile, outside of the towns—absolutely nothing done worthwhile—that is not done by the hand of that patient laborer."[7]

Give Mr. Davis credit for this: He told the truth. And so do his contemporaries. As officials of the Northwest Treeplanters and Farmworkers United Union told the people of Oregon on October 30, 1998, "Without Mexican farm workers, legal or not, the rest of us would not eat."[8]

Turning a blind eye to illegal aliens has always included not only Mexicans, but also a wide variety of other ethnic groups. For example, leaders of the Irish Immigration Reform Movement pleaded with Congress (in 1987) to provide more visas for their brethren; that was the only way to stop "discriminating" against the 150,000 Irish nationals and the estimated 90,000 Poles "forced to live in the shadows as illegal aliens." Add to these the estimated (as of 1997) 335,000 illegal El Salvadorans, the 105,000 Haitians, the 165,000 Guatemalans, and the 95,000 Filipinos[9] and, without even including the illegal Chinese, Vietnamese, and Dominicans, you develop a Polaroid snapshot of those who live and work in the shadows of American life.

Living a lie is scary for the illegals; but it's even more frightening for the rest of us. Our contradictions—or lack of information—hide reality; and if we are ever to deal with the issues raised by the interviews that began this book, we need, like Mr. Davis in 1920, to perceive the world that is actually there.

- Since U.S. immigration laws were dramatically transformed in 1965, more than 23 million legal immigrants have arrived in the United States. Documents at the Kennedy and Johnson libraries indicate that government officials never meant to welcome the world. As Attorney General Katzenbach told Congress on February 10, 1965, the new law was designed primarily to eliminate the institutionalized "evils" and "cruelties" of the 1924 and 1952 immigration acts. Architects of the new bill only included features like first come, first serve "in large part because of the injustices under the old system."[10] The ethnic mix of U.S. society was *forever changed* as a result of the unintended consequences of introducing our professed ideals (e.g., all people are created equal) to the laws of the land.

- Whether legal or illegal, immigration to the United States is part of a worldwide process. It is fueled by factors like greed, poverty, family ties and networks, the nature of capitalism, and economic change. It is these changes, for example, that make high- and low-skilled jobs a plentiful source of employment for immigrants working in Paris and San Diego, Tokyo and Chicago, Brussels and Miami.

- Millions of immigrants live in the United States because of the consistently neglected consequences of U.S. foreign policy. Whether it's the one million Cubans or the one million Vietnamese, you can't grasp their presence in the United States without recalling the Cold War that brought these "boat people" to U.S. shores.

- Roughly 20 percent of the El Salvadoran people now live in the United States.[11] Their continuing presence is intimately linked to President Reagan's handling of civil wars in Central America.

This list could be extended. The presence of Cambodians, Guatemalans, Nicaraguans, Dominicans, and Hmong cannot be separated from the consequences of U.S. foreign policy. Like that of legal and illegal Mexicans, the presence of Jamaicans and Barbadians is intimately linked to U.S. agriculture's—and other industries—need for cheap, disposable labor.

As we trace the history of recent immigration to the United States, let's start with a request and a conclusion. Do not blame the newcomers. In the year 2000, primary responsibility for the ethnic composition of the United

States rests squarely on the shoulders of at least five generations of U.S. political and economic interests.

CHICKENS COMING HOME TO ROOST

National Origins Law of 1924

On December 27, 1923, Congressman John Miller (D., Washington) gave his colleagues a lecture on "old," "new," and "weak" blood. Miller opened with a conclusion. "We are fairly settled with the Chinese; they cannot come; they understand it; we understand it."

Asked if he knew anything about the smuggling of Chinese from Canada to Washington, Miller said, "Oh, yes. Everyone does more or less." However, "There is not near as much smuggling as formerly." The real problem was "the enormous number of other orientals coming to our country, the largest number being the Japanese."[12]

Miller stressed, "There is a sociological aspect of this thing, gentlemen: A Chinaman coming to this country remains a Chinaman. Oriental blood is old blood; the last blood in the world to change, and the hardest to change. You can change the blood of a nation which is a new blood and modernize it much more readily and easily; it responds much more quickly than the blood of the old nations."[13]

Congressman Elton Watkins (R., Oregon) wanted to know, "Is that not true of every race except the Nordic?" Miller said, "Yes, sir, you can modernize and Americanize the citizens of Northern Europe; they are new blood in the world. But the blood of the Orient is the oldest blood, the hardest to change."[14]

Luckily, "not one (Chinaman) out of a thousand marries a white woman." But the races did occasionally mix—"a Japanese frequently wants to marry a white woman"—and, as Miller instructed his colleagues, "A half caste is a failure in most cases; there are some exceptions. The half-caste Indian is a failure; the half-caste black man is very likely to be a failure; but the half-caste oriental is worse. He seems in the majority of cases to inherit the vices of both races and the virtues of neither. It makes, as a general rule, a bad product."[15]

By excluding "orientals" the United States prevented the manufacture of damaged goods. This was beneficial in any case but especially important in 1923 because "I believe scientists agree that the white blood is the weakest in the world and the most easily tainted; and the half caste as a general rule partakes more of the other race in his temperament than he does of the white race."

Miller's logic challenged Charles Darwin. If only the fittest survived, how did the "weak"-blooded whites manage to achieve anything of significance? Was old blood tired blood? Was weak blood, so easily "tainted," better blood? And if "the half-caste oriental was more of an oriental than he was a white man," wasn't old blood stronger than new? Or, was new blood better, because, like a shiny Model T, it had just come off the human assembly line?

In 1923 no one asked these questions. On the contrary, Miller's colleagues politely listened as he summarized the justification for the new immigration law. "The perpetuity of the institutions of a country depends upon the passing from one generation to another of the full blood; that is the way great institutions are perpetuated."[16]

However candidly, Congressman Miller expressed an anxiety shared by the architects of the 1924 immigration act.[17] Albert Johnson, chair of the House Committee on Immigration and Naturalization, warned that "the people of the country when they see the aliens creeping up in New York City like locusts a block or two at a time, have reason for apprehension." And Congressman William Vaile of Colorado told a story about an alligator and a cat. "The cat looked the alligator over the very moment the alligator was brought into the house. The alligator snapped at the cat frequently; and the alligator kept growing larger and larger. The cat did not grow. And finally, one day the alligator killed the cat."[18]

Congress decided to act before the alligator opened its jaws. Indeed, despite witnesses who complained that the law blatantly discriminated against Chinese and Greeks, Japanese and Italians, Poles and Russians,[19] the House Committee earnestly explained that the new law imposed strict quotas on countries like Italy primarily because it was the "new seed" that discriminated against the old.

Congress offered these figures. From 1871 to 1880, "the total number of immigrants into the United States from Western Europe was 2,080,266 while the total from Southern and Eastern Europe was only 181,638." But, from 1897 to 1914, the "old immigration" was nearly three million, the "new immigration" more than ten million.[20] The alligator was growing quite large and, as this Congress never forgot, the alligator had a family.

Then and now the U.S. immigration laws established preferences for the immediate relatives of naturalized citizens and "certain declarants." Husbands, wives, and others came to entry points like Ellis Island outside the overall quota set by law. The intention was noble, to allow families to unite. But, given the 3-to-1 ratio of new to old immigrants, the former would quickly swallow the latter unless the law forever stopped "the endless chain of relatives."

The House Committee therefore stressed that "herein lies one of the prime reasons for reduction of quota to 2 percent and establishment of base for quota on the 1890 census." In the future the United States had to figure a country's yearly quota of new immigration based on 2 percent of its total in 1890 (thus Britain got 62,458 slots, Italy 3,912, Greece 47, and China and Japan 0[21]); if Congress set a base line of 1910 or 1920, it guaranteed the "future pyramiding" that built, on American soil, ever-expanding monuments to Southern and Eastern Europe. Thus, House leaders proposed that new citizens could bring in orphaned nieces and nephews, but if they had parents, "stay home," and give the same message to grandma and grandpa. They would be "denied admission as 'nonquota' immigrants in order to prevent future appeals for admission from lines running to the grandparents."[22]

In the name of equalizing conditions for the old seed, Congress successfully sterilized the new seed. Until 1965 Italians and Greeks with money always managed to get Congressmen to pass "special bills" for their special friends, but for virtually all "orientals" and most Southern and Eastern Europeans, the new law was a brick wall. After 1927 the law parceled out 150,000 immigration slots in proportion to the distribution of national origins in the white population of the United States in 1920.[23] The overall quotas for nations like Italy and Greece were not markedly changed. Even world wars never demolished the law, and even the most principled criticism never moved his colleagues to heed the pleas of the Honorable Emanuel Celler.

McCarran-Walter Act of 1952

Representing a congressional district in Brooklyn, New York, Emanuel Celler entered Congress in 1923. He challenged the national origins system when it was first introduced, and he once again voiced his principled opposition as Congress debated, in March of 1951, major revisions of the nation's immigration, naturalization, and nationality laws. "Suffice it to say, national origins is dead as a dodo from a scientific standpoint. We had the best example of that in the Hitler regime, when we had the Herrenvolk and the Sklavenvolk, super race and slave race. That was the Hitler theory. Certainly it should be scotched in all scientific minds that one race is better than another race. Our history should certainly prove that."[24]

Despite history, Celler avoided a frontal attack on the national origins theory. His opponents easily had all the votes required to maintain restrictions, so Celler said, "I bow down to the inevitable." But, what about the unused quotas of Great Britain and Ireland? Year after year over 40 percent of the English quota "remained idle"; meanwhile, Congress found itself passing the "private bills" that made exceptions, and more exceptions, to the national origins restrictions. "I think the time has come when we should take a portion of these unused quotas and divide them equitably among those nations whose quotas are pitifully small. And they are pitifully small."[25]

Celler then explained how the small became smaller. In the original (1924) and proposed (1951) legislation, statutes specified that a country could use no more than 10 percent of its yearly quota in any one month. Spain, for example, had a quota of 252, yet if twenty-six Spaniards wanted to migrate in January, the twenty-sixth had to wait. While the law did allow a country to fulfill the remainder of its entire quota in November and December, Celler said to "see how the quotas of small countries who desperately need the quotas go to waste because of such a provision." Turkey had a quota of 226, but only 177 were used. Despite Spain's total of 252 immigration slots, only 63 were used in 1947 and only 189 in 1948.[26]

Celler wanted to "reckon how many quotas were not used, and then in the next years you would allocate among those countries having quotas less than seven thousand. That is all."[27] Congressman Francis Walter (D., Pennsylvania) said that "I think there is a very delicate question of foreign relations involved, diplomatic relations." Presumably Great Britain or Ireland would react angrily to the United States using their unused quotas. Celler responded that when Congress "whittled away" at the already tiny quotas, Congressional knife work also threatened our ties with nations like Italy and Greece. But, sensing that he was once again spitting in the wind, Celler turned to "what might be deemed a discrimination against the colored people."[28]

In the 1924 legislation no quotas existed against immigrants with origins in the Western Hemisphere. Especially after the U.S. military occupation of Haiti (1915–1934) and the Dominican Republic (1916–1924),[29] the United States received heated criticism from its Southern neighbors. So, in what would later be called the Good Neighbor Policy, the United States theoretically opened its doors to anyone in the Western Hemisphere.

What bothered Celler—and his Brooklyn constituents—was a new quota for the British colonies of Jamaica and Trinidad. In the 1924 law, immigrants from these colonies entered under the British quota. That was the largest total by far, so the 1951 law proposed that all colonies and non–self-governing territories shall have a quota of 100. Even that number was further restricted, for example, 30 of the 100 slots went to parents of Jamaicans or Trinidadians who were *already* U.S. citizens. Celler argued, "I think we ought to hesitate long before we take that action. We do not do it with reference to any other landmass in the Western Hemisphere. We do it just for those two. And it might be deemed a discrimination against the colored people. I think they have a right to claim discrimination because the colored folks come from those areas."[30]

Indeed they did! As laborers in Florida and Connecticut, West Indians engaged in the "stoop and squat" work that put sugar on America's tables and cigars in a congressman's mouth. One Connecticut tobacco grower even told Senator Paul Douglas of Illinois (in February of 1952) how important the low-wage West Indians were: "I think probably agriculture in the State of Connecticut would be nonexistent if the price rose to where it would attract the (U.S.) labor."[31]

Like Mexicans on the West Coast, Jamaicans (and Puerto Ricans) proved to be indispensable on the East Coast. In Hartford, farmers welcomed them to pick tobacco, while in Washington Congress easily passed the McCarran-

Walter Act of 1952. In vetoing the legislation President Truman proclaimed that the national quota system is "out of date . . . unrealistic . . . inadequate . . . discriminates deliberately and intentionally . . . is unworthy of our ideals and traditions . . . and repudiates our belief in the brotherhood of man."[32]

Congress quickly overrode the president's veto on March 25, 1952. Old restrictions against new and "colored" blood remained in force until President Kennedy courageously decided to act on his ideals—and the timely death (in 1963) of Congressman Francis Walter. As chair of the House's Committee on Immigration and Naturalization, Walter was the one man who might have toppled the white knights of Camelot.

Immigration and Nationality Act of 1965

First stop for the Kennedy men was the office of Emanuel Celler. As chair of the House Judiciary Committee, Celler helped captain the disposition of all immigration issues. After forty years of spirited resistance to the national origins system, his support seemed certain, yet the Kennedy staffers wisely chose not to take him for granted. As a sign of respect Celler received one of the first congressional briefings about the president's proposals. During the meeting Celler obligingly scanned the legislative outline that existed in the spring of 1963; despite the lack of specifics, Celler appeared "reasonably pleased with the bill." Precise details would be worked out over time; meanwhile Emanuel Celler offered both principled as well as practical support.[33]

Problems developed when Kennedy staffers stumbled over the neglected ego of Congressman Michael Feighan (D., Ohio). As new chair of the House Subcommittee on Immigration and Naturalization, Feighan "felt slighted, I think, that we had gone to see Celler before we went to see him. He made us absolutely no promises about whether he would support it or whether he was sympathetic. In fact, he seemed very nettled and irritated and unfriendly."[34]

The president's men decided to, as they say in Columbia, "chupa medias" (suck socks). Assistant Attorney General Norbert Schlei said that "I explained to him [Congressman Feighan] that we were there to get his ideas and nothing was final, that we had gone to see Mr. Celler first out of feeling that that was the proper thing to do—you go to see the Chairman of the full committee first and then go to the Chairman of the subcommittee." Feighan also received assurances that "Celler had nothing whatsoever to do with the development of the bill"; Schlei and his colleagues "went to see him, we told him about it, but I'll bet you that he could not give a precise description of what's in it."[35]

Did Feighan buy this line? Apparently not. Schlei said that our stroking "may have mollified Mr. Feighan some but he seemed very cool."[36] In fact, Congressman Feighan would place both reasonable and unreasonable stumbling blocks before the immigration bill for the next two years.

Doorway to the World

It's a wonderful cartoon. Strapped to the side of the torch held by the Statue of Liberty, President Kennedy uses a bellows to blow life into Ms. Liberty's flame. While the flame is flickering in the drawing, the determination in the president's eyes assures all that he will relight the way for the world's huddled masses.[37]

Appearing in the *Kansas City Star* on July 29, 1963, the cartoon depicted one response to the formal congressional submission of the president's bill. As the editors of the *Bayonne Times* stressed, "While this country is engaged in a great struggle to eliminate discrimination among its citizens . . . it is only fitting that the United States cut through the racial curtain that has separated us from peoples throughout the world."[38]

Other papers defended the national origins system. The New Orleans *Times-Picayune* wrote that "in spite of much propaganda to the contrary, the United States has one of the most liberal immigration and naturalization laws in the world"; moreover, "unassimilated minority groups are easy pickings for the unscrupulous politician." This sentiment was shared by the *Times-Press* in Illinois: "No people, regardless of northern or southern Europe or elsewhere around the world, have a legitimate complaint of the present immigration plan of the United States. It is time we assume a role of enlightened selfishness, with the idea that charity begins at home."[39]

A third response to the President's message was surprise. In Lubbock, Texas, the *Avalanche Journal* wrote that "millions of Americans must have rubbed their eyes when they read of the plan the President submitted to lawmakers this week." In Santa Monica, *The Outlook* seemed equally confused. "One of the last causes that we would have expected President Kennedy to espouse at this time is that of ending quotas for immigration into this country . . . it's a strange kind of sentimentalism, we think, which makes John F. Kennedy long for a return to the melting pot of the decades between the Civil War and World War I."[40]

The Outlook was wrong. Instead of a longing for days gone by, it was idealism—mixed with a healthy dose of politics—that fueled the efforts of the president's closest immigration advisors. Officials at State, for example, thought that Congress remained wedded to the national origins system; Abba Schwartz therefore argued that, instead of embracing certain defeat, the president ought to seek the minor changes that could, with luck, open additional slots for Italians, Greeks, and Poles.

Mike Feldman (Deputy Special Counsel to the President) took the high road. In White House discussions he not only cited the pledge in the president's 1960 platform, he (and others) emphasized that "the national origins system was the only thing left in the law of the United States, really, that discriminated against people on the basis of their race or their place of birth.

And it was just something that we felt as a matter of principle the Administration should not be in a position of defending."[41]

While White House and Justice Department officials really wanted "to shoot at what we regarded as a major evil," they also needed to reelect the president. "The bill was a great boon in dealing with the Italian-Americans and Americans of Greek origin and all the—well . . . hyphenated groups and the organizations that were interested in the subject of immigration."

For the president the bill was a win, win proposition. He acted on the basis of theoretically all-American ideals. Even if the bill failed in Congress, "hyphenated" Americans would sing his praises all the way to the ballot box. That was a grand slam for any politician so, when the bill died in the 1963 Congress, the president expected to resurrect it in 1964, the year of his presumed reelection.

Death stopped John F. Kennedy; however perversely, it helped his immigration bill. As the fiery rhetoric of Malcolm X suggested, "The chickens were coming home to roost." Too many seeds of hate had produced a vile mix, yet, besides more violence, the president's assassination also fueled laudable efforts to introduce our professed ideals to the laws of the land. Segregation and exclusion, separate water fountains, and "pitifully small" quotas marked two sides of the same coin. In 1964 and 1965 Congress rushed to make up for the past. As we today experience the immigration consequences of those transforming efforts, recall that the details of the new immigration law were required primarily because of what Malcolm X correctly called an institutionalized "climate of hate."[42]

In his oral interview for the Kennedy Library, Norbert Schlei said "one of the great problems of getting a bill passed that would abolish the national origins quota system was to think up some system that would not produce chaos to take its place."[43] For example, all concerned agreed that already-established preferences for family members and skilled labor made sense. Many of the close relatives would be consumers who bought American goods rather than workers who took American jobs; meanwhile, unions could not balk if new immigrants imported skills urgently needed by the United States.

The sticky issue was how to let migrants in without using a system rooted in national origins. Schlei says that "the idea that we came up with—and I think essentially this was my idea—we should start with 'first come, first served' because that's an unanswerably fair kind of a basis." In essence, if Americans truly believed that all men were created equal, the only principled choice was to say yes to anyone who walked through the immigration door. "We arrived at the conclusion that there should be a worldwide preference system and that quota immigration should be on a first-come, first-served basis within the preference categories."[44]

With one problem solved, another remained on the president's plate. What about the waiting lines produced by forty years of nonstop discrimination? In the legislative guidebook presented to every congressman—the copy in the Johnson Library is labeled "Road to Final Passage"—the anonymous authors focused on size and location. The waiting line was over 800,000 immigrants long. Almost 60 percent of these folks came from four countries—Italy, Greece, Poland, and Portugal—and "by far the largest component of the world-wide waiting list was European."[45]

Critics—especially "the rural Congressmen"—could relax. As if an ad subliminally flashed on a movie screen, readers of "Road to Final Passage" could rest assured that most new immigrants would still hail from Europe. But "if first come first served were allowed, if that system were allowed to dictate the entire quota immigration policy, we would get ninety percent of our quota immigration from Italy; we would get about 8 percent from Greece, and we would get the other two percent from Poland and Portugal."[46]

That was politically intolerable in forums like the United Nations; how, for example, could U.S. diplomats tout the virtues of brotherhood when, in 1965, the Chinese quota (of 100) was already mortgaged until 2008?[47] Similar mortgages existed all over the world. Once you also added in important allies like Germany and Great Britain, "it became apparent that the system needed some other features in order to have it meet fairly and practically the problems that faced us—in large part because of the injustices under the old system."[48]

Feature One stipulated a five-year phase in of the new law. In that manner countries with no present problems (i.e., England and Ireland) averted a "sudden, instant impact" on their immigration possibilities.

Feature Two authorized the president, in consultation with Congress, to reserve 30 percent of the numbers in any one year for distribution to immigrants important to the national security of the United States. Events like the Soviet invasion of Hungary in 1956 and Castro's politics in Cuba were prime motivations for this immigration provision.

Feature Three—arguably the most important—put a "*maximum* limit" on the number of immigrants from any one country. Given the backlogs in Italy, Greece, Poland, and Portugal, the new law's architects argued "that if any one country got ten percent of the total authorized immigration from the entire world, it was fair to impose a limit at that point. Additionally, the new law also required that the rest of the quota numbers be distributed to other countries."[49]

Combined with preferences for close relatives and first come, first served, Feature Three deserves credit for forever changing the ethnic composition of the American people. Any country on earth was now entitled to 10 percent of the U.S. immigration quota and, over and above that fixed total, immigrants could quickly bring in a wide variety of close relatives, who over time could bring in their mothers, fathers, sisters, brothers, husbands, wives, children. . . .

The extraordinary paradox is that to eliminate the evils and cruelties of national origins, the Kennedy/Johnson team sanctioned the "endless chain of relatives" feared by the designers of the 1924 legislation. For example, in 1996, 915,900 immigrants were admitted to the United States. Over 65 percent were "family sponsored immigrants," and 50 percent of those family-sponsored immigrants—over 300,000 people—came as the immediate relatives of U.S. citizens. They entered the United States over and above the statutory limit imposed by Congress.

One conclusion is that both God and the government work in mysterious ways. Another is that none of the president's men wanted or predicted our contemporary result; instead, they confidently assured Congress—in March of 1965—that the effects of the new legislation would be both limited and short term.

Before the House of Representatives, Attorney General Nicholas Katzenbach tried to be specific. "The countries of southern Europe, southeastern Europe, Italy, Greece, Portugal, Spain and also Poland. Those countries would be the principal beneficiaries of the new bill." Katzenbach also stressed that the "total" increase in immigration would be no more than seventy to eighty thousand people—and that included the relatives that would come outside the specific total set by Congress.[50]

Congressman Feighan was worried. While he apparently accepted the attorney general's sincerity, he nevertheless asked if the Justice Department would oppose "an annual ceiling." Katzenbach said, "Yes." He stressed that Congress could always change the total number if Justice's estimates proved to be incorrect. But, while noting that his estimate might be 30 or 35 thousand off the mark, Katzenbach emphasized that "it cannot be very far wrong."[51]

Why? Because the president's men felt that their immigration bill rested on scientific knowledge. It was "the first that ever was formulated, that was checked out in terms of its statistical impact, that was systematically worked out to see if it was practical."[52]

Besides noble ideals, the president's men also shared an air of arrogance. Thus, Norbert Schlei told the Senate "that we anticipate that at the end of five years there will be no preference waiting list in the world, with the possible exception of Italy. That means that we will have no relatives, no people who want to rejoin their relatives, who are being kept out."[53]

Senator Sam Ervin (D., North Carolina) asked about prophets. "Do you not agree with me that it takes a man with prophetic powers to foretell what would happen under this bill with respect to applications for immigration to the United States after the expiration of the five years?"

While Schlei agreed that the "prediction becomes less certain as you go into the future," he wanted "to add this fact. That the impact of registrations is *bound to be limited* because at all times the number, about two-thirds of the people, a minimum of two-thirds of the people would come in under this system will be preference immigrants who will either be people of extraordinary attainments or they will be relatives of American citizens" (emphasis added).[54]

Ervin refused to let go. He expressed serious concern about unlimited immigration from "the Eastern Hemisphere," using India as a prime example.

Ervin: "If my recollection is right India has approximately, at this time, about 450 million people."

Schlei: "I think that is right."

Ervin: "India has a minimum quota now, do they not?"

Schlei: "I believe they do, yes, sir."

Ervin: "Is anybody that gifted with enough prophetic foresight to foretell how many people from India are going to apply for admission to this country as immigrants when they are assured that we have abolished all discrimination by immigration laws?"

Schlei: "No, sir, but I can foretell that there will be a relatively limited number of people who will qualify."[55]

Schlei missed, and Ervin perceived the endless chain of relatives for the same reason: Both men were arrogant. But, where Schlei's conceit rested on his presumed powers of prediction, Ervin's arrogance revolved around a profound sense of national and racial superiority. Ervin championed what men like Katzenbach called evil; and, in the process, Senator Sam Ervin raised crucial questions about the meaning of the United States of America.

Throughout the Senate hearings Senator Ervin emphasized that he supported the restrictions imposed by the national origins system. "With all due respect to those who cast aspersions on it, the purpose is to bring to the United States people who have relatives here in a national origins sense, who have made contributions to our population and contributions to our development. I believe that we ought to give preference to those who have made such contributions to America and not put them on exactly the same basis as people who have made very little or no contribution to our population and no contribution to our development."[56]

Ervin used Greeks and Africans as an example of why he favored restrictions; "As far as the people of Hellenic descent are concerned it is much easier for the United States to assimilate 11 percent in new population each year if they come from the same nationalities which have contributed in a substantial manner to the population of the United States."[57]

The Africans were different. Ervin admitted that he was treading on soft ground—"since I live below the Mason-Dixon line, I should not refer to the Congo, because people immediately say I am full of prejudice"—but he nevertheless cited the testimony of his secretary. "A wide reader," she told the Senator that when the Belgians gave the Congo independence, people thought freedom and liberty came in a package. "Now you certainly agree with me that people that have that idea of freedom and democracy are not quite as ready to be assimilated into American life as people who come from a civilized nation like Greece or France or England or any of other older nations."

While no one pressed Ervin on the age of African nations or the implied civilized/barbaric dichotomy, Senator Hiram Fong (D., Hawaii) artfully challenged his colleague in this manner. "Following the line of reasoning of Senator Ervin, if we were to adopt his theory, then we would certainly have to open up immigration to a lot of African nations, would we not? We have eleven percent of our population who are of Negroid ancestry."[58]

One of the problems with reading reports of congressional hearings is that expressions and tone of voice are hidden from view. Nevertheless, when Fong got the witness to admit that, "yes," you would have to admit Africans because of their contributions, Ervin interrupted: "If you will pardon me, Senator Fong, you would not have to do anything of the kind. I stand for the nationality system, and it would be on the basis of the nations who have their representatives in this country."[59]

No wonder Ralph Ellison wrote the *Invisible Man*! Ervin totally disregarded the contributions of 20 million African Americans, as he continued to champion his philosophy with passion. In one instance Ms. Rosalind Frame of Savannah, Georgia, explained the origins of the Asia Pacific Triangle. In this section of the national origins legislation, "If a person is indigenous to the Pacific or to Asia, he must be charged to that area when seeking entry to our nation." Thus, a Chinese or Japanese person born in Brazil would nevertheless be charged to the Japanese or Chinese quota.

Ms. Frame asked, "Why was it necessary to impose the Asia Pacific Triangle?" The answer was birth rates. "The Chinese reproduce at the rate of more than three times the average American Caucasian." Thus, "I also present here a short sheet showing the overall character of expected immigrants under the proposed administration bill . . . within a forty year period (which all of us might live to see) there will be 114 million Red Chinese without considering the children of the one million Chinese already living within the United States. This figure of 114 million is 57 percent of our present population."[60]

Senator Ervin listened to this and Mrs. Frame's other explanations of U.S. and world immigration policies. Finally, he asked, "Mrs. Frame, is it correct to conclude from your testimony that your research and study indicates that the McCarran-Walter Act (the 1952 legislation) discriminates against the admission of no immigrant on account of his race or on account of his religion or on account of his place of origin?"

Mrs. Frame agreed, which moved Senator Ervin to end with this question. "So, instead of being a discriminatory law on immigration as it is pictured to be it is the least discriminatory of all the immigration laws of any country on the face of the earth that you have studied?" Mrs. Frame: "That is a fact."[61]

Senator Sam Ervin represented—and represents—millions of Americans.[62] We changed the laws but failed to reach a consensus about the meaning of the United States of America. The result is that in 1999 more than 9 percent of the American people are foreign born; meanwhile, 95 percent of all U.S. residents live in places that have less than 9 percent foreign-born residents.[63]

We remain a people divided—by geography and by the beliefs and values of men like Senator Sam Ervin.

Final Passage

Did the president want to cut a deal? After "extensive discussions" with Congressman Michael Feighan, "there is only one issue between us that could block agreement." Would Feature Three—the 10 percent limit on immigration from any one country—cover the Western Hemisphere? Feighan said, "Our bill would leave the Western Hemisphere outside the quota system—as it now is."[64]

The president and his advisors were caught in a contradiction. As Feighan and Congressman Peter Rodino stressed during the House hearings, "Mr. Attorney General, in retaining a nonquota status for the Western Hemisphere, would that not be discrimination? Now it is certainly a privilege, which is not given to any other country outside the Western Hemisphere. It is a privilege based on the accident of birth." Why was one form of discrimination better than another? Why was it evil to effectively exclude immigrants from the Asia Pacific Triangle, but acceptable to show preference for countries like Argentina and the newly independent nations of Trinidad and Jamaica?[65]

In public Katzenbach "respectfully disagreed." What Feighan missed was that the nonquota status of the Western Hemisphere was never intended as a form of discrimination against anyone. Instead, the United States was *including* more immigrants because of foreign policy considerations. Pressed yet again by Feighan, Katzenbach reluctantly conceded that "it is conceivable to make the argument that it is favoritism in theory. I do not think you can say it is favoritism in fact."[66]

Of course it was. But, as the president heard in a May 8, 1965 memo, Secretary of State Rusk felt "that if we go along with Feighan we will vex and dumbfound our Latin American friends, who will now be sure we are in final retreat from Pan Americanism. The immigration project, on top of [the April 29, 1965, U.S. military intervention in] Santo Domingo, will be, in the opinion of Rusk too much too quick for them to take."[67]

Feighan needed to remember the Good Neighbor Policy. If that memory failed to produce an agreement, Norbert Schlei nevertheless suggested no compromise. Immigrants had to prove they would never be a public charge, and the Secretary of Labor could exclude anyone who threatened American working conditions. Thus, the grant of nonquota status meant nothing because "there are a great many restrictions having to do with health, security, etc. Taken together, these restrictions can be so administered as to keep immigration from the Western Hemisphere at almost any desired level."[68]

Based on documents at the Kennedy and Johnson libraries, Schlei's stark cynicism is out of character. Moreover, the ability to administratively close the door on immigrants we supposedly have embraced had nothing to do with Congressman Feighan's insight. He legitimately criticized the administration's "favoritism" based on place of birth (i.e., the Western Hemisphere), and the president and his subordinates simply disregarded his criticism.

Ultimately the Senate resolved this dispute by siding with both Congressman Feighan and the secretary of state! With no preference categories or country quotas, the Senate's final version of the law imposed a ceiling on Western Hemisphere immigration but delayed imposition of the ceiling until a commission decided whether the secretary of state's dire predictions proved to be accurate.

In October 1965 the new immigration law passed by an overwhelming majority in the House and by a voice vote in the Senate. As Schlei later boasted, "They didn't even count because it was obvious that it had passed."[69]

Results of the New Immigration Law

Despite a variety of major and minor modifications over the last thirty-three years, U.S. immigration policy continues to be shaped by the principles established in 1965. Under the umbrella of the six or more specific preferences for family members and priority occupations, immigrants still generally arrive on a first come, first served basis. As of 1996, the cap on the number of visas from any one country has been raised to 28,016, but the law still puts a firm limit on the number of individuals who can legally migrate from any one country in any one year.

One of the 1965 law's conspicuous consequences has been a marked increase in the diversity of newcomers:

- From 1820 to 1860, 95 percent of all immigrants came from Northern and Western Europe. The total number of immigrants equaled more than five million people.

- Between 1901 and 1930, Southern and Eastern Europe accounted for almost 70 percent of all U.S. immigrants. The total number of immigrants equaled 18.6 million.

- Between 1931 and 1960 41 percent of the immigrants came from Northern and Western Europe, 40 percent from Southern and Eastern Europe (remember the "special bills" always passed by Congress), and 15 percent from Latin America. The total number of immigrants equaled slightly more than four million men, women, and children.

- Between 1966 and 1997 more than 23 million immigrants arrived in the United States. The percentage from all of Europe hovers around the 15–17 percent mark; Asia (including the large number of refugees from countries like Vietnam and Cambodia) now accounts for roughly 37 percent of all immigrants, and Latin America and the Caribbean produce another approximately 40 percent of all U.S. immigration.[70]

- Mexico alone provides 12.5 percent of all new immigrants; other major sources of new immigration include the Philippines (which often ranks second), Russia, Vietnam, El Salvador, China, the Dominican Republic, India, Korea, Jamaica, Poland, and Haiti.[71]

- In 1910 14.7 percent of the U.S. population was foreign born; the figure in 1970 was 4.8 percent; the figure in late 1996 was 9.3 percent.

- Immigrants are geographically concentrated. Six states—California (23%), New York (18%), Florida (9%), Texas (7%), New Jersey (6%), and Illinois (5%)—contain almost 70 percent of the immigrant population.

- Finally, the new law has produced waiting lines every bit as long as the ones that existed in 1965 for Italians and Greeks. For example, the waiting line for Filipino professionals is roughly sixteen years long, and the Filipino line for the brothers and sisters of U.S. citizens was last calculated at 12.5 years.

Full Circle: Diversity Immigrants

The preceding statistics scare many Americans. In *Alien Nation*, Peter Brimelow (a senior editor of *Forbes* magazine and a naturalized immigrant from England) recently wrote, "The American nation has always had a specific ethnic core. And that core has been white."[72] While white is not an ethnic group, Brimelow, like Senator Ervin in 1965, expresses a provocative concern about the present and future shading of the American people. Indeed, despite census figures that indicate that (as of September 1997) 83 percent of the American people were still labeled white, critics like Brimelow bemoan the "inundation" of an "indefinite number of foreigners." Presumably they will consume the light racial core, with results that are as ominous as the White Identity movement that fuels many contemporary militia groups.[73]

As early as 1989, Congress was also worried about the ethnic makeup of the new immigrants. But, instead of using the white/black dichotomy, Congress talked of seeds: old ones, new ones, and the proper mix required to allow old seed immigrants to once again produce new Americans. "It is a question," said Senator Edward Kennedy (D., Massachusetts), "of how we correct an unexpected imbalance stemming from the 1965 Act—the inadvertent restriction on immigration from the old seed sources of our heritage."[74]

Senator Kennedy noted that, as far back as 1981, Congress received indications that "old seed" immigrants experienced problems entering the United States. First, the preferences established by law favored those with needed skills and/or relatives in the United States. Second, as the 1965 debates made clear, groups like the Irish and English had rarely used the huge quotas deliberately assigned to their nations in 1924. Old seeds therefore lacked the immigrant base required to bring in close relatives. Finally, even after the 1965 laws opened America's door to the world, many Northern Europeans continued to stay home. By 1980, poorer members of the original heritage groups did finally want to come to the United States, yet they still lacked either the skills mandated by the laws or relatives who had themselves recently migrated to America.

The mayor of Boston, Raymond L. Flynn, explained that in the face of these discriminatory restrictions, Irish nationals now broke the law. However, instead of suggesting that these illegal immigrants be arrested and deported, Flynn told Congress that "it is wrong that literally tens of thousands of young people from Ireland and other nations must today live shadow-like existences in our nation's largest cities . . . it is wrong that they must exist only from day to day without access to health insurance . . . it is wrong above all because this is not the American way, and it is equally intolerable for me that many of the victims of the current bad law include thousands from Italy, Haiti, and other countries as well."[75]

Haiti! Was Flynn suggesting that Haitians qualified as old seed? Or that the United States allow illegal Haitians the same rights as illegal Irish and Italians? On the rights issue Flynn seemed to say yes. But when it came to a specific plea he focused on the Irish. They were 8 percent of the U.S. immigration mix in 1950 and only <u>two-tenths of one percent</u> since 1965. "How is that situation fair?" (emphasis in original).[76] What was Congress going to do to restore the balance for old seed immigrants?

The State Department proposed this solution: *It would use the old national origin prejudices to help reverse the consequences of eliminating the old national origin prejudices.* Officials explained that certain—mainly European—countries had been "adversely affected" by the 1965 immigration law. To admit an additional 50,000 immigrants each year, the State Department devised a formula based on migration at the time when the national origin prejudices still determined who entered the United States. Government officials totaled the number of immigrants between 1953 and 1965 and compared that to the number of immigrants from 1965 to 1985. Ireland, for example, had 6,853 immigrants in the first period and only 1,500 in the second.

By this reasoning Ireland had been adversely affected; and one part of any solution was a point system for potential immigrants. In the bill before Congress people from Great Britain, Ireland, France, Germany, Italy, or Poland would receive thirty points for their place of birth and another ten points if they spoke English. While a person also got ten points for a high school diploma and another twenty points for having a job offer in place, the focus on national origins provoked a strong response from those with bad memories.[77]

Attorney Steve W. Chu expressed his concerns. He understood the old seed, "political considerations" moving the legislation, yet the forty-point head start offered to the English and Irish immigrants assured anything but equal opportunity. Given the same skills and education, a European would be chosen before a person from Korea or Japan. To Chu, "this (1987) bill definitely gives the flavor of being anti-Asian or pro-European."[78]

Lawrence Fuchs (a member of the 1981 Select Commission on Immigration) said that, given the cap on immigration from any one country, the bill was a form of "affirmative action" for European countries. He recommended dropping the category of "adversely affected country"; the United States should seek individuals as immigrants "because they were desirable for their attributes as persons." New Americans should never be selected because of their national or ethnic backgrounds.[79]

While critics initially blocked the 50,000 new slots for old seeds, senators like Edward Kennedy and Patrick Moynihan still strongly supported the resurrection of national origin prejudices. By late 1989 the program had received a new name—"diversity immigrants"—with the hope that by mentally linking the legislation to programs that benefited minorities, critics would overlook the legislation's 1924 roots.

Before Congress, advocates of the bill proved to be their own worst enemies. As Donald Martin, national political coordinator of the Irish Immigration Reform Movement, told the House of Representatives, "There is no question that the diversity visas or the alternative replenishment visas (another new label) are not fair and balanced by themselves; they are not meant to be. However, . . . they create some balance against a system which is currently heavily weighted against many countries in the world."[80]

Once again the Asian-American community immediately raised its voice in protest. In a long legal brief submitted by a coalition of Asian groups, the attorneys argued that the 1965 law was not heavily weighted against certain countries. On the contrary, *"many applicants from low demand countries were given the same access and opportunity to apply for visas but chose not to or deselected themselves when visas became available"* (emphasis in original). The system was first come, first served, and the cap on immigration from any one country assured more ethnic diversity than at any other period in U.S. history.

Thus, the proposed 50,000 new slots for mostly European immigrants should be rejected because the legislation assumed that certain nationalities were more desirable than others. It thereby disregarded a fundamental U.S. consensus against discrimination on the basis of nationality or ethnicity. Most depressing of all, the bill "was bound to result in ethnic tension and conflict within the United States."[81]

Congress chose to ignore the Asian and other critics of "replenishment." Arguing that thirty-four countries (Haiti was not one of them) experienced adverse affects as a result of the 1965 legislation, Congress established (in 1990) a transitional "diversity" program for three years, from 1992 through 1994. The law allowed 40,000 new slots a year for these diversity immigrants, traveling full circle from 1965, the law "reserved a minimum of 40 percent of the 120,000 visas issued over the three year period for natives of Ireland."[82]

The law succeeded. In 1994, for example, Poland (17,495), Ireland (16,344), and the United Kingdom (3,050) grabbed the lion's share of the new diversity visas. Equally important, these immigrants could soon bring in their relatives, assuring the never-ending replenishment of the old seed heritage. As David Martin summed it up for the House of Representatives when he testified in 1989, "The Irish Immigration Reform Movement sees dealing with the issues of diversity as an additive process. In other words, we don't seek to attack in any way the family preference system. Our grievance against the family preference system is that we are not in it and won't be without the Congress helping us."[83]

Full, Full Circle

Congress soon reversed its reversal of the national origin prejudices. The permanent diversity program established in 1995 eliminated the specific 40 percent preference for Ireland and mandated instead 50,000 additional visas for the entire world. Any specific country received a maximum of 3,850 visas; in addition, big senders like Poland, the United Kingdom, and South Korea did *not* qualify for any of the new diversity visas. Overall, Africa got 43 percent of the diversity openings, Europe's share equaled 46 percent, and Oceania got .017 percent of the new diversity visas.[84]

To an outsider, Congress seemed to be drinking. In reality, senators and representatives remained, as in 1965, prisoners of the professed ideals of the American people.

- "Diversity" preferences based on place of birth clashed with our supposed belief in equal opportunity for any and all individuals.

- Affirmative action might make some sense when it helped groups like women, the handicapped, and African Americans. However, affirmative action for Northern Europeans made no sense to Asians who, deliberately excluded for a good part of the twentieth century, still represented less than 4 percent of the American people in 1998.

- If all people are created equal, how can Africa be excluded from the list of world regions providing the immigrant diversity that the United States supposedly requires?

Congress answered these questions by trying, as in 1965, to bring the immigration laws into line with our professed ideals. While the result will undoubtedly be a more colorful America than ever before, instead of a consensus about our immigration ideals, Congress—reflecting the nation—is as confused today as it was in 1965. With one hand it deliberately invites new immigrants from nations like Nigeria and Ethiopia, as it substantially increases (in the 1990s) the number of close relatives permitted to come to America. With its other hand Congress removes (in 1996 legislation) many of the social benefits to which legal immigrants have long been entitled. As a result of these policies, Congress helps create a negative atmosphere against the people whom it is simultaneously inviting to California or New York.

Meanwhile, even though roughly 50 percent of all illegal immigrants first enter the United States legally (e.g., with a student or work-related visa), Congress demanded that the INS focus its efforts on Mexico. The number of Border Patrol agents has tripled (from 2,100 in 1982 to 6,900 as of late 1997), with a full 92 percent of the agents stationed along the Southwest border. As of December 1997, the GAO says there is no evidence that the small army of agents has reduced the illegal flow from Mexico, not to mention the rest of the world.[85]

What shall we do with our America? One contemporary answer is to close the nation's doors and restrict even further the rights of people who are not part of the "white ethnic core." Another is to postpone an answer and first try to understand, besides the policies of Congress, the economic and political factors that propel millions of people to the same place: the United States of America.

NOTES

1. President Lyndon Johnson Library, Austin, Texas, White House Central Files, Legislative Background—Immigration Law, 1965, Box 1, Road to Final Passage, pp. B6–B7.

2. Joel Dyer, *Harvest of Rage: Why Oklahoma City Is Only the Beginning* (Boulder: Westview Press, 1997).

3. U.S. Government Accounting Office, *H-2A Agricultural Guestworker Program*, GAO/HEHS-98-20 (Washington, DC: GPO, December 31, 1997), especially p. 49.

4. See, for example, *Rural Migration News* 4, no. 2 (April 1998): 11; for the same thing only different, see *Migratory Labor*, Hearings Before the Subcommittee on Labor and Labor Management Relations, Senate, 82nd Congress, 1952, especially pages 244–245; for the acceptance of illegal immigrants, see pp. 70–71.

5. U.S. Government Accounting Office, *Illegal Immigration: Southwest Border Strategy*, GAO/GGD-98-21 (Washington, DC: GPO, December 11, 1997), p. 6.

6. Ibid., pp. 22–23; on the number of illegal immigrants, see *Rural Migration News* 3, no. 2 (April 1997): 18; for the percentage of illegal farm workers, see U.S.

Department of Labor, "Legal Status," *A Profile of U.S. Farm Workers* (Washington, DC: GPO, April 1997).

7. *Temporary Admission of Illiterate Mexican Laborers*, Hearings Before the Committee on Immigration and Naturalization, House of Representatives, 66th Congress, 2nd session (Washington, DC: GPO, 1920), p. 80.

8. *Rural Migration News* 5, no. 1 (January 1999): 13, on the Web edition of this exemplary periodical.

9. For the Irish and Polish figures, see *Legal Immigration Reforms*, Hearings Before the Senate Subcommittee on Immigration and Refugee Affairs, 100th Congress, first session (Washington, DC: GPO, 1987), pp. 507–508; for the other figures, see Bob Warren, *Illegal Immigrants in California*, U.S. Commission on Immigration Reform (Washington, DC: GPO, February 21, 1997); pp. 2–3.

10. *Immigration*, Hearings before the Senate Subcommittee on Immigration and Naturalization, 89th Congress, 1st session March 1965, p. 256; for Katzenbach's statement see President Lyndon Johnson Library, White House Central Files, Container 1, Legislative Background—Immigration Law, 1965.

11. Augustín Escobar Latapí, Emigration Dynamics in Mexico, Central America and the Caribbean, *International Organization for Migration*, p. 2, accessed at ⟨www.iom.int/doc/Conference/L.A.html⟩.

12. *Restriction of Immigration*, Hearings Before the Committee on Immigration and Naturalization, House of Representatives, 68th Congress, first session (Washington, DC: GPO, 1924), pp. 96–97.

13. Ibid., p. 107.

14. Ibid.

15. Ibid.

16. Ibid., p. 108.

17. See, for example, the discussion of the races in *Immigration from Latin America, the West Indies and Canada*, Hearings Before the Committee on Immigration and Naturalization, House, 68th Congress, 2nd session, March 3, 1925 (Washington, DC: GPO, 1925).

18. Ibid.; for Johnson's comment, see p. 475; for Vaile's story, see p. 477.

19. See, for example, ibid., pp. 285–315. This was the highly critical testimony of Attorney Louis Marshall; also Dr. Alvin Johnson, Director of the New School for Social Research, pp. 519–523.

20. Ibid., p. 16.

21. Ibid., pp. 286–287.

22. Ibid., pp. 14–16; for a superb history of the legislation and the period, see John Higham, *Strangers in the Land* (New Brunswick, NJ: Rutgers University Press, 1963).

23. Ibid., Higham, p. 324.

24. *Revision of Immigration, Naturalization, and Nationality Laws*, Joint Hearings Before the Subcommittees on the Judiciary, Congress of the United States, 82nd Congress, first session (Washington, DC: GPO, 1951), p. 352.

25. Ibid.

26. Ibid., p. 354.

27. Ibid., p. 353.

28. Ibid., p. 357.

29. See, e.g., Ronald Fernandez, *Cruising the Caribbean: U.S. Influence and Intervention in the Twentieth Century* (Monroe, ME: Common Courage, 1994).

30. *Revision of Immigration, Naturalization and Nationality Laws*, 1951, p. 357; see, too, Robert Pastor, "The Impact of U.S. Immigration Policy on Caribbean Emigration: Does It Matter?" in Barry Levine, ed., *The Caribbean Exodus* (New York: Praeger, 1987), pp. 242–259.

31. *Migratory Labor*, Hearings Before the Subcommittee on Labor and Labor Management Relations, Senate, 82nd Congress, second session (Washington, DC: GPO, 1952), p. 605.

32. President John F. Kennedy Library, Papers of W. Willard Wirtz, Box 92; document is from the Democratic National Committee, "The Gates Must Be Left Open," page 2.

33. Kennedy Library, Oral History Interview with Norbert A. Schlei, 1968, see especially pp. 38–39. Schlei was an important figure in guiding the legislation through Congress. His influence is also apparent from documents at the President Lyndon Johnson Library. Finally his oral history interview matches what he told Congress in the public hearings.

34. Ibid., pp. 38–39.

35. Ibid., p. 39.

36. Ibid.

37. *Kansas City Star*, July 29, 1963; the clipping appears at the Kennedy Library, Papers of Abba Schwartz, Box 6.

38. Ibid., *Bayonne Times*, July 27, 1963.

39. Ibid., Papers of Abba Schwartz, Box 6.

40. Ibid., Box 6. The files contain roughly one hundred editorials and stories about reaction to the president's immigration ideas.

41. Interview with Schlei, p. 38.

42. See, for example, James H. Cone, *Martin and Malcolm: A Dream or a Nightmare* (New York: Orbis Books, 1996), especially chapter 7.

43. Interview with Schlei, p. 36.

44. *Immigration*, Hearing Before the Subcommittee on Immigration and Naturalization, Senate, 89th Congress, first session (Washington, DC: GPO, 1965), pp. 255–256; also, interview with Schlei, p. 36.

45. President Lyndon Johnson Library, Legislative Background—Immigration Law, 1965, Box Number 1; the quotes are from page 41 of "Road to Final Passage."

46. *Immigration*, p. 256.

47. *Immigration*, Committee on the Judiciary, House, Hearings before Subcommittee No. 1, House of Representatives, 89th Congress, first session (Washington, DC: GPO, 1965), p. 54.

48. See Schlei's Congressional Testimony in *Immigration*, Senate, 1965, p. 256.

49. Ibid.

50. *Immigration*, Committee on the Judiciary, House, 1965, p. 23.

51. Ibid., p. 40.

52. Interview with Schlei, p. 40.

53. *Immigration*, Senate, 1965, p. 258.

54. Ibid., p. 267.

55. Ibid., p. 279.

56. Ibid., p. 387.

57. Ibid., p. 389.

58. Ibid., pp. 389–390.

59. Ibid., p. 390.

60. Ibid., pp. 810–811.

61. Ibid., p. 818.

62. See, for example, Peter Brimelow, *Alien Nation: Common Sense About America's Immigration Disaster* (New York: Random House, 1995); for a capsule analysis of the White Identity movement, see Morris Dees, *Gathering Storm* (New York: Harper, 1997), or Jess Walker, *Every Knee Shall Bow* (New York: Harper, 1996).

63. See *Managing Migration in the Twenty-first Century*, edited by Philip Martin, Kai Hailbronner, and Thomas Straubhaar, pp. 10–11; available at migration news, ⟨www.migrationnews.com⟩.

64. President Lyndon Johnson Library, White House Central Files, FG135-9, Box 184; the quotes are from a memo to the president by Norbert Schlei. The memo is dated May 7, 1965.

65. *Immigration*, Committee on the Judiciary, House, 1965, pp. 41–42; for Peter Rodino's comments, see p. 22.

66. Ibid., p. 43.

67. Johnson Library, White House Central Files, Box 184; this is from page 1 of a memo to the president dated May 8, 1965.

68. Ibid., Schlei's memo to the president, dated May 7, 1965, p. 2.

69. Interview with Schlei, p. 40.

70. The numbers were drawn from three sources: *U.S. Immigration Policy and the National Interest*, Final Report of the Select Commission on Immigration and Refugee Policy, March 1981, especially pp. 186–192, reprinted in *Legal Migration Reforms*, Hearings Before the Subcommittee on Immigration and Refugee Affairs, Senate, 100th Congress, first session, 1987; David E. Simcox, ed., *U.S. Immigration in the 1980's* (Boulder: Westview, 1988), pp. 15–17; Roger G. Kramer, *Developments in International Migration to the United States*, the United States report for the Continuous Reporting System on Migration of the Organization for Economic Cooperation and Development, October 28, 1996, esp. p. 10, ⟨www.migration.ucdavis.ed⟩.

71. See, for example, Brimelow, *Alien Nation*, appendix 2.

72. Ibid., p. 10.

73. *Resident Population of the United States, Estimates by Sex, Race and Hispanic Origin*, U.S. Census Bureau (Washington, DC: GPO, September 1997).

74. *Immigration Reform*, Hearings Before the Subcommittee on Immigration and Refugee Affairs, Senate, 101st Congress, first session (Washington, DC: GPO, 1989), p. 2.

75. *Legal Immigration Reforms*, Hearings Before the Subcommittee on Immigration and Refugee Affairs, Senate, 100th Congress, first session (Washington, DC: GPO, 1987), pp. 68–69.

76. Ibid., p. 70.

77. Ibid., pp. 10–11, 118–119.

78. Ibid., p. 11–12.

79. Ibid., p. 180.

80. *Immigration Act of 1989*, Hearings Before the Subcommittee on Immigration, Refugees and International Law, House of Representatives, 101st Congress, first session, September 1989, p. 219.

81. Ibid., p. 604, 626–628.

82. Immigration and Naturalization Service, *Provisions of the Immigration Act of 1990*, p. 3, ⟨www.ins.usdoj.gov/stats/annual/fy95/120.html⟩.

83. *Immigration Act of 1989*, Part One, p. 270.

84. Immigration and Naturalization Service, *Visa Lottery/Diversity Immigrants*, pp. 1–4, ⟨www.streefland.com/lottery.htm⟩.

85. GAO, *Illegal Immigration: Southwest Border Strategy*, pp. 6–7.

2

Empires and Serfs: Migrant Labor in the United States

"It is a form of economic slavery . . . this country is capable of stopping labor traffic in wetbacks if we have the moral will to do it, but that has not been demonstrated to date, and I criticize both governments for this kind of economic slavery."
                                    —Wayne Morse (D., Oregon), Senate, 1952[1]

GOLD AND SILVER PAYROLLS

Who built the Panama Canal? As a boy in a Brooklyn Catholic school, I always got the right answer. Colonel George W. Goethals built the Panama Canal. He did it with such force and intelligence that even though Goethals (and Colonel William Gorgas) needed simultaneously to eliminate yellow fever and malaria, the Canal nevertheless opened ahead of schedule. Nuns devotedly assured my friends and me that in 1914 the world stood in awe before yet another manifestation of American genius.

Excavating the openings for the locks required men to move 175 million cubic yards of earth. Even Goethals couldn't shovel that much dirt, so Secretary of War Taft seriously considered Chinese labor. While Canal officials assured him that coolies had docilely built the railroads that crisscrossed the United States, Taft ultimately decided to reject more temporary Chinese labor. "Peonage or coolieism, which shortly stated is slavery by debt, is as much in conflict with the thirteenth amendment of the constitution as the usual form of slavery."[2]

What to do? With all the force of his commanding personality, President Roosevelt had ordered Taft to "make the dirt fly." The Secretary of War trumpeted a call for Southern Europeans. Canal officials brought in 500

Spaniards who, along with other whites, became the "dependable nucleus" of the Panama labor force. Meanwhile, Negroes acted as the "floating supply" of disposable manpower. But, instead of importing Negroes from the United States, the Roosevelt Administration avoided new charges of slavery by relying on the colonial subjects of the British Empire.

In Jamaica and Barbados the people who literally built the Panama Canal met two types of labor recruiters. In villages throughout the island one fellow rounded up the young men who wanted to make large amounts of money. At the docks the village recruiters received "several dollars" for every able-bodied man they delivered; then, after automatically rejecting those with venereal disease, doctors performed a cursory exam of lungs, eyes, hearts, and joints. If a fellow received a passing grade, canal recruiters moved him to the ship. There he received a new nickname, "decker," because for the five to thirteen days the trip to Colon normally took, the men lived on deck.[3]

Officially Canal recruiters brought 31,000 British subjects to make the dirt fly. Women were supposedly excluded, yet tens of thousands soon joined their husbands, other relatives, and friends. Today, in a potent manifestation of the axiom that there is nothing more permanent then a temporary worker,[4] Panama and other Central American nations still contain "colonies" of West Indian people.

As in the past, tension exists between Panamanians and their guest workers; however, discrimination today pales in comparison to the practices of Goethals and his colleagues. To segregate one group of workers from another, Goethals established "gold" and "silver" payrolls. White Americans, "other" whites, and Panamanians with good jobs were treated like gold. "All other persons not covered above" found themselves on the silver payroll. They received less pay for the same work, their children attended schools that were separate and quite unequal, and the general tenor of Canal relations, well into the 1940s, is best summed up in this remark: "Any Northerner can say 'nigger' as glibly as a Carolinian and growl if one of them steps on his shadow."[5]

This history matters for at least three reasons. One, Americans often read our past through the prism of arrogance and individuality. "What America touches, she makes holy," said Woodrow Wilson,[6] and too often we believe the hype as we render historically *invisible* the consistently indispensable role of invited (and uninvited) immigrants.

A cynic might argue that it is much easier to celebrate Goethals than face his (and his president's) ghastly exploitation of West Indian people. But, whatever the psychological dynamics, the Canal's shadow reaches to states like California, New Mexico, Arizona, and, of course, Texas. As Corpus Christi farmer Fred Roberts told the House of Representatives in 1920, "White men moved into that country and mixed with the Mexicans that were already there . . . we have always enjoyed the privileges of obtaining this labor. We have followed the course of least resistance. We have put an empire in cultivation and made prosperous farms and prosperous farms in that country is based on plenty of labor."[7]

A second significance of the Canal is that, besides Mexicans, many of the ethnic groups most actively disdained in the twentieth century came to the United States because they received an eager invitation from U.S. economic interests. In 1866 many of the Chinese recruited to build the railroads worked all winter in snow tunnels; when jubilant executives celebrated the opening of the transcontinental railroad—"one of the most remarkable engineering feats of the time"—no Chinese received invitations to the ceremonies that celebrated America's achievement.[8]

A large number of the earliest Japanese and Korean immigrants met recruiters who wanted them to stoop and squat, not on vegetable farms in California, but on the sugar plantations of Hawaii. Growers continually played one ethnicity off against the other, so much so that when the United States received Puerto Rico and the Philippines as "war booty" from the Spanish, U.S. growers recruited thousands of Puerto Ricans and Filipinos to compete with the Japanese and Koreans. One result was ethnic conflict; another, wages fit for temporary labor.[9]

Meanwhile, West Indians worked so well in the Canal Zone that, along with farmers, the U.S. government invited thousands of them to help win World War II. Jamaicans harvested cranberries in Wisconsin, manufactured flashlights for soldiers in New Jersey, and cut cane in the Florida Everglades. Soon, men who had had no experience of Southern hospitality traveled in pairs as a shield against hatred. "Interestingly, the strategy worked and through it we gradually began to earn the cooperation, if not the respect, of the white cane growers at Canal Point. They called us 'the smart Jamaican niggers.' "[10]

In 1999 Jamaicans still cut cane in Florida, but they no longer harvest tobacco for Connecticut growers. Dominicans do that work now, while a community of roughly 60,000 West Indians soldiers on in Hartford. Invisible to those who live in the surrounding suburbs, West Indians are nevertheless a source of fleeting interest when, each year, they sponsor parades to celebrate their day of independence from British rule.[11]

A final reason to recall the Canal is a page-one story in the June 15, 1998, edition of the *New York Times*. Titled "Asia's Crisis Upsets Rising Efforts to Confront Blight of Sweatshops," it focuses on "factories that might have emerged from the pages of Dickens." In Far Eastern nations that eagerly imported temporary migrants—Thailand, Korea, and Indonesia—"aliens" compete with the locals. One consequence is people willing to endure any conditions for the biggest paycheck of all, survival.[12]

We are not alone. In Panama in 1910 and Indonesia in 2000, the world is on the move. One United Nations estimate says that, besides the many millions who have already naturalized, 100 million additional people now live outside their countries of citizenship.[13] This is migration with so much force and intensity that to comprehend America, we must first understand the global, the structural forces that continually nurture new (and old) immigrations. Other things being equal, these structural factors insure that the new streams will continue despite the best efforts of even sincere policymakers; moreover, in time, the new streams will become as self-sustaining as the West Indian communities in Connecticut, New York, Florida, and Panama.[14]

PLANES, PARACHUTES, AND PEOPLE

The Italian law seemed so impotent that even a daily dose of Viagra would erect no barriers against immigrants. On November 16, 1995, Prime Minister Lamberto Dini issued an emergency decree giving Italian authorities the right to expel from Italy, within six to ten days, illegal aliens who committed crimes. Officials dutifully served the expulsion orders at once, yet only one-sixth of the illegals agreed to leave the country. That left Italy with a mountain of alien criminals and another half million illegal immigrants on top of the lawbreakers. The political opposition, after loudly trashing the prime minister, offered this solution: Forcibly round up the immigrants, load them on to military transport planes, and, when they were above sending nations like Senegal or Albania, order them to pull the ripcord. These immigrants were parachuting home.[15]

Like so many of the rest of us, politicians have a short memory. Italy, for example, boasted the largest number of recorded emigrants in the world from 1876 to 1976. An estimated 26 million Italians left to live in places like Argentina and Brazil, the United States, and Australia. Cities like Sydney sometimes boasted more residents from a particular Italian village than the village itself; and in 1998 West Germany contains, besides two million Turks and 356,000 Greeks, more than 570,000 Italian immigrants.[16]

Explanations of past and contemporary immigration often begin with what scholars call "push" and "pull" factors. The idea is that variables like joblessness or poverty motivate people to emigrate and a desire for cheap and disposable labor moves host countries to welcome—at least initially—the immigrants. While it's anything but that simple, the push/pull dichotomy nevertheless serves as a point of departure, especially if we reverse course and start with pull instead of push.[17]

Take Europe. Until the mid-1960s more people left Europe than immigrated to it. In the 1950s Europe lost 2.7 million citizens to migration. The 1960s reversed that trend, and in recent decades the figures look like this: In the 1970s, the positive immigration balance (not counting "irregular" residents) reached 1.9 million people, in the 1980s the figure was 1.6 million, and in the 1990s it reached the 1.5 million mark in 1995.[18]

One principal reason people came is that they were invited—by no less than the governments of the host countries. Especially in the 1960s, Germany and France (for example) signed government-to-government agreements with poorer European neighbors; this started the theoretically "temporary" flow of Greeks, Italians, Spanish, and Turkish migrants. In time both agricultural and construction interests, among others, recruited labor "in the colonies." Britain received a large number of West Indians, Belgium saw Moroccans flock to its borders, and France welcomed Algerians. Eventually, Spain's economic successes made it not only a net importer of temporary labor from the Western Sahara, but a principal transit point from Africa to any nation in the European Economic Community.[19]

Europe, the United States, and parts of Asia share many of the structural variables that produce invitations to supposedly temporary immigrants. In an almost unique situation, the United States welcomed more than half a million Puerto Rican immigrants during the 1950s. The situation is peculiar because, even though Puerto Rico is a colony, under U.S. law the Puerto Ricans are not counted as immigrants; they are instead "citizens by statute."[20] These factors include low birthrates in the industrialized nations coupled with a need for more workers in growing economies. Throughout the world the unskilled "temps" do the "dirty, dangerous, and demanding" work that is often shunned by the nationals of countries that have moved up the economic ladder. Thailand, which still occupies a low rung on that ladder, has nevertheless reserved agriculture and fishing jobs for immigrants. Thais "don't do that kind of work."[21]

Another shared experience—linked to the push side of the equation—occurs when nearby countries (e.g., Turkey and Germany, Mexico and the United States, Japan and the Philippines) have high birthrates and much lower rates of prosperity. There then exists a decided advantage for those who seek labor. The temps are cheap and, if illegal, there is no need for employers to pay anything from Social Security to other "required" benefits. Especially in Belgian, French, and U.S. agriculture, the temps are only needed for the short harvest season. As in the building of the Panama Canal, workers "float" in and, with luck, they sink in somebody else's community.[22]

The push side of the equation of course includes poverty; for example, about 10 percent of the Dominican people, 750,000 men, women, children, have migrated since 1985.[23] Yet the push also derives, not "just" from desperation or hunger, but from a man or woman's supposedly laudable desire to "amass capital." Many people come with absolutely no intention of staying. In the literature their label is "sojourner"; it implies a short, pleasant visit, while the reality is a stay that often includes years of hard labor. Studies of Mexican immigrants show that they leave roughly *ninety cents* of every dollar they earn in the United States. In American eyes the 10 percent "profit" is a pittance; to someone with ambition it's a new start in the Old World.[24]

Besides poverty and ambition, people are encouraged to leave home—they are pushed out—by their own governments. In countries like Bangladesh, Jamaica, and the Philippines, high birthrates, linked to the pull from "advanced" economies, make people a superb, plentiful, and relatively inexhaustible natural resource for developing nations. Remittances—the money immigrants send back to their countries of origin—reached $70 billion a year in the 1990s; only oil accounts for more aggregate international and financial transactions.[25] Policymakers in developing nations often want their citizens to leave, send back their earnings, and not return home.

Listen to this story from a colleague in Jamaica. He lived and labored in England—as the decently paid administrator of a social work agency—for many years. He missed home, and he could no longer tolerate the racism he experienced in England on an everyday basis. Lincoln came home, expecting to find a nation that would welcome his financial sacrifice and genuine desire to live with the Jamaican people. Trouble is, officials in the government wanted him to stay abroad. His remittance checks produced more economic growth than his presence in the homeland.

A final point about the push/pull dynamic is this: The global economy changes so quickly it's hard for our everyday conceptions about immigration to maintain a link to reality. For example, the dominant stereotype of a labor immigrant remains that of a poor, uneducated family man. Listen, however, to the February 1998 Congressional testimony of Dr. T. J. Rodgers, president and CEO of the Cypress Semiconductor Corporation. Rodgers wanted the right to "import" more temporary labor but, instead of illiterate peasants, he sought those with advanced education and cutting-edge skills. Fully 37 percent of Cypress's engineers claimed immigrant status; this is "a typical situation at high-tech companies . . . because Cypress cannot find enough skilled workers to fulfill its maximum growth potential." In fact, in an industry survey more than 70 percent of the companies identified the lack of skilled workers "as the leading barrier to their growth and competitiveness."[26]

Back to Yogi Berra! But it's not really déjà vu all over again. Because however much Rodgers sounds like strawberry growers sounding the SOS of potentially rotting crops, the CEO from Silicon Valley is alerting us to a structural variable that now unites push and pull factors at the high end of advanced industrial economies. India, for example, has a number of engineers ready and willing to work abroad; and, using recruiting agencies that do nothing but bring those engineers to California or Paris, Rodgers and global colleagues hire temporary workers, at lower wages. Like the Moroccan in Belgian agriculture, these folks are also disposable; and sometimes they do return home, a burden to no one but the local labor they may displace. But, just as often, the high-tech temps overstay their visas and work for Dr. Rodgers or a variety of other advanced industrial organizations.[27]

All over the globe the demand-pull, supply-push factors are dynamic rather than static; agriculture's need for the unskilled may fall while Microsoft seeks out "Third World" engineers with viable master's degrees. Or, as in California, the demand for low- and high-tech labor may be equally strong. Thus, a policymaker spends billions spitting in the wind of illegal immigration at the border, while thousands of well-educated (initially legal) immigrants smilingly walk through the airport doors. (Recall that roughly 50 percent of all illegal immigrants entered the United States legally.)

Controlling legal and illegal labor migration is much harder than it looks. On the one hand, national and local politicians in search of votes sometimes use the immigrant as a societal punching bag while they simultaneously accept handsome campaign contributions from employers trying to import more legal and illegal immigrants. On the other hand, the push/pull dynamic makes it very difficult for even sincere policymakers to design effective strategies because one variable may lose its effectiveness over time. For example, the legally authorized immigration of hundreds of thousands of Mexicans from 1943 to 1964 has now been replaced by two "new" variables. One is the "informal" (i.e., by word of mouth, under the table) employment recruitment that is found in France as well as the United States. The other is a social network, a variable of such importance that it requires a separate analysis.[28]

NETWORKS

Juan Chanax succeeded. His point of departure was the highlands of Guatemala, his goal the United States. He arrived in Houston, Texas, in 1978, and his hard-working efforts in a local chain of upscale supermarkets so impressed his bosses that they slowly replaced their traditional workers—Chicanos and African Americans—with Mayans from Juan's distant village. "First my relatives came," said Juan, "and then my friends came, and then the friends of my relatives and then the relatives of my friends and then the friends of my friends' relatives came. And now those who remained in Totonicapán are sending their children."[29]

Juan became a one-man employment agency. Apparently the other original staff talked back to customers. If someone treated a clerk with arrogance or condescension, he refused to "take the crap." Mayans were different. They docilely fit the employment description of the supermarket chain—"we hire cheerful servants"—which left the door wide open for the informal recruiting that produced a self-sustaining network of new Mayan migrants.[30]

The network is self-sustaining because, whether it's Algerians in France, Thais in Israel,[31] or Mayans in the United States, the employment network simultaneously increases the dependency of the distant village and the host country employer. With such cheerful servants, why would the supermarket chain hire anyone else but Mayans? With money coming back to the village, people rely on the remittances for survival and/or the much higher standard of living they now enjoy. If the supermarket chain downsizes, that could easily mean *more* people trying to migrate to the United States for the work that sustains their community's "forever-changed" expectations. "People contemplating entry into the labor force literally do not consider other options; they expect to migrate frequently in the course of their lives and assume they can go whenever they wish."[32]

Social networks also create ripple effects that extend beyond the employer and the employee. In developing nations with scarce resources and, as in Mexico, institutionalized corruption, officials tend to neglect areas that survive off remittances from abroad. One result is a village or region that becomes more dependent than ever on labor migration.

Another ripple effect occurs when a network's "monopoly" of work at particular farms, hotels, restaurants, and factories pushes out the local labor force. Say it's a Mexican manager and the language on the factory floor is Spanish; by definition English-only speakers need not apply. Or, since the labor migrants often reduce both wages and an employer's overhead costs (e.g., for a personnel department), they displace the locals who can no longer compete, for example, in cleaning office buildings in Los Angeles. Whatever the case, when the locals are displaced both remittances home and employer dependence increase.[33]

The network feeds on itself. Once established, it fuels migration with a force that can equal the pull/push dynamic. Throughout the world bankers are chasing the remittance money. In the Caribbean local banks compete with Western Union by establishing a network of automatic teller machines in the host and home countries. Western Union is bypassed as the person with money on deposit in New York simply transfers the remittance from one account to another. In Puerto Rico the 75,000 Dominican migrants use Banco Popular's teller machines—at a dollar a shot—to transfer money across the Mona Passage.

An arguably perverse manifestation of the network's ripple effects is one bank borrowing from another, using as collateral next year's remittances. In a deal recently negotiated with a number of European and U.S. investment banks, Banco Nacional de Mexico raised $206 million by "selling" the projected flow of remittances coming into the country via Western Union.[34]

Along with the pull/push dynamic, the networks that exist throughout the world assure legal and illegal labor migration streams to Europe, Asia, and the United States for the foreseeable future. Search for the proverbial chicken and egg in 1999 and you find instead an intermingling of variables that is often impossible to disentangle. However, it is feasible to trace the history of particular immigrant groups. That's essential here because any empathetic answer to the question, What Shall We Do with Our America? depends on an assessment of responsibility and an understanding—to the extent possible—of cause and effect.

It's both senseless and unfair to blame immigrants for contemporary problems if, as with the Turks, Greeks, and Italians in Germany, many of the labor migrants in the United States also received invitations from the central government and a host of eager employers. Moreover, if many of the variables that produce labor migration are at best hard to control, don't we need an overarching consensus that tries to accommodate, not the world we might want, but the one that is actually there?

In the following pages the focus is on Mexican Americans. Accounting for fully 27.2 percent of all U.S. immigrants,[35] Mexican Americans are by far the largest immigrant group in the United States. Their experience in many ways symbolizes that of other labor migrants to the United States. And, most important of all, Mexican Americans are an increasingly integral part of America's future. We ignore their past at our own peril because the enduring significance of Mexican Americans is already a fact of twenty-first-century life.

The First Americans

Nobody knows for sure but the best educated guess is that the word Chicano originated among rural Mexicans who received invitations to the United States—in 1942—from the federal government, from state governments, and from farmers throughout the nation. In truth many of the Mexicans "imported" during the war years actually claimed Indian origins; they spoke "Nahuatl," and when they tried to pronounce "Mexicanos," it apparently came out "Mesheecanos." This was shortened to Chicanos, and in its earliest uses the word carried a heavy load of ridicule; Chicano implied an illiterate mestizo who nevertheless represented, in U.S. eyes, the Mexican people.[36]

In the 1960s political activists in California and elsewhere used their imaginations and intelligence to inject new life into an old word. Chicano became such a badge of pride that men and women, shoulders raised, loudly used it to announce a new reality: A Chicano/a was "a Mexican-American with a non-Anglo image of himself." Chicanos eagerly embraced their Mexican, agricultural roots, and they bitterly resented the arrogance of Anglos who suggested that Chicanos originated in "underdeveloped nations." *Que mierda!* (What a bunch of crap!) Chicanos not only owned a culture that predated the Pilgrims, Chicanos gave life to the Aztecs.[37]

In Aztec mythology priests called the wondrous land of origin Aztlan. It contained groves of trees, along sparkling lakes, rivers and streams. Food arrived on "floating gardens," which gave life to corn, chilies, tomatoes, and beans. Geographically, Aztlan existed somewhere north of Mexico. While nobody knew its exact location, stories of splendor so captured the imagination of the Spanish invaders that, as early as 1524, historians discover the "conquistadors" in Texas, searching for the New World's Garden of Eden.

The Spanish never found Aztlan. The Chicanos did. Identifying the birthplace of the so-called Aztecs with the historical geography of the U.S. Southwest, Chicanos argued that they predated the Aztecs. In essence, since Aztlan apparently existed in what is today California, Arizona, New Mexico, and Texas, Chicanos "redefined themselves" as, simultaneously, the primordial Americans and the original Mexicans.[38]

Not bad for an "underdeveloped" people! And, if we postpone a discussion of Eden, not bad for an accurate analysis of which group came first in the Southwest. President Polk did, after all, acquire states like California as "war booty," and even growers in search of Mexican labor told Congress the truth about the deepest roots of Southwest culture and Southwest prosperity. As one Texas grower lectured the House in 1920, "Our entire industry, beginning, whenever it commenced, back in 1836, is absolutely and unconditionally based upon Mexican labor." And, in the same set of hearings, another stressed that "the Mexican in Texas has been there from the time of the Republic and before we were there."[39]

Finally, consider this 1926 congressional testimony from grower S. Maston Nixon. "If Mexican influence would have ruined a civilization, Texas would have been a Bolshevik Russia years ago, for our state used to be part of Mexico." However, "Texans who are thoroughly familiar with Mexican influence feel satisfied that they are fully capable of maintaining their superiority over the Mexican."[40]

This is a chicken-and-egg argument that can be settled: The Mexicans came first. They lost their original homeland in a war about America's manifest destiny,[41] a destiny that included—then and now—inherently contradictory agendas. On the one hand, politicians assured the American people that they labored under a God-inspired obligation to spread democracy throughout the North American continent. On the other hand, that destiny also included the economic agenda of transforming the conquered lands, that is, the agricultural Southwest.

But, suppose Congressman John C. Box (D., Texas) was correct? In a set of 1921 hearings titled "Imported Pauper Labor and Serfdom in America," Box argued that agricultural interests (and others) "wanted all restrictions removed which hinder the importation of alien laborers." Growers "want to bring the most ignorant, who are most easily handled 'like cattle' . . . and that which is bound to them or their customers or their industries, by contracts and conditions and practices destroying freedom and creating a kind of serfdom."[42]

Serfdom! In America! These were strong charges, especially from a Texas Congressman speaking in a Washington, D.C., building not far from the Lincoln Memorial. Box's colleagues nevertheless listened as he explained the inherent contradiction of promising freedom and democracy yet developing the Southwest via the servitude of illiterate migrants whom growers treated like cattle. As a courtesy, Congressman Box received permission to present the evidence; however, with great civility, his colleagues disregarded his assessment of the social status of Mexican immigrants.

By 1926, with more and more serfs entering the United States every day, Congressman John Box energetically sponsored legislation that threatened to seriously restrict the import of "alien labor."

The Congressional hearings that criticized the Box bill are important history for at least two reasons. One, they include—75 years ago—growers seeking *even more* Mexican labor for a wide variety of states—Minnesota and California, Texas and Iowa, Arizona and Michigan, Colorado, Wyoming, and Montana. Two, these hearings include Congress's answer to a question posed by farmer C. S. Brown of Phoenix, Arizona, in 1926. "Every race of people, either semi-civilized or uncivilized, would have sometime become civilized if they had not at some period of their development been stunted. And we feel, gentlemen, *that there has been born in the West an infant Empire. We feel that you are its legitimate father, now what shall we do?* Shall we let it grow up a dwarf, a hunchback, or shall we develop it to its full stature?" (emphasis added).[43]

Congress said, "Let it be a giant." And the giant grew to unparalleled proportions because of the people from Aztlan. Forget that, and you accept a myth—"Americans practice what they preach"—that will make it very hard for all of us to live together in the twenty-first century.

Serfdom in America

Let's start with the paternity suit. Farmer Brown argued that Congress fathered the development of Arizona agriculture because federal officials first funded and then engineered the Roosevelt reservoir. Brown said that, thanks to Congress, farmers in Arizona could now "warehouse our surplus water and the water that was used to destroy our crops and our dams and our river beds is now orderly marketed to ourselves through a process of cooperation with you and the government."[44]

In Europe citizens called that kind of cooperation socialism. In the United States it was government support for the free enterprise farmer. Brown, for example, told the House that "that little act of yours, gentlemen, aided us in transforming 260,000 acres of desert land into orchards and vineyards, fields of head lettuce, winter peas, cantaloupes, and other types of horticulture."[45]

This sounded like the "floating garden" of Atzlan. However, in Arizona the green garden subsidized by Uncle Sam could easily wither and die without stoop and squat labor. Farmer Brown stressed that while he pleaded with locals to work his fields, "white people" not only refused to pick for the wages offered, "they won't pick it at all." Brown needed Mexicans, and he argued that his labor needs always trumped the fears expressed by Chair (of the House Committee on Immigration and Naturalization) Albert Johnson. "I am in mortal fear that the United States will come all too soon to tenant farming and the creation of a peasantry of its own. I see that coming on, and as I think of it I realize that the Nation . . . cannot hope to escape the farm situations of the old country."[46]

Johnson's concerns masked a reservoir of crocodile tears. Call it a peasantry or an army of old-world serfs; either way, many Mexicans working in agriculture came to the United States via a huge loophole in the 1924 immigration law. Caving in to the demands of employers all over America, Johnson and his colleagues had defined Mexicans who crossed the border for a "temporary" stay as non-immigrants. Forget the visa. Just present a plausible explanation to the border patrol and you not only got into the United States, border officers happily facilitated your next visit by issuing "crossing cards" to you, the wife, and the kids. Just show the card the next time you entered the United States and there was no stopping at go. Pass right on to the fields of Farmer Brown, the mines in Pennsylvania, and the factories in Chicago.[47]

Since Johnson and his colleagues had said yes to "temporary" labor in 1924, farmers argued that the House of Representatives must now prevent the restrictions threatened by Congressman Box. Representing the Fresno County Chamber of Commerce, S. P. Frisselle declared that, like their colleagues in Arizona, farmers dutifully worked with the Department of Agriculture, "as well as our President." They had opened new lands to crops and diversified their produce "by following out the plans laid down" by officials of the federal government. Now, that same government wanted to take away with one hand what it had given with the other. "We must have, gentlemen, and we cannot exist without, manpower. . . . diversified farming needs must have manpower to succeed. Without it we will go back to the grain fields and the tractor."[48]

Frisselle sympathized with fears expressed by Congressman Box. In fact, sounding like California Governor Pete Wilson when he campaigned for Proposition 187 in 1995, Frisselle said that he appreciated the "social problem" that accompanied Mexican labor. "It is a serious one. It comes into our schools, it comes into our cities and it comes into our whole civilization in California." However, despite the "Mexican problem," Frisselle offered this bottom-line assessment of agriculture's government-assisted predicament. "We, gentlemen, are just as anxious as you not to build the civilization of California or any other western district upon a Mexican foundation. We take him because there is nothing else available. We have gone east, west and north and south and he is the only manpower available to us."[49]

While typical of the testimony offered in 1926,[50] these words are nevertheless a hard read. Frisselle openly and easily expressed his ugly mix of prejudice and cynicism because that was the conventional wisdom of the farmers and farm organizations represented in these hearings. For example, when one congressman asked if Frisselle favored "lifting the ban on the Japanese," the farmer said no. "The Japanese does not want to work for anybody else. He wants to work his own farm. In that he differs from the Mexican."

The Congressman pushed, "You say that the Japanese are inclined to become permanent residents and home owners, and that is what you want, and they are skilled laborers and that is what you want. Why is it, then, that they are not satisfactory?"[51]

Part of the answer involved raw prejudice. Frisselle agreed that farmers refused to accept Japanese people as permanent settlers in California.[52] But, even if the antipathy against the Japanese never existed, their skills and education still made them inappropriate for the needs of "diversified" agriculture. Above all, farmers sought a plentiful pool of cheap, unskilled, disposable labor to do the dirty, demanding, and dangerous work that anyone with a choice avoided like the plague.

Throughout the hearings farmers and representatives complained about the lure of the cities. Congressman Vincent moaned that "we get in laborers, we give a preference to farmers but the economic condition between the city and the country is such that it is just like a sponge. It takes these people to the city and then you are back with the same problem you had before, because they have gone to live in the city."[53]

However unintentionally, Congressman Vincent echoed the frustrations and complaints of farmers. In a nutshell, the nation faced a vicious dialectic. The partnership of government and agriculture helped farmers open new lands to new stoop and squat crops. That fueled the need for more Mexican labor but, in a theme that runs through these hearings, urban mining, railroad, and industrial interests lured workers from the fields. Migration to the cities therefore exacerbated the already dire need for labor, which was further exacerbated by the farmers' desire to make even more profits from the government/agriculture partnership.

Grower Nixon explained that in order for the agricultural empire to reach its full potential, Texas requested the government's help to put another 1.25 million acres of land in production. Problem was, "on this land there is a heavy growth of mesquite trees and various thorny undergrowth that require grubbing before the plow can be used . . . the land must be grubbed and the Mexican laborer is the only man that we have found that is adapted or will do this work."[54]

Follow Nixon's advice, and you put more pressure on the migrant labor supply, which already experienced great pressure from the success of government assistance and the perpetual lure of cities offering better-paying and/or less back-breaking jobs. In truth, only one thing temporarily helped the farmer to resolve his problems: more "temporary" Mexican labor. From all over the nation, farmers demanded that Congress vote down the restrictions proposed by Congressman Box. For anyone who harbored moral qualms about the use of serfs, Fred Cummings of Fort Collins, Colorado, offered this philosophical assessment: "There is always a class of labor that must be done by ignorant people . . . there is one class of people who do the work and another to supervise. The white people will not do this back work."[55]

White people did this; black people did that. But Mexicans, a distinctive mix of black and white, never fit into the racial dichotomy that dominated American thought. Mexicans therefore became an amorphous mass of "others." As laborers, Mexicans were turned by farmers and the U.S. government into serfs; as people, Mexicans were turned by the nation into something worse—a group so far outside the mental mainstream that Mexicans were, well, almost something.

Whatever their racial and ethnic status, Mexican workers got "pulled" into the United States by powerful economic and political interests. Poverty and politics (e.g., the Mexican revolution and its aftermath) certainly provided a platform from which people willingly moved to the United States but, as these hearings argue, the U.S. dialectic that ceaselessly fueled the need for more temporary labor already existed in 1926.

Also in existence were the beginnings of the social networks that gave additional, *independent* impetus to the movement of people. Records of money orders wired in July-August of 1926 show that Mexicans sent more than 23,000 "checks" totaling more than $2.5 million dollars in these two months; the figure for the year exceeded $13 million. California and Texas migrants sent the largest number of money orders, but substantial activity also occurred in Illinois, Indiana, Pennsylvania, Michigan, New York, Kansas, and Oregon.[56] The lure of the cities—and the ability to find work—was already a demonstrated fact of U.S. life in 1926. To further fuel the fires of Mexican migration Congress rejected the restrictions suggested by Congressman Box. Farmers got the workers they needed and, simultaneously, the general public received assurances that Congress meant to stop the workers to whom they had just given a green light.

Workers crossing the border got a label: "legal" or "illegal." Both types of migrants immediately received a job in a mine in Pennsylvania or a farm in Colorado, and the number of legal and illegal migrants was often the same. But, by using the label "illegal," Congress underlined who did—and who did not—possess cultural as well as political power.

The everyday meaning of the word illegal suggests someone—later a "wetback"—"who has entered the United States breaking the U.S. laws with the main purpose of doing something that will represent a cost or burden to the American people."[57] Forget that farmers repeatedly testified that the survival of Southwest agriculture depended on Mexican labor. Label the Mexican a criminal, and the moral onus shifted to the other side of the Rio Grande; meanwhile, a police force offered a public relations shield for those Americans who never approved the U.S. government's approval of Mexican labor migration.

Enter the border patrol. They caught the "bad guys," they did it in a way that, thanks to Congress, rarely interfered with Farmer Brown's need for labor. Testifying in 1928, Grover C. Wilmuth (District Director of Immigration, El Paso, Texas) explained the actual workings of the border patrol. You had your "local crossers" who lived in places like Juarez and worked in El Paso. Crossers came and went on a daily basis; they had visas and obeyed the laws.

Besides the crossers, Wilmuth also talked about regular immigrants. They possessed a visa and, like the crossers, they paid a head tax to work in the United States. But, instead of staying near the border, they went to Illinois, Indiana, or wherever else they could find work.

Category three—temporary visitors—was the class that generated the most interest from Congress. The 1924 law said that these "non-immigrants" received permission to enter the U.S. if they planned to conduct business or visit friends and relatives in America. Farm or other work was forbidden, but Congressman Schneider of Wisconsin didn't buy Wilmuth's explanations. So, "the fact of the matter is that this visiting immigrant from Mexico at the present time, who comes in as a visiting immigrant, does not come for that purpose at all but comes in here for the purpose of working and evading paying the head tax. Is that not true?"

Wilmuth: "With a goodly proportion of them that is true."

Schneider: "A great percentage of them?"

Wilmuth: "Yes, sir."[58]

Wilmuth also explained what happened when he and his colleagues actually apprehended an illegal Mexican immigrant. To avoid paying the required costs of transporting the person back to Mexico, Wilmuth permitted workers to "voluntarily return" to Mexico. But suppose, said Congressman Brigham, "the alien does not voluntarily return?" Wilmuth "turned him loose." You mean "turn him loose in the country?" "Absolutely," said Wilmuth, and that wasn't the worst of it.

In the final quarter of any year Wilmuth's deportation account lacked funds. If he picked up say 25 illegals, Wilmuth asked them to return, but if they refused, he just let them head on in.[59]

Congressman Vincent seemed surprised. Suppose, via the network, word got out that you once again lacked money? Wouldn't that start a year-end stampede of illegals? Vincent answered his own query with this apt summary of the situation of Mexican labor migrants in the 1920s: "The very fact that you had, say, a dozen Mexicans herded in some place and that you gave them a chance to go back to Mexico and they said they would not go, and then you very politely turned them loose, that would indicate to their mind that there was a screw loose somewhere, would it not?" Wilmuth replied, "Yes, sir; that is a natural inference."[60]

Economic Slavery*

Writers use a number of metaphors to portray the passage of people through time. History is a river that ebbs and flows. It's a circle that endlessly repeats itself. History is a mirror: Look into it and you may or may not like what you see.

One metaphor that comes to mind when an American analyzes the congressional history of Mexican labor migration to the United States is "toxic pool." Senators and congressmen routinely use words like slavery to describe the Mexican situation,[61] but as the century moves on, the man-made pool of toxic policies gets deeper and deeper. It is a bottomless pit that has never received federal environmental protection.

On November 23, 1942, Laurence Hewes, the regional director of the Farm Security Administration, told the Senate about a recent trip to Mexico. Along with representatives from a variety of other federal agencies, Hewes "took part in the formulation of a program for the selection and transportation of Mexican nationals to work as agricultural labor in the Western States."[62] No less than President Avila Camacho agreed to a binational accord that theoretically provided Mexicans with a variety of labor rights on the job as well as "guarantees of transportation, living expenses and repatriation." Meanwhile, U.S. farmers no longer needed to worry about losing workers to the war effort or better jobs. Recruited with help from two governments, Mexican workers signed a contract whose first provision was this: "The worker will be employed exclusively in agricultural work."[63]

Hewes happily reported that the first trainload of Mexican nationals arrived in Stockton and Sacramento on September 30. "It was a long trip— 42 hours from Mexico City to Juarez and another 48 hours to Stockton. The men went to work on the first day of October, I believe."[64]

The first "braceros" (from the Spanish *brazo*, for "arm") inaugurated a program that legally admitted the legally inadmissible![65] In giving its imprimatur to *contract labor*, Congress discovered a problem of its own making, the Anti-Alien Contract Labor Law of 1885. Sponsored by groups like the Knights of Labor, this fifty-seven-year-old law rested on a sharp distinction between voluntary migration and the shipment, "as so many cattle, of large numbers of degraded, ignorant, brutal . . . foreign serfs." As America wanted none of the latter, the legislation explicitly forbid the entry of more, especially Chinese coolies, on American soil.[66]

Congress squared this circle by discovering a loophole in the 1917 immigration law. The small print—Proviso Nine of Section Three—gave the attorney general the right to "issue rules" that could admit "otherwise inadmissible aliens." In 1942 this translated into an order to the INS: "For

---

As a small step toward redefining the issue of Mexican migration I will, for the remainder of this book, use the phrase "unauthorized migrant" in place of "illegal migrant."

Braceros in the United States

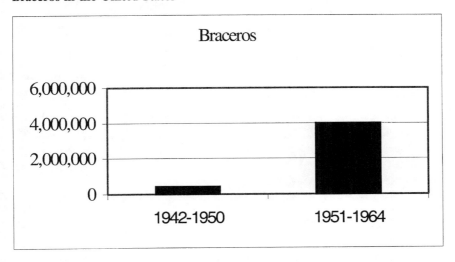

such time and under such conditions" as the commissioner deemed appropriate, the INS could admit the inadmissible.[67]

Even into Texas. Under the terms of the bilateral agreement the Mexican government stipulated that braceros could not work in the Longhorn State. Besides horrible working conditions, many Texans discriminated against Mexicans—in schools, stores, restaurants—with all the force used against African Americans. The Mexican government said no, but in 1943 the INS nevertheless helped recruit as many as 1,500 workers a day for Texas growers.[68]

Complaints from the Mexican government eventually stopped this INS recruitment of migrant workers for Texas. However, in a variety of forms, a contract labor program designed to provide temporary workers during World War II lasted through the early years of the Vietnam War. From 1942 to 1950, over 430,000 workers signed on as twentieth-century "chattel."[69]

From 1951 to 1964 the number of braceros skyrocketed faster than Sputnik I. Fully four million men and women[70] entered in little more than a decade. As in the 1920s, they refused to stay on the farms when the lure of unauthorized work in the cities continued to beckon. As Senator Aiken of Vermont warned his colleagues in 1952, any law that absolved farmers of responsibility for hiring illegal workers must also absolve employers in the cities. Why? "Because I have a suspicion that there may be more aliens illegally employed in the cities of the United States than there are on the farms."[71]

While the dialectic of the 1920s continued unabated, the fuel for the massive march of migrants still came from agriculture. Beginning in 1947, when the wartime law expired, farmers flocked to Washington and made

their case for the continuation of a good thing: an army of workers brought
to their gates, not by smugglers or hired agents, but by officials of the U.S.
Immigration and Naturalization Service.[72]

Listen, for example, to George Pickering, president of the Yuma Producers Cooperative Association, in 1949: "During the war the War Food Administration brought them in and delivered them to us, took care of them,
and when we were through with them, they took them away." In 1949 the
INS provided the workers, but whatever government agency got the job
done, "our need for these Mexicans is acute." Domestic workers refused to
labor in Pickering's fields because "the type of crops we raise, especially the
vegetables, require a lot of stoop labor. That is men who stoop over and
work with a little short-handled hoe. They thin these crops, hoe them for
weeds and harvest them stooping over."[73]

In California the issue was heat. Agricultural Commissioner B. A. Harrigan testified, "I have lived in Imperial County for a good many years. I can
say that historically the desert areas have depended *entirely* on the Mexicans
to stand the intense heat in those areas" (emphasis added). Unfortunately
Mexicans sometimes "got too old to do stoop labor" and their children took
skilled and unskilled jobs in the cities. Thus, "about every twenty years . . .
we find it necessary to have a new blood transfusion, so to speak, to get a
new supply of stoop labor."[74]

If nothing else, B. A. Harrigan was an honest man, making his case to a
Congress that never hesitated to provide something as lifesaving as a blood
transfusion. Not to be outdone, the INS went a step further and actually
performed medical magic throughout the Southwest. In the 1949 agreements
between Mexico and the United States, one provision requested that, in
hiring new braceros, preference be given to unauthorized Mexicans *already
working* in the United States.

Cynics called this operation "drying out the wetback." Whereas the 1942
agreements accepted the admission of inadmissible contract labor, the 1949
accords meant to legalize workers who already had admitted themselves!
Meanwhile, via the network grapevine, word got out that the easiest way to
get legal contract work was to go illegal. Cross the border, let the INS know
your status, and, presto, you joined family and friends whom the INS had
also dried out. Thus, between 1947 and 1949, almost twice as many unauthorized Mexicans—already working in the United States—became braceros
as those who were actually "imported" from Mexico for temporary work.[75]

Once again, somebody had a "screw loose." Legislators like Senator Paul
Douglas of Illinois urged his colleagues to go to the source: Hold employers
responsible for their behavior and put them in jail for a year "for each alien
in respect to whom any violation" of the proposed law occurred.

This suggestion did little to effectively sever the structural roots of the
pull/push/network dialectic. Even when all the legal ducks were in order,
the government's postwar support for the bracero contract labor program

significantly increased the dependence of U.S. employers on Mexican migrants and, simultaneously, the dependence of Mexican villages on the wages braceros earned. As in the 1920s the process fed on itself.[76]

Douglas nevertheless scared employers throughout the Southwest. Growers with substantial farms faced a century or more in jail for hiring unauthorized immigrants. By labeling both farm and city employers as criminals, Douglas forthrightly challenged America's conventional wisdom about Mexican migration. In the words of Senator Hubert Humphrey, "We have been so used to bleeding the people of Mexico for cheap labor that it has become a habit for some people."[77]

Humphrey actually argued, "I think that the Government is a party to a crime that is going on."[78] This was radical indeed. Before employers assumed any responsibility for their behavior, they had friendly senators pull a fast one on their colleagues. As Senator Aiken noted, "I have had no opportunity to read the bill; but, with the assurances that its (employer) provisions are equitable, I have no objection."[79]

THE MIDCENTURY WATERSHED

Point man for this legislative sleight of hand was Senator Mark Kilgore of West Virginia. On February 5, 1952, he stressed the need for expeditious passage of a bill recently amended by the Department of Agriculture, INS officials, and the agricultural organizations. "The bill was really drafted by them," and the Senate had to pass it because new agreements between the United States and Mexico could not be signed until the Senate agreed with changes made by those seeking to avoid "a very severe hardship" for farmers.

Senator Lehman seemed angry. When Kilgore remarked that "perhaps the distinguished Senator from New York has not read all the provisions of the bill?" Lehman answered, "I could not have read all of it because I did not see the bill until a few minutes ago."[80] Senator Douglas called Kilgore's request "a most incredible situation"; the bill, "which is hot off the press, so to speak," said it was a felony to "harbor" an illegal alien but not a felony to hire an illegal alien "if the normal practices of the employment are followed."[81]

This sounded like the doublespeak of George Orwell's recently published book, *1984*. You could hire a person, house him, and feed him—but that was not harboring, because the employer "does not make any special effort to conceal him." Kilgore understood that his distinction seemed hard to discern, but he nevertheless believed that the Senate had no right "to punish employers who were used to a long practice of carelessness which we had allowed to develop."[82]

By this reasoning two wrongs made a right—or at least the farmer's right to hire unauthorized aliens in the normal fashion. For example, Kilgore noted that "practically every State in the Union has had the wetback problem

. . . because they are wetbacks *they can be kept in a state of peonage*" (emphasis added).[83] The way to end the peonage was to allow farmers who had hired illegals in the past to continue doing it in the present. "The mere fact of having them in his employment shall not, under the meaning of the words, be classed as harboring."[84]

History calls this exception to the rule "the Texas proviso." In reality Kilgore slipped through provisos. The bill drafted by the trinity of the Department of Agriculture, the INS, and agricultural interests also changed the rules about who could issue a warrant to search a farm or factory. Kilgore said the bill as originally drafted used the term "supervisory personnel." That meant officers familiar with a particular locale or a particular employer could issue their own search warrants. In the Kilgore version of the law only the four district directors of the INS and their three assistants could issue a warrant. In addition, the warrants needed to precisely specify "the time of day or night at which the warrant may be executed."[85]

Senator Humphrey then emphasized, for the record, that the changes "severely limited" any chance the bill had to deal effectively with the "wetback problem." Just that morning he listened to Archbishop Robert Lucey, of San Antonio, Texas, "testify about the miserable, deplorable conditions which exist in the migratory-labor field; it is something which is shocking and revealing."[86]

Just as revealing were the workings of the United States Senate. Humphrey, for example, added to his remarks with this: "The wetback problem stands as a blight and a shame on the American Republic." Then, after more of the same, the senator said, "Mr. President, I have no objection to the consideration of this bill."[87]

Senator Paul Douglas, however, threatened to submit an amendment stipulating that employers who hired unauthorized aliens committed a felony. This was "too strict" for Senator McFarland of Arizona. He understood the objections of his "distinguished friend" from Illinois, but would his friend please grasp that "the bill was taken up by the Senate today with the understanding, of course, that it would be passed as it is and there would not be a great deal of controversy."[88]

Douglas nevertheless submitted his amendment, with this final score: 69 against the amendment and 12 for some semblance of decency in a body that had just overwhelmingly endorsed continued peonage for the next generation of Mexican migrants.[89]

In public the INS ballyhooed Operation Wetback, a program that in 1954 deported more than one million Mexican migrants. Americans watching "Uncle Miltie" on TV could presumably feel secure because the wetbacks had been turned back; meanwhile, Uncle Sam helped bring in an average four hundred thousand braceros a year between 1955 and 1960.[90] These men came as additions to the hundreds of thousands of unauthorized Mexicans who continued to be hired (but never harbored). In the 1950s, the cycle of

Sustaining Dependency on Mexican Labor

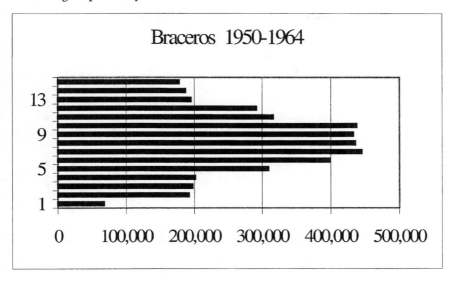

dependency between farmers and migrants thus continued with more force than ever.

While the statistics are important, they can numb us to the experience of the migrant and to the gargantuan greed and inhumanity of America's empire builders. This line is written after a long examination of the senatorial papers of Lyndon Johnson. All files are available at the President Johnson Library in Austin, Texas. They contain box after box of telegrams and letters virtually all pleading for the same thing: Keep the braceros coming, and keep the bloody Department of Labor off our backs.

Two communications, almost a decade apart, indicate the growers' single-minded pursuit of their needs. The first is a 1951 editorial called "A Mistaken Look." It appears under a picture of a straw-hatted bracero stooping to pick cotton in a Texas field. The unnamed editorialist lashed out at *Look Magazine*, which had printed an article sympathetic to workers. The diatribe sent to Johnson stressed that you "could pay five dollars a hundred and still couldn't get enough of the so-called organized labor to pick one bale of valley cotton." As only the Mexicans would do it, "We wish Look and labor and congress and the immigration department all would take a vacation for the next three months. We've got to get our cotton picked."[91]

When federal authorities tried to take the fingerprints of those cotton pickers, the men and women's hands often contained so many scratches that their prints were "unclassifiable." Cotton picking had temporarily erased an indelible part of the Mexican's humanity.[92]

The second example is a letter written to Senator Johnson on April 9,

1958, that originated in Muleshoe, Texas. W. T. Millen wanted to "figure out some way to get Mexican Bracero Labor." He told Johnson that he had "steady native labor the year around." But what about picking periods? "It would not be feasible to uproot men and families from big cities such as Dallas just to take care of our labor problems during peak seasons."

It would be very expensive and we do not have the proper housing facilities to accommodate them besides. With the Bracero labor we can procure them as we need them, and can put several hands in a room that would not accommodate a family. They will do a type of work such as irrigating and hand labor that the American who is used to high wages will not do . . . it seems ironical to us, the farmer . . . to be forced by organized labor, to hire men that have priced themselves out of business, thereby creating greater hardships on the farmer.

So please see if something can be done to right this injustice being imposed on the farmer.

Your friend,
W.T. Millen
Pres. Bailey Co. Farm Bureau[93]

Permanent Non-Permanent Residents

Secretary of Labor Willard Wirtz took pride in his successful efforts to terminate the bracero program. Years of lobbying had produced not only the cessation of government-sponsored contract labor in 1964, but as Wirtz saw it, the actual end of migratory workers as a part of U.S. life.

In a confidential report sent to the White House in October of 1966, Secretary Wirtz made his case to the president. "The ultimate structure of a Great Society has no place in it for a roving group of a million and a half people spending their lives moving from one part of the country to another." This "kind of life" destroyed any chance for assimilation because it eliminated any chance for a sense of community. In addition, "it made family life an impossibility or a nightmare"; it provided no opportunity for the proper education of children and that "engrained" the poverty that undermined any chance for a Great Society.[94]

The good news appeared in the form of a prediction: "Migratory labor will taper off rapidly as a source of agricultural labor supply and will virtually disappear within the next ten to fifteen years."[95] Wirtz partially based his prediction on an understandable faith in technology. For example, as the bracero program came to a halt, the Department of Agriculture used federal and state funds to subsidize university research focusing on the mechanization of the tomato industry. This succeeded so brilliantly that in one decade California tomato growers did a gigantic about face. In 1960 "all processing tomatoes were picked by hand; in 1970 none were."[96]

Wirtz made sense. He reasoned that growers forced to pay higher wages because of a reduced or unreliable labor supply would use machines to eliminate people. In the short term the capital costs seemed excessive; but in the long term the growers assured themselves of both profits and workplace peace of mind.

The rub was the real world. Suppose, for example, that nobody ever enforced the already weak sanctions against employers who hired unauthorized workers. Suppose that farmers used labor contractors over and under the table to provide workers who received, at best, verbal guarantees of their rights and wages. Finally, suppose that the U.S. government permitted an abundant supply of both authorized and unauthorized labor to cross the border and break the farmworker strikes that could have produced the changes Wirtz predicted?

Under these conditions, farmers could go either way. Mechanize? Use the Mexicans? It was a judgment call so quickly decided in favor of the Mexicans that Senator Walter Mondale held hearings in 1969. Titled "Migrant and Seasonal Farmworker Powerlessness," the hearings suggested that, instead of the mechanized future predicted in Washington, workers would experience a world with sharp echoes of the Texas provisos of 1952.

Mondale spoke at his own hearings. Explaining a trip to the Mexican-American border, the senator discussed baptismal certificates as proof of U.S. citizenship. "I had never heard of this until I went down to the border myself and stood and watched people come across. Forty-five percent of them produced baptismal certificates and they are coming through there so fast that if they bothered to check one out of every 20 of them, they would have Mexicans backed up to Mexico City."[97]

James Hennessy, the executive assistant to the director of the INS, agreed that "a baptismal record is obviously not the best primary proof of birth in the United States." This was especially so when the certificates looked as fresh as just-printed counterfeit money! Mondale said, "I saw persons 18 or 20 years of age, who had crisp baptismal certificates. A Catholic priest told me it was a major problem in and around the border area."[98]

It was not only a major problem. It was a major business. The INS actually established a "fraudulent documents center" to serve as a "repository for documents used by Mexican aliens to support false claims to U.S. citizenship." In 1969 Hennessy offered no indication of the number of counterfeit documents in the agency's possession, but he did say, "For the seventh consecutive year there was an increase in the number of claims to false citizenship encountered by the border patrol."[99]

This admission moved Senator Murphy of California to ask if more fraud occurred after the end of the bracero program. Hennessy reminded the senator that during the twenty-some years of the contract labor system, many Mexicans were in fact born in the United States. After the "large wetback drive occurred in the 1950's" these folks returned to Mexico, and the use of baptismal certificates made some sense from that perspective. Presumably they were born in America, yet baptized at home.

While Hennessy never actually answered the question about rates of fraud, he did reluctantly admit that the wetback problem appeared worse than ever.[100] In truth, the only thing wet about the mass march of migrants witnessed by Senator Mondale was the ink on their baptismal certificates. The INS seemed to be working for the growers, especially when researchers announced these astounding statistics: Of the real U.S. citizens who crossed the Mexican border, fully 34 percent *"had never lived in the United States."* Of the real green-card holders (i.e., the supposedly permanent resident aliens), 44.6 percent had *"never lived in the United States."*[101]

These figures represented the latest manifestation of the "commuters" first perceived in 1926. However, by 1969, the INS included so many perks for Mexican commuters that farmers got what they always wanted: seasonal help who left when they finished their work. In this environment growers with savvy saw no reason to mechanize.

Consider for example the "permanent nonpermanent resident." The phrase is admittedly confusing but not nearly as perplexing as INS enforcement of its own rules and regulations. The INS gave green cards to individuals who it knew would never live in the United States. This was the permanent nonpermanent resident. Then, in a unique manifestation of the relative pyramiding feared by Congress in 1924, the INS allowed cardholders "to secure visas for members of their families, even though no one has any current plans to live in the United States."[102]

Add up the exceptions—the newly baptized, the nonresident citizens, the permanent nonpermanent resident aliens, their relatives, and the relatives of their relatives—and you get a good idea why farmers saw no reason to use machines instead of people. Remember, too, that despite the INS green light to the green-card holders, unauthorized immigrants continued to arrive with such force that by 1977, the INS apprehended almost as many illegal aliens (1,033,427) as it did when the all-time high was achieved in 1954 (1,089,583).[103]

Some congressmen screamed "uncle." Peter Rodino, chair of the House Judiciary Committee, said in 1975, "This wholesale violation of the law disrupts the legal and orderly flow of aliens into the United States, and threatens the integrity of our system of immigration."[104]

What integrity? In concert with growers and a *wide variety* of other employers (e.g., hotels, restaurants, construction firms), the INS parted the waters at the Mexican border by waving through the mass of migrants waving absurdly fraudulent documents. Meanwhile, whenever the chorus of criticism reached serious proportions, Senator James Eastland (chair of the Senate's Judiciary Committee) refused even to hold hearings. For example, with support from President Nixon and President Ford, congressional critics demanded the serious employer sanctions first suggested by Senator Paul Douglas in 1952. But, instead of trying to ram through a bill no one read, under Eastland the senators received nothing except the stone wall of silence erected by a senator who grew even more cotton than the constituents writing to Senator Lyndon Johnson.[105]

By 1981 congressmen like Dan Lungren of California openly admitted the truth: "I grew up in Southern California. I can tell you the number of people who have undocumenteds working in their neighborhood, who have them working in their companies. *I don't happen to come from an agricultural area so I don't know about that.* But to me the joke we play on the American people and the joke we play on the person here legally is to pretend the problem doesn't exist. It exists all over" (emphasis added).[106]

Mexicans even received an invitation from Mickey Mouse! Disneyland was chock full of unauthorized workers.[107] Congress therefore faced at least two very different options. It could try to achieve a measure of social harmony by asking the nation to face up to its own contradictions and hypocrisies. Or, Congress could try to stop the migration that, as Congressman Lungren argued, was both desired and institutionalized.

Congress chose to stop the migration. Serious efforts began in 1981 but no legislation reached the floor of Congress until employers received assurances that the Texas provisos would be replaced by a series of affirmative actions. Chambers of commerce from throughout the nation had converged on Washington, demanding that employers not be held accountable for "unknowingly" hiring illegal workers.[108]

In 1952 you could hire but never harbor. After 1986, you could hire with no question of harboring because the new law—the Immigration Reform and Control Act—released employers from any obligation to check the authenticity of documents presented by new workers. Confronted by an INS agent, the employer simply presented his or her "affirmative defense," which went something like, "I filled out the required paperwork. The documents looked real. What do you want from me?"

Employers didn't stop there. As in 1926 the INS received so little funding for enforcement that in 1988 it checked out less than one-fifth of 1 percent of the nation's employers. Even then, the INS never wanted to appear too aggressive. Thus, "in order to demonstrate that the INS is not engaging selective enforcement of the law," fully 25 percent of the "raids" occurred on a random basis. Critics instantly pointed out that tips, leads, and investigations might be a better way to catch employers; in an apparent response the INS increased to 40 percent the number of random raids.[109]

Criminologists note that for laws to work as a deterrent to crime, officials must link the severity of punishment to the certainty of enforcement. One without the other is a cart without a horse. Thus, as with the legislation passed in 1952, the Immigration Control and Reform Act contained so many enforcement loopholes that wags suggested a person had a better chance of winning the lottery than being arrested for hiring illegal workers.

Meanwhile, the 1986 law also guaranteed more Mexican immigrants than ever before. It did this by "drying out" two different groups of anauthorized workers. The first included 1.7 million people who lived and worked in the United States before January 1, 1982. These folks became permanent resident aliens, with the right to bring in just as many relatives as Indian, Japanese, Irish, or Polish immigrants.

SAWS (Special Agricultural Workers) included 1.1 million migrants who completed ninety days of farm work in 1985–1986. SAWS got into the act because growers pushed—at the last minute—for their inclusion. Indeed, growers did such a good job helping to write this part of the law that, instead of the onus being on the worker, it was shifted to the government. Washington needed to prove the alien was lying, and it did such a bad job "that as many as two out of three people who were granted legal status did not in fact qualify." Of course, SAWS did have fraudulent documents, presumably provided by the same people who manufactured baptismal certificates.[110]

Reform in 1986 yet again repeated twentieth-century history. With nearly 3 million people instantly transformed, Mexican (and Caribbean) migrants soon argued, as their relatives did in 1950, that the best way to become legal was to go illegal. Cross the border and you too could participate in one of America's periodic amnesty programs.

These policies backfire with such force because they root themselves in a halfhearted acceptance of reality. In 1950 and in 1986 Congress belatedly recognized the permanent presence of millions of unauthorized Mexican migrants. So far, so good. But, in simultaneously gutting the employer sanctions law, Congress also assured the need for yet another amnesty in the future. After all, if Congressman (later Attorney General of California) Dan Lungren is correct about the people in his neighborhood, the pull/push/network dynamic will nurture even deeper roots for what is already a century of both authorized and unauthorized Mexican migration to the United States.

It's like the war on drugs. Blame and police the Latin American supplier as you continue to demand what the supplier supplies.

The chart is one way of indicating the dramatic increase in unauthorized Mexican migrants. But, of the 2.7 million people, "only" an estimated 600,000 unauthorized migrants (approximately 94 percent of them Mexicans) work in agriculture.[111] The rest make your clothes, wash your car, clean your office, manicure your lawn, care for your children at home, care for your aged parents in nursing facilities, or dig the hole for your pool. In California all-American types hire a Mexican from a group waiting on a street corner and then treat him in this fashion. They agree to pay upon completion, pick the fellow up for eight days running, and on the ninth day the Californian has a hole in his backyard and the Mexican a hole in his wallet. In the words of a local attorney, "It's horrible but it's absolutely endemic here. It's mind-blowing."[112]

In Renton, Washington, 3,000 Mexicans moved to the city over the last thirty years. One result is that 150 restaurants rely on the small Mexican

The Rise in Unauthorized Mexican Migration

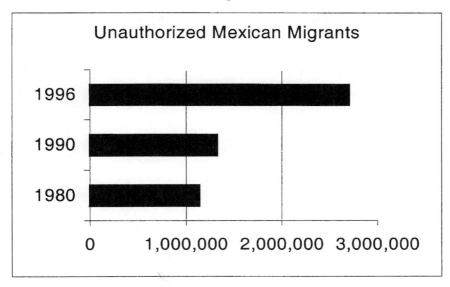

Unauthorized Mexican Migrants

1996	
1990	
1980	

0   1,000,000   2,000,000   3,000,000

town of Cuautla for a work force that includes both authorized and unauthorized labor.[113]

As another example, consider the meatpacking and poultry-producing industries. In Dodge City, Kansas, most of the Latinos arrived after 1990 and were hired by the local offshoot of Cargill Foods. Human resources manager Jim Maher says he recruits via his current employees; one relative tells another, and you soon have a labor force of "authorized" workers.[114]

Based in Arkansas, Tyson Foods offers work that is so disagreeable the company experiences an average 73 percent turnover in its eighty-four chicken-producing plants in twenty-one states. Thus, while Tyson recruits by word of mouth, it also uses labor recruiters based in the Rio Grande Valley. Tyson's preference is for "newly arrived" Mexicans at a cost of $150 to $250 a head.[115]

A Government Accounting Office report published in 1998 outlines the spread of new meatpacking plants throughout states like Iowa and Nebraska. Once again, the work is so awful that the high turnover rate results in the hiring of a workforce that is roughly 25 percent unauthorized. Most of these workers are Mexican, and they are blamed not only for the quality of their fraudulent documents (i.e., the affirmative defense) but also for the social problems that Mexican and other migrants "produce." School officials complain about students with limited English proficiency, and "everyone" complains about the tax dollars being used to underwrite both authorized and unauthorized migrants.[116]

One final example. Atlanta's 1996 Olympic Games became such a mecca for unauthorized Mexican workers that someone could have put a "made in Mexico" sign on many of the sports facilities.[117]

Swat the Hyphen

During World War I the United States witnessed powerful social movements to both "Americanize the Immigrant" and "Swat the Hyphen." The former sought to produce 100 percent Americans, while the latter focused on threats that moved immigrants to stop speaking "foreign" languages in public.[118]

Contemporary versions of a "Swat the Hyphen" movement go by different names: Proposition 187 in California and the U.S. government's "Illegal Immigration Reform and Immigrant Responsibility Act of 1996."[119] Another example is this suggestion from a Latino writer: "The most decisive action against illegal immigration needs to be taken within the barrios themselves." Because the unauthorized depress wages and "provoke" both suspicion and animosity among many Americans, Latinos need to police themselves. The three million "legalized" in 1986 must forget their own unauthorized roots and, free of charge, guard the barrios against any friends or family who seek to enter the United States in an unauthorized fashion.[120]

This astonishing suggestion adds a new meaning to swatting the Mexican. At once it accepts the criminal label, asks Latinos to be a homefront border patrol, guarantees agonizing personal and family conflicts if they do so, and even assigns a backstage role to the proven villains: U.S. political and economic authorities.

Targeting and penalizing the immigrant is both easy and futile. Easy because it transfers responsibility to Mexicans for what is an all-American problem. Futile because legislation like the immigration act of 1996 does not deal effectively with the two monumental issues that refuse to go away.

The first issue is structural. The pull/push/network dynamic is such a powerful force that despite billions spent on border control, migrants still make it through an estimated 70 percent of the time. Meanwhile, more migrants than ever try to enter before the border really tightens up, and others never even return to Mexico. They just remain in America as a permanent addition to the pool of unauthorized migrants.[121]

Strategies to effectively counter the pull/push dynamic do exist. Serious change is possible; for example, let's use the money migrant families now pay to smugglers to establish a binational agency focusing on the development of human and material infrastructure in Mexico. Link these funds to U.S. withholding taxes set aside for migrant-related projects and you provide the beginnings of a serious attack on the push side of the equation.[122]

The literature is full of other suggestions and possibilities (see chapter 9). What links them is a focus on structure and a refusal to waste any more time targeting Mexicans for the consequences of a perpetual national desire: cheap and disposable labor.

The second problem—What Shall We Do with Our America?—is more serious. As of mid 1999 the United States contained roughly 18 million Mexicans *who are also Americans*. In addition, the pool of almost 3 million legalized in 1986 is naturalizing at a much faster pace than ever before. Men and women, fathers and mothers are responding to efforts that deny permanent residents access to social services; they are becoming U.S. citizens and, in the process, gaining the right to bring in their close relatives who will bring in their close relatives who. . . .

Mexicans are a permanent and increasingly important part of American life. For any chance of social harmony Mexicans need to be a vital part of any effort to establish a national consensus about the meaning of the United States of America. But, given the history detailed in this chapter, why would a sane Mexican want to embrace U.S. society?

As a nation we must walk into the twenty-first century on the basis of a corrected past. In short, primary responsibility for the physical presence and economic condition of Mexicans in the United States rests with five generations of U.S. policymakers.

Accept that fact and we can begin to talk about a spiritual consensus for the next century. Reject it and you exclude—before the conversation even begins—the many millions of Chicanos who, living in Aztlan, remember the real history of the American Southwest.

Postscript: The Puerto Ricans, Citizens by Statute

Nearly 3 million Puerto Ricans live in the United States. Almost 4 million live on the island. All are U.S. citizens, but those who reside in Puerto Rico cannot vote in a federal election, have no voting representation in Congress, and *are* subject to the U.S. draft. Meanwhile, in a nation that speaks Spanish, the federal courts in Puerto Rico mandate the use of English. Since only an estimated 25 percent of the Puerto Ricans living on the island are fully bilingual, no islander ever receives a jury of his or her peers in a federal court. By definition, solely Spanish-speaking islanders are ineligible for federal jury duty. They therefore link arms with the prominent attorneys who refuse to practice in a federal court because they doubt their English-language abilities or, even more important, because they deny the political right of the United States to make Puerto Ricans speak a foreign language in "their" court system.

Puerto Rico is unique. It is the oldest colony on earth, owned by the oldest representative democracy on earth.[123] As Senator Henry Jackson publicly told Puerto Rican legislators in 1974, the island "became a part of the United States by an act of conquest." Equally important, since 1898 Congress has always claimed plenary or absolute power over Puerto Rico because, as Article Four, Section Three, of the U.S. Constitution stresses, Congress makes *all* needful rules and regulations for U.S. territories.[124]

The contradiction is that, whether in 1898 or 1998, Congress also refuses to accept, with its absolute power, primary responsibility for the bizarre consequences of one hundred years of U.S. political, economic, and military control of Puerto Rico and its people. For example, the U.S. naval base at Roosevelt Roads is not only the largest (in land area) in the world, it is also the only place in the Atlantic Ocean where the United States and Nato forces practice war in an unrestricted sense. Congress has never indicated what will happen to the Navy and Army bases that encompass roughly 14 percent of the island's acreage, and Congress has also repeatedly refused to allow a status vote in Puerto Rico that would accept the expressed will of the island's electorate.[125]

The result is a state of limbo. The second largest group of Latinos in the United States—and that is without the nearly 4 million Puerto Ricans on the island!—could easily become aliens in their own country, or, if Puerto Rico became a state, the 4 million islanders would instantly have seven congressional representatives and two U.S. senators. States like Vermont, Connecticut, Rhode Island, Montana, Wyoming, New Hampshire, and Delaware would take a congressional back seat to the 4 million Puerto Ricans in the Caribbean and the 3 million on the mainland.

It's a morass made in Washington, D.C. It's discussed in a chapter focusing on undocumented migration because the peculiar U.S. citizenship of Puerto Ricans now offers them a future as uncertain as that of the millions of Chicanos who also live in the shadows of U.S. life.

Puerto Ricans are citizens by statute. When, in 1914, "the agitation for independence" was quite intense, Congress held hearings on the future of Puerto Rico. Secretary of War Lindsay Garrison represented the Wilson administration when he testified, "As I understand the situation . . . there is no suggestion that Puerto Rico should not be connected with the United States for all time. And that we should not in the fullest measure be responsible for it as we are for any other thing that is under our flag."[126]

Congress made Puerto Ricans U.S. citizens to emphatically underline that Puerto Rico was a "permanent possession of the United States."[127] In response, Puerto Rico's elected representatives unanimously refused U.S. citizenship, and Congress then disregarded their expressed desires. Puerto Ricans became citizens by congressional statute in April of 1917. Indeed, as Woodrow Wilson brainstormed about a League of Nations that would offer self-determination to the world, he told the Puerto Ricans, "We welcome the new citizen, not as a stranger, but as one entering his father's house."[128]

Congress has never relinquished the sense of paternalism so openly expressed by President Wilson. Congressman Fred Crawford and his colleagues publicly and casually discussed our "subjects" in Puerto Rico as late as 1949,[129] and as recently as October of 1998 Congress once again refused to endorse a status vote that would abide by the democratical will of the Puerto Rican people.

Nobody knows where we go from here. And *nobody* knows what the Puerto Rican people do or do not want. That is so because the status vote in Puerto Rico will change with the conditions set by Congress. For example, in an April 7, 1998, meeting with Representative Nancy Johnson of Connecticut, the congresswoman indicated that for Puerto Rico to be granted statehood, islanders needed to produce a significant majority (say 65% to 70% of the votes) in favor of formal integration into the United States of America. In addition Puerto Ricans also needed to understand that they could speak Spanish in their churches or clubs but that English would be the medium of instruction in the school and political systems. Like every other state, Puerto Ricans would "melt" into U.S. culture, or they could continue to bask in the Caribbean's sun.[130]

Congressional conditions like these are quite unlikely to produce a vote in favor of statehood. The specifics are the key to any ultimate vote of the Puerto Rican people, and that vote is impossible to accurately predict until and unless Congress specifies the exact nature of statehood, independence, or continued colonial status. For example, Congresswoman Johnson also indicated that, if granted independence, Puerto Ricans who lost their U.S. citizenship could also be permitted to enter and leave the United States whenever they pleased. In addition, given the century of control by Washington and its lawmakers, Congress owed at least twenty-five years of significant economic assistance to the island.

Under those conditions Puerto Ricans could conceivably vote for independence. Congress must offer precise details if any vote is to actually produce social and political peace. So, until Congress acts or Puerto Ricans produce a political crisis that resembles Northern Ireland, the second largest Latino group in the United States impatiently waits for a resolution of its "immigrant" status and its potential role in the political and cultural future of the United States of America.

NOTES

1. *Migratory Labor*, Hearings before the Subcommittee on Labor and Labor Management Relations, Senate, 82nd Congress, second session, Part One (Washington, DC: GPO, 1952), p. 73.

2. Michael Conniff, *Black Labor on a White Canal, Panama, 1904–1981* (Pittsburgh: University of Pittsburgh Press, 1985), p. 25; on Chinese labor on the railroads see, for example, Roger Daniels, *Asian America: Chinese and Japanese in the United States Since 1850* (Seattle: University of Washington Press, 1988).

3. Conniff, *Black Labor*, pp. 26–27.

4. See, for example, Philip Martin, "Network Recruitment and Labor Displace-

ment," in David Simcox, ed., *U.S. Immigration in the 1980's* (Boulder: Westview, 1988).

    5. Conniff, *Black Labor*, pp. 34–35.

    6. Quoted in Robert Nisbet, *The Present Age: Progress and Anarchy in Modern America* (New York: Harper and Row, 1988), p. 29.

    7. *Temporary Admission of Illiterate Mexican Laborers*, Hearings before the Committee on Immigration and Naturalization, House of Representatives, 66th Congress, second session (Washington, DC: GPO, 1920), pp. 48–49.

    8. Sucheng Chan, *Asian Americans: An Interpretive History* (New York: Twayne, 1991), p. 31.

    9. Ibid., especially pp. 38–42.

    10. Leoford C. Williams, *Journey into Diplomacy: A Black Man's Shocking Discovery* (Washington, DC: Northeast Publishing House, 1996); on the issue of hate, see John Howard Griffin, *Black Like Me* (New York: Signet Books, 1961). His discussion of the "hate stare" is especially poignant.

    11. On Jamaicans in Florida, see Alec Wilkinson, *Big Sugar: Seasons in the Cane Fields of Florida* (New York: Vintage Books, 1990).

    12. Nicholas Kristoff, "Asia's Crisis Upsets Rising Effort to Confront Blight of Sweatshops," *New York Times*, June 15, 1998.

    13. Nicholas Van Hear, *Migration Displacement and Social Integration*, Occasional Paper Number 9, United Nations Research Institute for Social Development, World Summit for Social Development, 1994, p. 7.

    14. For fine essays about these structural variables, see Wayne Cornelius, *The Structural Embeddedness of Demand for Migrant Labor in California and Japan*, 1998, ⟨www.migration.ucdavis.edu⟩; Douglas Massey, Luin Goldring, and Jorge Durand, "Continuities in Transnational Migration: An Analysis of Nineteen Mexican Communities," *American Journal of Sociology* 99, no. 6 (May 1994); 1492–1533. On global issues, see Kenichi Ohmae, *The End of the Nation State: The Rise of Regional Economies* (New York: Free Press, 1995); and William Greider, *One World, Ready or Not: The Manic Logic of Global Capitalism* (New York: Simon and Schuster, 1997).

    15. *Migration News* 2, no. 12 (December 1995): 17, ⟨www.migration.ucdavis.edu⟩.

    16. See Rudolph Vecoli, "The Italian Diaspora, 1876–1976," in Robin Cohen, ed., *The Cambridge Survey of World Migration* (London: Cambridge University Press, 1995), pp. 114–122, especially p. 114; Thomas Sowell, *Migrations and Cultures* (New York: Basic Books, 1996), p. 145; for the numbers of immigrants see *Migration News* 3, no. 8 (August 1996): 19.

    17. See, for example, Agustin Escobar Latapi, Philip Martin, Gustavo Lopez Castro, and Katherine Donato, *Factors That Influence Migration*, U.S. Commission on Immigration Reform (Washington, DC: GPO, 1997).

    18. Rainer Mynz, *Where Did They All Come From: Typology and Geography of European Mass Migration in the Twentieth Century*, European Population Conference, Milan, Italy, September 1995, p. 9.

    19. Anthony Apostolides, *Intra-European Temporary Migration of Labor During 1961–1975: Magnitudes and Effects*, ⟨www.igc.apc.org/intacad/immi9.html⟩; also, Wayne A. Cornelius, Philip Martin, and James F. Hollifield, ed., *Controlling Immigration: A Global Perspective* (Stanford, CA: Stanford University Press, 1994).

    20. See, for example, Ronald Fernandez, *The Disenchanted Island: Puerto Rico and the United States in the Twentieth Century*, 2nd ed. (New York: Praeger, 1996).

21. See *Migration News* 5, no. 2 (February 1998): 29.

22. On Belgium, see Marcelo M. Suarez-Orozco, "Anxious Neighbors: Belgium and Its Immigrant Minorities," in Cornelius, Martin, and Hollifield, eds., *Controlling Immigration*, pp. 237–271; on France, see Mark J. Miller, *Western European Strategies to Deter Unwanted Migration*, U.S. Commission on Immigration Reform (Washington, DC: GPO, 1996), esp. pp. 32–34.

23. *Migration News* 3, no. 11 (November 1996): 13–14.

24. Gustavo Verduzco and Kurt Unger, *Impacts of Migration in Mexico*, U.S. Commission on Immigration Reform (Washington, DC: GPO, 1996), p. 428.

25. See Van Hear, *Migration Displacement*, p. 15.

26. Senate Judiciary Committee, *Immigration: The View from Silicon Valley*, February 25, 1998, p. 7, ⟨www.senate.gov/~judiciary/rodgers.htm⟩.

27. See Michael Smith, *The New High-Tech Braceros? Who Is the Employer? What Is the Problem?*, U.S. Commission on Immigration Reform (Washington, DC: GPO, 1996).

28. Escobar Latapi et al., *Factors*, p. 170.

29. Roberto Suro, *Strangers Among Us: How Latino Immigration Is Transforming America* (New York: Alfred A. Knopf, 1998), p. 32.

30. Ibid., p. 46.

31. *Migration News* 5, no. 5 (May 1998): 37.

32. See Massey et al., "Continuities," p. 1500.

33. These last paragraphs are drawn from Martin, "Network Recruitment and Labor Displacement," pp. 67–91, esp. pp. 70–71.

34. Michael Teitelbaum and Sharon Stanton Russell, Potentials, Paradoxes and Realities: Economic Development and the Future of International Migration, *Migration News* web page (1996) <www.migration.ucdavis.edu/mn/mntxt.html>, 1996, p. 6.

35. Jennifer Glick and Jennifer Van Hook, *The Mexican-Origin Population of the United States in the Twentieth Century*, U.S. Commission on Immigration Reform (Washington, DC: GPO, 1996), p. 574.

36. Are Chicanos the Same As Mexicans? *The Azteca Web Page* (1997) ⟨www.azteca.net/aztec/chicano.html⟩; also George Sanchez, *Becoming Mexican American* (New York: Oxford University Press, 1993).

37. Earl Shorris, *Latinos: A Biography of a People* (New York: W.W. Norton, 1992), p. 101.

38. Rudolfo Anaya and Francisco Lomeli, eds., *Aztlan: Essays on the Chicano Homeland* (Albuquerque: El Norte Press, 1989); on the redefining of origins, see J. Jorge Klor de Alva, "The Invention of Ethnic Origins and the Negotiation of Latino Identity, 1969–1981," in Mary Romero, Pierette Hondagneu-Sotelo, and Vilma Ortiz, eds., *Challenging Fronteras* (New York: Routledge, 1997), pp. 55–74, esp. pp. 60–61.

39. See *Temporary Admission*, pp. 61, 80.

40. *Seasonal Agricultural Workers from Mexico*, Hearings Before the Committee on Immigration and Naturalization, House of Representatives, 69th Congress, first session (Washington, DC: GPO, 1926), pp. 45–46.

41. See, for example, Frederick Merk, *Manifest Destiny and Mission in U.S. History* (New York: Vintage, 1972); Albert K. Weinberg, *Manifest Destiny* (Baltimore: Johns Hopkins, 1935); Walter La Faber, *The New Empire* (Ithaca: Cornell University Press, 1963).

42. *Imported Pauper Labor and Serfdom in America*, Hearings before the Committee on Immigration and Naturalization, House of Representatives, 67th Congress, first session (Washington, DC: GPO, 1921), p. 6.

43. *Seasonal Agricultural Laborers from Mexico*, p. 34.

44. Ibid., p. 32.

45. Ibid., p. 33.

46. Ibid., p. 35 for Brown and p. 39 for Johnson.

47. *Immigration Border Patrol*, Hearings before the Committee on Immigration and Naturalization, House of Representatives, 70th Congress, first session (Washington, DC: GPO, 1928), esp. pp. 18–19.

48. *Seasonal Agricultural Laborers from Mexico*, p. 6.

49. Ibid., p. 7.

50. Ibid.; see, for example, the testimony of Fred Cummings of Fort Collins, Colorado, esp. pp. 62–64.

51. Ibid., for the first quote see p. 9; for the second, p. 17.

52. Ibid., p. 18.

53. Ibid., p. 40.

54. Ibid., p. 41.

55. Ibid., pp. 62–64.

56. Manuel Gamio, *Mexican Immigration to the United States* (New York: Arno Press, 1969), pp. 4–5. The original edition of this book was published in 1930.

57. This paragraph is firmly based on Jorge Bustamante, *Some Thoughts on Perceptions and Policies, Mexico–United States Labor Migration Flows*, U.S. Commission on Immigration Reform (Washington, DC: GPO, 1996), esp. p. 831.

58. *Immigration Border Patrol*, pp. 32–33.

59. Ibid., pp. 8–9.

60. Ibid., p. 10.

61. *Migratory Labor*, Hearings Before the Subcommittee on Labor and Labor Management Relations, Senate, 82nd Congress, second session, Part One (Washington, DC: GPO, 1952); e.g., p. 73 for the comments of Senator Morse or p. 68 for those of Senator Humphrey.

62. *Investigation of Western Farm Labor Conditions*, Hearings Before the Special Subcommittee to Investigate Farm Labor Conditions in the West, Senate, 77th Congress, second session (Washington, DC: GPO, 1942), p. 3.

63. Ibid., p. 11.

64. Ibid., p. 5.

65. I am drawing heavily here on the superb history by Kitty Calavita, *Inside the State: The Bracero Program, Immigration and the I.N.S.* (New York: Routledge, 1989), p. 22; see, too, Alfredo Mirande, *Gringo Justice* (Notre Dame: University of Notre Dame, 1987).

66. See John Higham, *Strangers in the Land* (New Brunswick, NJ: Rutgers University Press, 1963), esp. pp. 48–49.

67. Calavita, *Inside the State*, p. 23.

68. Ibid.

69. See Congressman Dan Lungren, in *Immigration Reform*, Hearings Before the Subcommittee on Immigration, Refugees and International Law, House of Representatives, 97th Congress, first session (Washington, DC: GPO, 1981), p. 48.

70. Mirande, *Gringo Justice*, p. 125.

71. *Congressional Record*, 82nd Congress, second session, 1952, 98, Pt. 1:792.

72. Calavita, *Inside the State*, p. 3.

73. *Admission of Foreign Agricultural Workers*, Hearing Before a Subcommittee of the Judiciary, Senate, 81st Congress, first session (Washington, DC: GPO, 1949), pp. 11–12.

74. Ibid., p. 13.

75. Calavita, *Inside the State*, p. 28.

76. Ibid., p. 108, 130.

77. *Migratory Labor*, 1952, p. 68.

78. Ibid., p. 13.

79. *Congressional Record*, p. 792.

80. Ibid., p. 795.

81. Ibid., Lehman, p. 795; Douglas, p. 798.

82. Ibid., p. 794.

83. Ibid., p. 793.

84. Ibid., p. 794.

85. Ibid., p. 793.

86. Ibid.

87. Ibid., p. 794.

88. Ibid., p. 798.

89. Calavita, *Inside the State*, 69.

90. Ibid., p. 218.

91. President Lyndon Johnson Library, Austin, Texas, U.S. Senate, 1949–1961, Legislative Files, 1950–1952, Container 233.

92. The fingerprint story is from Calavita, *Inside the State*, p. 63.

93. Johnson Library, U.S. Senate, 1949–1961, Subject Files, 1958, Container 605.

94. Johnson Library, White House Aides—Gaither, Box 363; the report is dated October, 31, 1966, see p. 2.

95. Ibid., p. 2.

96. Philip Martin, *Mexican Immigrant Workers and U.S. Food Expenditures*, U.S. Commission on Immigration Reform (Washington, DC: GPO, 1996), p. 874.

97. *Migrant and Seasonal Farmworker Powerlessness*, Hearings Before the Subcommittee on Migratory Labor, Senate, 91st Congress, first and second sessions, Part 5-A (Washington, DC: GPO, 1969), p. 1973.

98. Ibid., p. 1974.

99. Ibid., p. 1974–1975.

100. Ibid., p. 1975.

101. Ibid., p. 2205.

102. Ibid., p. 2307.

103. *U.S. Immigration Law and Policy, 1952–1979*, A Report to the Committee of the Judiciary, Senate, 96th Congress, first session (Washington, DC: GPO, 1979), p. 71.

104. Ibid., p. 72.

105. See Kitty Calavita, "U.S. Immigration and Policy Responses: The Limits of Legislation," in Cornelius, Martin, and Hollifield, eds., *Controlling Immigration*, pp. 65–66.

106. *Immigration Reform*, House, 1981, pp. 82–83.

107. As late as January of 1996, Disney received, potentially, the largest fines for "improper paperwork" on 1,200 new hires. See *Migration News* 3, no. 1 (January 1996): p. 6.

108. Calavita, "U.S. Immigration" p. 66.

109. Ibid., p. 70.

110. *Migration News* 1, no. 6 (June 1994): 2.

111. See "Demographics," *A Profile of U.S. Farm Workers* (Washington, DC: U.S. Department of Labor, April 1997), p. 1. This report is based on data from the National Agricultural Workers Survey.

112. Sanford Ungar, *Fresh Blood: The New American Immigrants* (Urbana: University of Illinois Press, 1998), p. 169.

113. *Rural Migration News* 2, no. 2 (April 1996): 2.

114. *Rural Migration News* 4, no. 2 (April 1998): 3.

115. Ibid., p. 4.

116. *Community Development: Changes in Nebraska's and Iowa's Counties with Large Meatpacking Plant Workforces*, Government Accounting Office (Letter Report, 2/27/98/ GAO/RCED-98–62) (Washington, DC: GPO) pp. 4, 7.

117. *Migration News* 3, no. 8 (August 1996): p. 8.

118. Ray H. Abrams, *Preachers Present Arms* (New York: Round Table Press, 1933), p. 117.

119. On Proposition 187 see Philip Martin, *Proposition 187 in California, Factors That Influence Migration*, U.S. Commission on Immigration Reform (Washington, DC: GPO, 1996), pp. 897–901; the 1996 Report of the Commission can be downloaded from the INS homepage: ⟨www.ins.usdoj.gov⟩.

120. See Suro, *Strangers Among Us*, pp. 277–278.

121. Douglas Massey, "March of Folly: U.S. Immigration Policy After Nafta," *The American Prospect*, no. 37 (March-April 1998): 22–33.

122. This suggestion is Douglas Massey's; see ibid., pp. 14–16.

123. Ronald Fernandez, *The Disenchanted Island*, 2nd ed. (Westport: Praeger, 1996).

124. See White House Central Files, ST 51–2; Papers of President Richard Nixon, Nixon Project, Alexandria, Virginia. This is from a White House memo of April 30, 1974.

125. Fernandez, *Disenchanted Island*, especially chapters 6 and 7.

126. See A Civil Government for Puerto Rico, Hearings Before the Committee on Insular Affairs, House, 63rd Congress, second session, February 26, 1914, p. 31.

127. This theme is repeated again and again in the 1914 hearings, ibid. See, especially, Chairman Jones, p. 55.

128. See Arthur S. Link, ed., *The Papers of Woodrow Wilson*, vol. 41 (Princeton: Princeton University Press), pp. 515–516.

129. Congressional Record, House of Representatives, 81st Congress, first session, May 5, 1949, p. 5709; see also p. 5708.

130. I attended a meeting with the Congresswoman in her New Britain, Connecticut, congressional offices.

3

Refugees and Other Aliens

"I think the Federal government is a damn welsher when it comes to refugees—a huge welsher."
—Congressman David Obey, August 1, 1996[1]

UNINTENDED CONSEQUENCES

One of capitalism's hallmarks is the inescapable exposure of one capitalist to the competitive efforts of another. Whether it's light bulbs, phones, or computer chips, all market shares are assailable because, by definition, a good capitalist searches for a competitor's vulnerabilities and pounces on any weaknesses that expose the other company's profits.[2]

Competition among capitalists is allegedly beneficial to everyone. But, how about fierce and global competition for refugees? Suppose, as Senator Alan Simpson worried in August of 1995, advocacy groups in need of clients so distort legal standards that people disguised as refugees are entering the United States "largely from pressure, pure pressure, from special groups using special leverage."

To Simpson, a real refugee "truly has no hope of safe return, they will be killed if they return to their homeland." How could many of the recent arrivals from the Soviet Union be called refugees? "We have them waiting for a year or a year-and-a-half until they decide to come. That can't be a refugee. You can't be a refugee when you have six months or a year or eighteen months to sort it out as to where you are going to go."[3]

Senator Simpson had a problem. He was trying to be reasonable. But reason often had no place in the global marketplace for refugees. VOLAGS (private resettlement agencies) generally received a stipulated amount for each person they could pressure the president and Congress to bring to U.S. shores. To sustain and grow their businesses, agencies combed the world for new opportunities.[4] Sometimes, as in the senator's example, VOLAGS stretched the word refugee so far it broke; at other times the standard of a death threat made way for a river of tears. Who, for example, could say no to the Amerasians?

The horrible plight of these (now over 75,000) children and adolescents fathered by American servicemen during the Vietnam War created what John Shade, former director of the Pearl Buck Foundation, called "tremendous competition among the voluntary agencies. We all wanted to get back into Vietnam."[5]

And they did. But not without stiff resistance from the U.S. State Department. Negotiating for the children meant recognition on some level of the Vietnamese government. U.S. officials refused that with such force that despite $2 million in hand and a commitment of luxury liners to transport the children, Shade's board of directors nevertheless responded to pressure from Washington. In 1985 the Pearl Buck Foundation canceled a voyage for 8,000 Amerasians and used the $2 million to build a "fancy new building in Bucks County."[6]

Fueled by both compassion and the competing voluntary agencies, public pressure continued to build—in spite of the State Department. On one level Amerasians elicited genuine sympathy because they symbolized people's awful ability to be cruel to one another. Called half-breeds in Vietnam, the children allegedly polluted "God's chosen people—the Vietnamese—with monkey genes."[7] Thus, the children were often abandoned and always subjected to ridicule. Like a scar on a person's nose, Amerasians perpetually reminded their Vietnamese (and American) neighbors of what both wanted to forget—twenty years of war and dreadful death and destruction from U.S. and Vietnamese military forces.

In the United States Amerasians also epitomized the hallowed obligations Americans willingly shouldered because of the unintended consequences of U.S. foreign policy. Whether Cuban or El Salvadoran, Vietnamese or Nicaraguan, Cambodian or Hmong, the refugees Senator Simpson normally labeled legitimate often came from countries in the midst of wars instigated, assisted, or perpetuated by U.S. covert or overt military action.

Admittedly Amerasians never fit into the pure refugee category. Helpless victims best described their situation. But add to that helplessness the moral responsibility accepted by Americans of all political persuasions and you get the Amerasian Homecoming Act of 1987. Suddenly the children had a home, and they could even bring their families.

The family side of the equation set off another form of fierce competition. Vietnamese who wanted to come to America "adopted" children who lived with no one; or they traveled to rural areas, rounded up Amerasians, and tried to pass them off as blood relatives. In Saigon "the fraud was out of hand"; so, along with the children of war, America's new refugees included adults who would, once in America, again abandon the already abandoned children.[8]

By 1994 the GAO reported that Amerasians arrived in the United States with three strikes called before they even came to bat. In general the children—actually adolescents—possessed no more than a sixth-grade education, no marketable skills, and no proficiency in English. A successful entry into American life required a tremendous amount of training, yet the federal government mandated that the agencies make the kids self-sufficient as fast as possible. In the GAO sample, only 37 percent attended some English-language courses, 23 percent enrolled in high school, and 14 percent received some job training. The only thing the youngsters really possessed was the deadend jobs that allowed the agencies to claim success in Washington. These kids, like all good Americans, supposedly paid their own way.[9]

Meanwhile communities throughout the nation voiced complaints like this one posed by Lee Pevsner, the director of Housing and Transportation in Merced, California. Speaking before a House Committee in 1994 Pevsner noted that the federal government's Office of Refugee Resettlement "had been grossly inadequate in its estimation of what Southeast Asian refugees need." He did not want to go through that history "but the language skills they brought to this country, the educational skills they brought to this country, *to expect them to be employable in a short length of time is totally irrational*" (emphasis added).[10]

Pevsner complained that the government added insult to irrationality by "increasingly cutting back on the amount of time in which there would be 100% Federal participation. I think it is down to four months. So, to me, nobody was trying to figure out what was going on, the Feds were trying to bail from their responsibilities."[11]

Mr. Pevsner correctly pinpointed not only a nationwide phenomenon, but also one of its principal causes. In small towns and large cities throughout the United States, it seemed impossible to separate increasingly vitriolic attacks on foreigners from the "feds'" refusal to accept human and financial responsibility for the consequences of its actions.

Forget jobs for a second. Many of these youngsters instantly received three negative identities from U.S. culture: black, Amerasian, and foreigner. This generally equaled such a heavy load of negative information that even a well-educated person, seconded by a close and loving family, would have a hard time adjusting to U.S. society. These kids received instead continuing discrimination from members of their own community and this kind of homecoming from the Veterans Administration: Look for your father and know that the VA would "take all precautions to protect the veteran from unwanted and embarrassing disclosures."[12]

God never favored the Amerasians, who involuntarily represent all recent refugees because they are arriving in the United States at the worst possible time. Despite fourteen years of complaints from senators like Alan Simpson the "feds" now say yes to more refugees (and humanitarian admissions) than ever before. Meanwhile money is provided for less time in a decade when local communities loudly complain about the financial, educational, and criminal consequences of a flood of immigrants, "illegals," *and* uninvited (except by Washington and the VOLAGS) refugees. One result of the controversy is that, like the undocumented Mexicans, Amerasians get blamed even though they also possess an engraved invitation from powerful political and economic interests.

The only certainty is that the "pure pressure" on Washington continues to mount. Tap into one of the search engines on the Internet, type Amerasian, and in late 1998 you receive a long list of references, all referring to "Famas," or Filipino Amerasians. As a letter to President Clinton pleads, "Let us think about the 50,000 Amerasian children in the Philippines who have been abandoned and neglected by their U.S. serviceman fathers." Federal law extended to Korean and Laotian Amerasians the same rights granted to the Vietnamese Amerasians. But because the Philippines was never designated an actual war zone, these youngsters lack any right to a U.S. homecoming. Thus, in concert with the VOLAGS, Philippine organizations pressure the president and Congress to admit even more refugees who, when they arrive, will actually be humanitarian admissions.[13]

What is going on? How did we get from a world in 1961 where refugees were a very real exception to the immigration rules to a world where, despite a mandated limit of 50,000 refugees a year, Congress now averages 100 thousand refugees a year in the 1990s?[14]

Just as important, why are we shortchanging the new refugees when the one group that is always cited as a model—the Cuban refugees—received almost *twenty-five* years of federal assistance for a dazzling array of community support programs? As Congressman William Natcher noted in 1978 appropriations hearings, the seventeen-year-old Cuban program was being phased out over six years, the three-year-old Indo-Chinese program over four years. "Do you (the U.S. agency representative) get any feedback from the States about the inequity of having different phase-out schedules for the two programs, Cuban refugees and Indo-Chinese, any complaints?"

The answer: "There has not been any appreciable complaint, Mr. Chairman."[15]

THE ACTION STORY

Reading federal statutes requires both patience and a clear mind. Caffeine is a welcome companion because federal statutes appear to be written in a language that defies understanding. Read them once; read them twice. You think you may understand, but you need the caffeine to remain awake for yet another try at translating the law.

The surprise in refugee statutes is the clarity of the "parole" provision. As Congress stressed in 1953 and 1965, "The parole provisions were designed to authorize the Attorney General to act only in emergent, *individual* and isolated situations." These situations included the case of an alien who required immediate medical attention; they did not include "the immigration of classes or groups outside of the limit of the law," (emphasis added).[16]

President Eisenhower was the first to "break" the law when, in 1956, he paroled over 30,000 Hungarian refugees into the United States. This obviously disregarded the intent of the statute but, with the open arms reserved for those fleeing Communism, Washington welcomed the Hungarians as parolees for two years. Congress then passed a law that effectively sanctioned the president's "breaking" of Congress laws. In July of 1958 senators and representatives erased the parole status of 30,000 Hungarians; the new law made the Hungarians, as a group, permanent residents of the United States.[17]

The Cubans were different. As early as 1938 aides told President Roosevelt that President Batista was both ignorant and corrupt. The CIA told President Truman in 1948 that (with Batista out of power) corruption existed throughout the government and "the National police now includes gangsters." In 1958 senators discussed in executive session the results of President Batista's 1952 coup d'etat. It was such a disaster that, as Senator Aiken of Vermont lamented, "They talk against him on the street; the man who flies the plane is against him, everybody is against him."[18]

Finally, on February 18, 1960, Assistant Secretary of State Roy Rubottom told the Senate (again in executive session) that "I think many Americans, if not most Americans, realized that there was some room for change, indeed perhaps for some social and political revolution in Cuba."[19]

Washington faced a terrible dilemma. How could it embrace the men and women who had aided, abetted, and participated in a generation of political dictatorships, gangsters in the National police, and such widespread corruption that it cut a path of bribes from Santiago to Havana, from one end of the island to the other?

President Kennedy responded by imitating the script of a play by Luigi Pirandello: "It is true if you say so." Thus, not a week after he took office, President Kennedy instructed Abraham Ribicoff (Secretary of Health, Education, and Welfare) to fly to Miami. As the president's personal representative, Ribicoff was to put all the power and wealth of the federal government at the disposal of the more than 66,000 Cubans already in the United States. "I want you to make concrete my concern and sympathy for those who have been forced from their homes in Cuba. . . . I want to re-emphasize most strongly the tradition of the United States as a humanitarian sanctuary, and the many times it has extended its hand and material help to those who are *exiles for conscience's sake*" (emphasis added).[20]

Documents in one presidential library after another indicate that the Cubans in political and economic power cut down their enemies as cleanly as a worker uses a machete to cut cane.[21] Castro did exactly the same thing, but the president's transformation of the nature of the Cuban exiles underlines an important point about all refugees. Law is in the background; up front is political policy. Thus, the Cubans became "freedom fighters" as President John F. Kennedy "adopted wholesale a policy of paroling the refugees into the United States." By the middle of 1962 over 60,000 Cubans received paroles; the prominent nature of the earliest exiles was such that, as the president stressed, "three-fourths of the faculty at the University of Havana are reported to be in South Florida at the present time" (i.e., February 3, 1961).[22]

Over the years the nature of the exiles would allegedly change. One "confidential" report from U.S. officials in Miami noted that the arrivals on the plane of January 25, 1963, included "just the dregs of Cuban society." Not only did passengers fight with one another, "it was apparent that many of them were would be Castristas, neophyte Communists or genuine Castro agents." The flight of February 1, 1963, included "the worst collection of human beings it has ever been my misfortune to encounter. . . . There were some who were obviously physical wrecks, there were a number of mentally deficient . . . in addition there were extremely low class people, there were almost illiterate negroes, and there were self admitted Fidelistas."[23]

At the White House all turned into freedom fighters entitled to the longest-lasting and most generous refugee benefits in U.S. history. In his February 2, 1961, report to the president, Secretary Ribicoff listed the first things that would be done:

1. A program of financial help to needy families to be "administered through existing Federal, State and local channels, based upon the standards used in the communities involved."

2. Essential health service, "supplemented by child health, public health services and other arrangements as needed through Federal support of established public agencies."

3. Federal financial assistance for local schools "and additional funding for needed temporary classroom construction."

4. Federal loans to Cuban students in American colleges and universities who had—or would soon—exhaust their resources.

5. Federal financial assistance for language training, skill refresher courses, orientation and vocational training for Cuban refugees.

6. Retraining for the large number of "doctors, lawyers, engineers, dentists, architects, nurses, agronomists and others." All would hopefully receive special training at the University of Miami so that they could be licensed in the United States as soon as was possible.[24]

In 1962 Congress passed special legislation to fund these programs. Indeed, not until a six-year phase-out started in 1978 did the federal government seriously question its extraordinary financial responsibilities to Cuban refugees and to the state, city, and voluntary agencies that actually carried out the plans of the federal government.[25]

Cuban Refugee Program

Fiscal Year	Obligations in $Millions
1961	4.1
1962	38.5
1963	56.0
1964	46.0
1965	32.5
1966	35.8
1967	45.6
1968	55.2
1969	70.6
1970	87.4
1971	112.1
1972	136.7
1973	143.7
1974	114.8
1975	84.2
1976	103.3
1977	80.5
1978	55.5

Those plans included financial assistance that extended well beyond normal forms of civilian aid. A National Security File memo at the Kennedy Library stressed that "*only the Cubans, among all the postwar refugee groups have a reasonable expectation of returning to their homeland within a short span of time*" (emphasis in original).[26] The United States therefore subsidized— with under-the-table funding—a wide variety of counterrevolutionary organizations. Recently declassified (in 1996) documents provide partial payroll figures for at least eight separate organizations. Brigade members of the Cuban Revolutionary Council received monthly checks. Even when an "elder statesman" moved to the sidelines, White House officials "agreed to take care of him personally." Meanwhile, Washington paid (as of April 1963) $25,000 a month in rent for the Miami headquarters of the Student Revolutionary Directorate and donated another $51,000 for "under guidance" activities of the students. It also turned over $5,000 (monthly? quarterly?) to the Cuban Women's Crusade, who "directed propaganda to the Cuban domestic population."[27]

In a memo to CIA Director John McCone, Edward R. Murrow (then head of the U.S. Information Agency) offered his suggestions "regarding the use of Cuban exiles in broadcasts beamed to Cuba." Murrow argued against appeals to "open rebellion." Instead the programs needed to focus on everything from work slowdowns to "relatively safe forms of sabotage. Specific examples of the activities urged would be putting glass and nails on the highways, leaving water running in public buildings, putting sand in machinery, wasting electricity, taking sick leave from work, damaging sugar stalks during the harvest, etc."[28]

Since thousands of people longed to leave the island, how could Morrow be sure that a row of nails never blew out the tires—and the lives—of Cuban democrats? In the struggle against Castro, the end justified the means. Long before Richard Nixon took office in 1968, a liberal Democratic president handsomely paid Cuban exiles for a grab bag of dirty tricks.

With both overt and covert payments, Cuban exiles received incredible financial and political assistance from Congress and the president. This help gave a powerful jump-start to an already well-educated community; but, instead of seeing federal assistance disappear after two or three years, the Cuban community saw it rise to new heights under the direction of President Lyndon Johnson. He called it "creative federalism," and he got creative, not only for the new Cubans fleeing their homeland but also for the citizens of Florida who threatened to storm the Bastille and demand a freedom of their own: no more Cuban refugees.[29]

After the Cuban missile crisis of October 1962, commercial flights between Cuba and the United States ended. Almost immediately "the number of paroles dropped sharply and consisted of those refugees who crossed the Straits of Florida in small boats." Then (in December of 1962) came the more than 1,000 Bay of Pigs invasion prisoners and, after that, a small number of people who managed to leave in small boats.[30]

As if operating a spigot, Fidel Castro once again opened the migration door with a public announcement in October of 1965. He would permit "all" who sought to leave Cuba for the United States to depart. While that was wonderful news for the Cuban exiles, Castro—not for the last time!—put tremendous pressure on the White House. The dictator in Havana could flood U.S. shores with more paroles than anyone imagined and, at the height of the Cold War, the White House could never say no.

On the contrary, the president publicly and proudly assured an audience on Liberty Island (on October 3, 1965) that "the dedication of America to our traditions as an asylum for the oppressed is going to be upheld." Meanwhile, backstage, the president's staff "had come up with the idea (on October 14) that the preoccupation of Florida authorities with the anticipated flow of Cuban refugees might be eased if the Congress were to act at this session on a pending bill providing federal assistance for the construction of a new exposition and trade center (INTERAMA) in the Miami area."[31]

The president's men established the "Federal Task Force for Greater Miami." Chaired by Secretary of Health, Education and Welfare John Gardner, the task force received a specific mission from the president: "We must make a concerted effort to help the Miami community in a number of ways, making the fullest possible use of existing Federal programs to maintain and stimulate economic growth in the Miami area and to avoid an undue additional burden on the community as a result of the influx of refugees."[32]

This made great sense for all concerned. Instead of the short-term, relatively hands-off policy adopted for the Amerasians in the 1990s, the federal government under President Johnson acted in a variety of enormously creative ways. Much of this funding never appeared in the Cuban Refugee Program statistics already cited; this assistance nevertheless offered tremendous help to Cuban refugees and to the Florida communities that, without prior approval, received an order to welcome with open arms another hundred thousand Cubans.

1. Miami received designation as an economic development area; this made it eligible for grants and loans under the Public Works and Economic Development Act of 1965.

2. With a first grant of $75,000, Washington established a Small Business Development Center. Gardner told the president that "it was housed in the offices of the local community action agency, adding further to the multiple services that low-income people can obtain there."

3. Authorization of a $2 million Headstart program, plus another $1.5 million for mobile and permanent classrooms.

4. Under the title of healthcare, a $50,000 grant "to explain the Federal program of Medical Insurance to old people eligible for optional benefits under Medicare." A $60,000 grant for "Child Spacing, a project making family planning services available to 5000 low income families."

5. Under the title of "Action Through Education," a $2.5 million loan to the University of Miami for a science building and a grant of $1.3 million to construct the facility. Barry College got $650,000 for library construction, and Miami Dade Junior College received $1 million "for construction purposes."

Called "the Action Story" the list of projects extends for twelve detailed pages. From sewer and water facilities to vocational rehabilitation, from low-cost housing to a special $750,000 grant for the control of (among other things) venereal disease, Miami became a Great Society special project.[33] Gardner skillfully had all the pieces in place by June of 1966, and this assistance would complement, through the Nixon administration, the special funds for the special Cuban Refugee Program.

The only problem was the parole law. While it specifically referred to emergency assistance to individuals, the airlift's earliest efforts extended to another one hundred thousand people. Following the precedents set by presidents Eisenhower and Kennedy, Lyndon Johnson claimed wide discretionary powers. He argued "that the Cuban airlift program represented an administrative exercise of the parole feature of the immigration law. Under it, the number of refugees who may come to the United States from Cuba was unlimited," and the president planned to continue this "unrestricted, humanitarian admission program" for as far as the eye could see.[34]

Congress not only seconded the president's efforts, it enacted special legislation (in 1966) to eliminate the lingering concerns of Cuban parolees. Immigration laws then stipulated that a person could be removed from parole status and admitted for permanent residence only if he or she left the country and applied for readmission on an immigrant basis. Since Cuban parolees understandably argued that this was either impossible or inconvenient, Congress "adjusted" the status of any Cuban who arrived after January 1, 1959. All became permanent residents after two years (later one year) in the United States; these Cubans "were counted against the overall ceiling of 120,000 on Western Hemisphere immigration until 1976, an action subsequently declared illegal by a U.S. district court."[35]

By the time Fidel Castro once again cut off flights in 1973, the airlift program alone accounted for more than 265,000 additional refugees. Overall more than six hundred thousand Cubans received parole from one president after another. Whether Democrat or Republican, liberal or conservative, each claimed wide discretionary power and each received approval from the same body—Congress—that in the late 1970s encountered yet another international emergency. This time the problem existed in Indochina, and this time Assistant Secretary of State Douglas Bennett forthrightly explained why the United States needed to offer parole to at least a half million Vietnamese, Cambodian, and Laotian "boat people."

"Our refugee policies seem to a large extent to be determined by our foreign policy blunders. The State Department views the Southeast Asia refugee situation as the result of U.S. involvement in that area and consequently reacts as though the U.S. is morally bound to atone for its blunders by accepting any and all persons displaced by the Communist takeover."[36]

CHAOS IN INDOCHINA

Saigon fell in April 1975. Over the next three years more than 145,000 Indochinese citizens received paroles from the only person actually authorized to grant it, the attorney general of the United States. Under the law the attorney general carried out the political/refugee policies of the president; and under the watchful and wary eyes of Congress, Griffin Bell answered for the increasingly controversial actions and ideals of Jimmy Carter.

Why were we carrying the refugee ball for the rest of the world? How many more men, women, and children waited in the camps of Thailand? And, since the ripple effects of the conflict had turned into a tidal wave of people, how did Bell plan to end, once and for all, the Vietnam War?

Griffin Bell began by honestly expressing both reservations and apprehensions. He agreed with Congressman Joshua Eilberg of Pennsylvania that "from a mere reading of the statute, it would appear that it was not intended to be used for large groups." Bell also knew "that we had let in 600,000 Cubans under that statute"; he was in the "delicate position" of having to respond to the huge refugee requests of the State Department "with very little statutory authority."

Bell ultimately closeted his reservations because "this is only the fourth time, I believe, this power has been exercised for groups, so we can't say there has been any abuse. But there could be. There could be. What you have to worry about in government and law is, set up a system so you can't have any abuses."[37]

That was exactly Congress's point. Representatives wanted to responsibly employ the checks and balances provisions of the constitution. Congressman Eilberg, for example, presented a letter from the Medical Director of Missoula County, Montana. Laotians now lived in Missoula and, over and above the problems of accepting a culture that accepted polygamy, Doctor William Norman sarcastically discussed other issues. "As the 'Great White Father' is taken with humanitarian fervor in this instance, I hope he will remember his poor children in Missoula and put some 'money where his mouth is' before the fact rather than haggle about it afterward."[38]

Congress voiced the anxieties of an already immigration-weary public. However, instead of a federal task force for Missoula, the Carter administration responded with answers like the following. Asked if the announcement of this new parole program didn't "spur the Vietnamese to take risks knowing that the United States would accept them," State Department officials said, "No way." Eilberg then stated that since "newer arrivals are extremely familiar with U.S. refugee programs," couldn't those programs be increasing the immigration everyone wanted to prevent? This time the response of Assistant Secretary of State Patricia Derian was, "Well, I suppose that it might be."[39]

In another sparring session Congressman Eilberg asked, "Do we have any idea how many relatives of refugees who have already been admitted still remain in Vietnam, including immediate families and extended families?" Derian said, "No." Eilberg persisted: "I'd like to know those figures so we can know where we are going further down the road."

Assistant Secretary Derian: "I was just asking if we had on a computer maybe somewhere in the list of questions we asked, whether this was included. But we don't have any indication of it, so it will just have to be a ballpark guess. And Jimmy the Greek does better than we do on that."[40]

The federal government knew as much as a Las Vegas odds maker. While this might seem like a strange or even bizarre admission, the written record contains no mention of either laughter or surprise. On the contrary, the discussion of future migration proceeded in a serious manner. Congress and the president simply sleepwalked into the future. Thus, as late as 1994 (34,248), 1995 (32,244), and 1996 (16,130), refugee admissions from Vietnam continued to march along at a brisk pace. The honest reservations of Griffin Bell or Joshua Eilberg never offered any competition to the testimony of men like William Colby, former Director of the CIA.

Colby emphasized that he refused to debate "the rights and wrongs of our many years of effort in Vietnam." His focus was a series of facts. Over many years our presidents, our Congress, and our people supported the Vietnam War. "The fact that some of the things we did, did not help, the fact that there were weaknesses on the Vietnamese side, the fact that we eventually withdrew our support, and the fact that the final result was defeat, in no way in my mind reduces the very personal commitment we made to the people of Vietnam." We "encouraged them" to fight. We "enabled" them to fight. We provided the "spirit" for their fight, and we must therefore accept the moral obligations—and refugee consequences—of our willingness to fight the Vietnam War.[41]

Colby stressed facts. Leonel Castillo (Commissioner of the INS) aimed for the patriotic jugular vein of every representative in the room. Had Congress seen the picture of the compass? It belonged to a U.S. soldier who apparently lost it in battle. Rescuers found the compass in a small boat full of people trying to sail 3,000 miles to Australia. Besides the compass the Vietnamese used a map (presumably) ripped out of an Army manual.[42]

The boat people were lost at sea and on the way to nowhere. A heartless person or nation might ignore its "special responsibilities" to the Vietnamese, but Castillo pleaded with Congress to expeditiously endorse what could be an open-ended commitment. He succeeded because Congress reluctantly agreed with his arguments. As America did fund and nurture the Vietnam War, both common decency and world opinion demanded that Congress scoop up the boat people—and the much larger mass of refugees who made their case via a competing group of voluntary agencies.

Castillo explained the "in-country" process. "Basically the voluntary agencies pick up the information and screen the refugees for the State Department. They turn dossiers over to the State Department representatives." U.S. officials then "carefully" examined the claims of each individual. Once people were accepted for parole status, the State Department provided medical examinations, transportation, and links to the same or other voluntary agencies that "sponsored" the Vietnamese when they arrived in the United States.[43]

This seemed reasonable, a happy marriage of public and private responsibility all in the service of humanitarian efforts. But what actually happened to the refugees when they came to California (37,947 Vietnamese as of April 1978), Texas (13,401), or Pennsylvania (7,431)?[44] Who paid the bills? What plans for language or skill training had been made? Did somebody contact the local communities that, as in Missoula, Montana, had to live with decisions made in Washington, D.C.? If not, how could people from such different cultures integrate themselves into U.S. society?

Here things got a little fuzzy. Hearings to admit the refugees occurred in January 1978. By April, Congress had admitted that, like the Carter Administration, it had no specific long-term plan for the refugees. However, it did express serious reservations about the financial costs of the refugees it had apparently agreed to accept. Congressman William Natcher of Kentucky noted that the camps in Thailand contained another hundred thousand people. "So, is there any feeling as to how far we can go in accepting additional refugees?" Government officials said, "Well, the proposal that has been addressed is on the basis of the U.S. accepting approximately 25,000 per year." With luck the Vietnamese would be dispersed throughout the entire county (Kentucky, for example, already had 1,070 Vietnamese), but these folks "followed the sun," which moved states like California to complain about the influx of boat people.[45]

Congress responded to these facts by embracing a contradiction. One hand welcomed more Vietnamese than ever before; the other approved a "phase-down" of support for Vietnamese boat people before they even arrived in the United States. Using the then seventeen-year commitment to the Cubans as a not-to-be-repeated precedent, Congress decided to place a firm limit on the extent of support any refugee would receive *from the federal government*. Thus, Congress "accomplished the phase-downs very largely by reductions in the level of reimbursement to the states for welfare and medical assistance."[46]

Critics argued that Congress wanted to claim electoral credit for boldly accepting the nation's moral responsibilities as it shamelessly shifted fiscal— not to mention everyday—responsibility to the states and localities where the Vietnamese actually lived. Congress answered its critics by chanting the mantra of self-sufficiency. In America people had to make it on their own; the Vietnamese therefore had to sink or swim, not in a boat bound for Australia, but in cities like Los Angeles, Houston, or Philadelphia.

In the spring of 1978 Congress agreed to cut off the first Vietnamese refugees in four years and the Cubans (who had real political muscle) in six years. Presumably all present and future refugees would assume responsibility for their own lives as quickly as humanly possible. If not, Congress offered this answer to the nation and the world: It passed the Refugee Act of 1980, a law that, among other things, tripled the *minimum* number of refugees permitted to enter the United States in any one year.

Refugee Act of 1980

Congress wanted to be rational. Since 1952, immigration law mandated a statutory limit of 17,500 on the number of refugees admitted in any one year. Yet the president and Congress had somehow accepted an average of roughly 50,000 refugees a year for the last thirty-four years. All concerned kept making exceptions to the rule, and they did it in such an ad hoc fashion that refugee policy bordered on the irrational. As the Honorable Dick Clark (U.S. Coordinator for Refugee Affairs) told the Senate, "The presentation to the Congress, the planning for the program, the budgeting for the program, and so forth, can never go forward until the decision to use the parole authority is made." But, as the Vietnamese boat people proved, parole decisions always occurred in the midst of an emergency. The inevitably unsatisfactory result was that Congress and the president stumbled along without a comprehensive policy fiscally rooted in real numbers and, most important, the lessons of the past.[47]

Ambassador Clark decided to go with the flow. He averaged the number of refugees admitted each year since World War II and then testified that 50,000 a year equaled "the so-called normal flow" of refugees. When senators obediently accepted this reasoning, 50,000 a year became the United States accepted *minimum* number of yearly refugees. However, in the event of another Cuba or Vietnam, Ambassador Clark assured the Senate that the new law gave the president the right to exceed 50,000 refugees if he determined that it was in the national interest. Naturally, Congress would always be consulted, but "if an emergency occurred after the beginning of the fiscal year," the president could potentially open the nation's doors to as many refugees as he or she saw fit.[48]

Barring the expected exceptions, the new law assumed that the president rationally planned for a normal flow of men, women, and children who, as the "important lessons" of the past proved, "had the greatest need for Federal assistance in the early years of the resettlement process."[49]

In his testimony Ambassador Clark never indicated what history he had in mind. The lesson from Cubans—a success story if there ever was one!—suggested the need for at least twenty years of sustained assistance. However, Clark underlined "that there should be a time limit (his suggestion was two years) on Federal support. To a degree this encourages refugees to adapt quickly, and it notifies both public and private agencies that Federal support for these programs would be of limited duration."[50]

To actually implement the president's plan the new law also established (in the then Department of Health, Education, and Welfare) an Office of Refugee Resettlement. This agency would prepare budgetary requests to Congress, "preserve and strengthen" the relationship between federal, state, and local governments, and do this with a specific mandate in mind: jobs for all refugees, the sooner the better.[51]

While no one questioned the ideal of self-sufficiency, Congressional critics did voice—at once—concerns about the mandate of limited federal assistance. Senator Simpson warned all listeners that "people of the states are very frustrated at the Federal government beginning a program, whatever it may be, with the states in full participation and then suddenly withdrawing and saying, 'here you are.' " So, what was Clark's answer to the governors, mayors, and municipalities who questioned the justice and rationality of the administration's plan?

Ambassador Clark stressed sympathy. He completely agreed that one could easily make a case for extending aid beyond two years. Actual refugees were, after all, anything but rubber-stamp-copies of one another. Some possessed an education; some did not. Some spoke English; most did not. Some longed to go home; some knew they could never do so. Some would immediately receive both financial and spiritual assistance from well-established ethnic communities (e.g., the Cubans); others were ethnic pioneers (e.g., the Hmong). Some refugees easily fit into Western schemes of racial, religious, and ethnic classification; others would be fish very much out of their cultural waters.[52]

Rationality demanded a flexible approach to refugee self-sufficiency. Clark grasped the obvious, but he nevertheless noted that "it was our feeling that, given the overwhelming budgetary pressures of the Government at this time, that (two years) was a reasonable point to stop."[53]

Like beauty, rationality is in the eye of the beholder. Thus, a Congress driven by budgetary concerns now institutionalized the contradiction first embraced with the Vietnamese boat people. After 1980 the United States would welcome more refugees than ever before as Washington simultaneously settled on a supposed maximum of three years of federal support, all focused on the narrow criterion of self-sufficiency.

No one asked if refugees would accept American political values, and no one discussed the apparent creation of two Americas. The first overflowed with brand new, original-language ethnic communities; the other contained the fourth or fifth generation of immigrants whose present attachment to ethnicity meant kielbasa instead of a hot dog, a green bagel on St. Patrick's day, or an Italian ice at a local religious festival.

Spiritual issues merited attention, but not from Congress. Instead, now finished with the issue of federal support, legislators decided to define the word *refugee*. In the original (1952) legislation the law not only limited the number of refugees, it also specified their geographical origins. Depart from a nation like Haiti and even with the threat of death looming, you never qualified as a refugee. But, come from a Communist nation or the Middle East (!), you could count as a person fleeing for your life.

Dictatorships waved a variety of ideological banners. Duvalier repressed his opponents just as mercilessly as Castro. In an attempt to open America's door to *anyone* fleeing persecution, Congress adopted the United Nations definition of a refugee. It now meant anyone "who was unable or unwilling" to return to his or her country of origin "because of persecution or a well founded fear of persecution on account of race, religion, nationality, or membership in a particular social or political group."[54]

Congress once again struggled to be rational and just. Since the new definition recognized persecution wherever it appeared, critics could no longer argue that the United States created ideological or geographical barriers for any group of legitimate refugees. Moreover, in an attempt to fully ascertain the truth or falsity of any particular claim, Congress expected to make all refugee decisions while applicants lived in *another* country. Thus, as in Thailand, only those who survived the screening process would be admitted to the United States as refugees.

Exceptions included those seeking asylum and any Cuban who made it to the United States. The former theoretically covered tiny numbers of ballet dancers or athletes who, performing in Boston or Los Angeles, decided to stay in the United States. The latter included a resurrection of the geographical and political exceptions Congress had just eliminated.

According to the Cuban Readjustment Act of 1966 parolees waited two years until they received refugee status. In the 1980 Refugee Act the waiting time became (in conference committee) one year. Equally important, other potential refugees needed to successfully pass the deliberately rigorous screening process; but, as Congressman Romano Mazzoli of Kentucky complained as late as 1994, the INS demanded "no standard of proof" from Cubans. "No nothing. You could have been a very rich person with a very comfortable life in Cuba, or you could have been a peasant who was hunted down by the Government. One way or another you can adjust under the Cuban Adjustment Act"—and the new 1980 exception to the supposedly universal standards adopted by Congress.[55]

Congressman Mazzoli was almost right. Under normal circumstances Cubans did receive what amounted to a procedural bye from the INS. As Deputy INS Commissioner Chris Sale told Congress, "Cuban adjustment is an exception, it is not even refugee processing. I mean it is just an opportunity for parole and adjustment (to permanent resident) in a year."[56]

But, once President Carter signed the new Refugee Act on March 17, 1980, he immediately confronted an almost unprecedented emergency. Fleeing from two Caribbean dictators, thousands of Haitian and Cuban boat people suddenly claimed to be refugees, not in another country, but on the beaches of Florida. President Carter got stuck with a political conundrum of the first order. In fact, when he asked Congress for assistance, documents in the Carter Library indicate that the president received these responses from members of his own party.

Senator Inouye of Hawaii said that "he was appalled that so many Cuban males would leave their families in Cuba to come to the United States, and he questioned the character of such people." Meanwhile, Senator Frank Church, a liberal Democrat from Idaho, suggested "that we put the Cubans on a destroyer and send them back, forcing them through the gates of Guantanamo if necessary. Senator Church did not want to discuss the options or relative merits of various strategies. He stated he could care less about them."[57]

129,000 Entrants

Who came first, the Haitians or the Cubans? Carter aides finally decided it didn't matter because, on June 20, 1980, the president confronted a situation no one could change. "To date about 114,000 Cubans and more than 15,000 Haitians have entered South Florida as 'boat people,' requiring an emergency response from the U.S. government and from the states, localities, and private voluntary agencies involved."[58]

The Cuban government started its exodus by removing guards posted at the Peruvian embassy. For more than a year small numbers of Cubans successfully sought asylum from both the Venezuelan and the Peruvian governments. But, when a Cuban guard died trying to prevent others from crashing into the embassy compound, the Castro government announced that anyone wanting to obtain a Peruvian passport was free to do so. Within days roughly 10,000 Cubans camped outside the compound. Among other things, health conditions worsened so that the Cuban government finally settled on a new strategy: All Cubans who wished to leave could board boats at the port of Mariel, a city 20 miles from Havana.[59]

Relatives of Cubans living in the United States could indeed leave, but the Castro government "forced acceptance of several non-relatives" for every family member taken on board. While criminals and the insane certainly formed part of the Mariel exodus, the Carter administration's final summary said this: "The Cubans are a heterogeneous group of people of wide age range and *wide range of reasons* for coming to the U.S. Some were political prisoners, many seek reunification with their relatives here, and many seek the greater *economic opportunities* and personal freedoms of our country" (emphasis added).[60]

The Haitians presented different problems. Aides told the President, "The regime in Haiti was, without question, as repressive as that in Cuba. Both countries were experiencing serious economic problems and there was no reason to *presume* that persons leaving Cuba did so for political reasons and those leaving Haiti did so for economic reasons" (emphasis in original).[61]

Despite this caution, INS officials continually concluded that Haitians left for economic reasons. One memo outlining the president's options indicated that, since 1970, the INS rejected fully 95 percent of Haitian claims for asylum. Actual deportation awaited the results of contentious litigation in a Florida federal court but any president acting on the facts presented by his aides faced a series of thoroughly unpalatable options.

If the president sent back the many thousands of Cubans who left for economic reasons, he would instantly be accused of forcing people into the belly of the Communist beast. On the other hand, if he acted on the truth—Duvalier was arguably even more repressive than Castro[62]—the president also faced certain opposition from Florida residents who refused to add "God knew how many" thousands of Haitians to the Miami mix. Equally important, in offering an unequivocal yes to the 15,000 Haitians, President Carter theoretically telegraphed a message of welcome to the masses queuing up in Port-au-Prince and other Haitian cities.[63]

Another problem was a presidential promise. On May 14, President Carter assured all listeners that "this nation is committed to evenhanded treatment for asylum applicants from all countries."[64] By definition this could never occur. The Cuban Adjustment Act already offered opportunities given to no other group. Despite protestations about stopping the flotilla from Mariel, Zbigniew Brzezinski and others reminded the president of his actual orders to commanders—"*modest* enforcement of our entry laws (fines and citations but few seizures and no attempt to block boats seeking to go to Cuba)" (emphasis in original).[65]

Political problems produced a political solution. On June 20, 1980, President Carter announced that all Cubans who arrived illegally in the United States between April 21 and June 19 and Haitians who had initiated INS proceedings as of June 19 would receive a special status. Neither refugees nor persons seeking asylum, the Cubans and Haitians became "entrants" (Status Pending for Six Months).

This artfully ambiguous word allegedly offered the Carter administration a perfect way out of its Caribbean dilemma. For example, even though the president had no intention of sending the vast majority of Cubans back,[66] using the word *entrant* for everyone supposedly guaranteed that Haitians and Cubans received the same treatment. Meanwhile, the president set no refugee or asylum precedents (remember the waiting line in Haiti or the Dominican Republic), and he also stopped the flow of migrants from both countries by announcing that June 20 marked a new beginning. The United States would now enforce its laws and send back those who arrived illegally.

Critics cried contradiction and capitulation. At a news conference Victor Palmieri (U.S. Coordinator for Refugee Affairs) answered questions about the status of other illegal immigrants. Why was it fair to make Cubans and Haitians entrants but not Mexicans? Palmieri said, "The answer is that we have a problem which is in the nature of an emergency problem in south

Florida."[67] By this reasoning, if the Mexicans once again stormed the Alamo, they would be welcomed by the United States as "entrants."

No one seemed satisfied, least of all John McMullan, executive editor of the *Miami Herald*. In a private briefing from Palmieri, McMullan asked why no one stopped the Cuban flotilla at once. "The ambassador countered that *had the boatlift been shut off* earlier there would have been *riots and disorders* by Cuban-Americans in the streets of Miami" (emphasis in original). That prompted this response from McMullan: "Are we to believe, then, that U.S. policy is being set not by law but by those who would flout it? And by listening to one segment of the community?"[68]

By surrendering to the Miami Cuban community, President Carter gave it *and* Fidel Castro more power. The dictator could open the boat-people spigot whenever he saw fit, and the now even stronger Cuban community would demand the same treatment offered to the Mariel flotilla. Meanwhile, by squeezing the Cuban economy with its blockade, the United States created economic conditions even more conducive to what it wanted to prevent: economic migrants who, because of the Cuban Adjustment Act, would be transformed instantly into political refugees.

As a final assault on reason and the humanitarian principles of refugee law, President Carter (and President Reagan) continued to offer economic, political, and military assistance to the Duvalier dictatorship. Thus, "Baby Doc" and General Cedras picked the people clean, killed or imprisoned anyone who got in their way, and often turned a blind eye to the boat people who, if they reached shore or a Coast Guard cutter, would still be presumed to be economic migrants. As Congressman Jerrold Nadler told his colleagues as late as June 1994, "We have the names of 20 rejectees who were later murdered, tortured or sexually assaulted." In fact, U.S. officials recently watched as "another eighty (rejected for political asylum) were observed being arrested on the dock, never mind how many were arrested later."[69]

The Central American Exodus

OTM. Instead of a secret code, the letters stood for "other than Mexican." Congressman Robert Garcia explained (in June 1985) that on a recent trip to Tijuana he closely examined the detention camps holding a large number of Central American men, women, and children. All had been caught trying to sneak into the United States, and all were segregated from the undocumented Mexican migrants because, as Congressman Garcia stressed, "I have no doubt that there is a direct relationship between the war in Central America and the number of refugees who come to this Nation."[70]

But, did the label refugee actually fit the El Salvadorans, Guatemalans, and Nicaraguans trying to enter one of America's many back doors? For example, the Reverend Sid Mohn of the United Church of Christ told Congress, "From our experience in the Midwest, we estimate that the number of Salvadorans residing in the city of Chicago number between 40,000 and 50,000." While most made the trek from where the civil contra war raged—rural El Salvador—they only settled in Chicago because word of mouth messages indicated that the windy city provided a warm welcome to Spanish speakers. As the Reverend Mohn testified, "The Central Americans utilize a well established historic Mexican migration route [see chapter 2] from Mexico to a large Mexican community in Chicago."[71]

So, did economics or politics motivate the Central American immigrants? Were they "undocumented migrants" or, as Congressman Garcia suggested, "undocumented refugees"? No such status existed, but Congress needed to define the problem at once, because even though no one knew how many Central Americans actually lived in the United States, a "crude guess" put the number of undocumented El Salvadorans at half a million. Add to that an estimated 100,000 Nicaraguans, plus another (estimated) 75,000 Guatemalans—most entering between 1979 and 1985[72]—and it became immediately clear why policymakers fought about which immigration label would be used for the Central Americans. As refugees, they would be entitled to all the benefits given to Vietnamese and Cubans. Equally important, once Congress gave the benefits, word-of-mouth messages would instantly produce the need for additional appropriations as well as additional detention pens at the Mexican border.

As a Puerto Rican, Congressman Garcia suggested he felt an affinity for the Central Americans.[73] He wanted the truth as a matter of ethnic conscience. Garcia therefore allowed Professor William Stanley (of MIT) to precisely answer the question, "Economic Migrants or Refugees from Violence?" Stanley began with a grisly comparison of who murdered more people. In the second half of 1982 guerrilla forces killed 26 people; El Salvadoran millitary and paramilitary "security forces" killed 1,000 civilians in 1979, 8,000 in 1980, and 14,000 in 1981. In the beastly competition for more murders of innocent people, the El Salvardoran government won hands down. "The vast majority of violence against the general population has been carried out by the Salvadoran military and by paramilitary death squads, both of which in many instances operate under a common leadership and involve the same personnel."[74]

Why did the people come to the United States? The State Department argued that if they left because of fear for their lives, El Salvadorans only needed to reach a safe haven in Mexico. Conceivably their first motive stemmed from fear, but once in Mexico, the State Department argued, the El Salvadorans *then* decided to take advantage of the Mexican network for economic reasons. For example, evidence showed that OTMs used the same human smugglers employed by undocumented Mexicans.

Professor Stanley countered with this argument. In sharp contrast to the wealthy Nicaraguan refugees living in some of Miami's finest homes, peasants who fled for political reasons lacked the resources required to remain away from their normal means of support. Peasants and other poor people needed work to survive. Moreover, since Mexico lacked jobs for its own people, the chances of work for outsiders appeared slim indeed.[75]

Ultimately Professor Stanley reached this conclusion: "The findings of this study provide strong empirical evidence, based on the actual behavior of Salvadorans, that fear of political violence is a major, and probably *the predominant motive* behind the decisions of Salvadorans to migrate to the United States since 1979" (emphasis in original).[76]

When religious and other witnesses also offered firsthand evidence that the Central Americans migrated "to escape the strife of their homelands,"[77] Congress and the president yet again faced the dilemma posed by the contrast between Cubans and Haitians. Certainly only his most virulent critics argued that Fidel Castro murdered 14,000 people a year; and even Iranians received political asylum 60 percent of the time. So how explain an acceptance rate for Nicaraguans of 10 percent and a rate for El Salvadorans of 3 percent?[78]

No one offered a satisfactory, factual explanation. As in Haiti, the anticipated economic costs of refugee status once again trumped even the most gruesome political violence. Thus, betwen 1981 and 1987 the State Department granted permanent resident status to 97 Central American refugees as it simultaneously said yes to 3,871 Iranians, 3,516 Thais, 2,853 Romanians, and 1,515 Ethiopians.[79]

The State Department did make one exception, however. Led by the ever more powerful Cuban American Foundation, Nicaraguans managed to get the Reagan Administration to temporarily reverse its policies. Perry Rivkind, Miami's INS director, suddenly decided (in April 1986), "I've always had difficulty viscerally with sending back people to a cowardly Communist government. The Sandinistas are exactly that."[80]

Rivkind's statement instantly produced such long lines that the INS Miami office established "weekend hours, outreach centers, and rules that dictated when people could apply on the basis of their birth month." In six short weeks 30,000 presumably undocumented Nicaraguan refugees applied for political asylum and, with the implicit assurance that they would support Republican candidates and causes, the State Department's approval rate jumped from 10 percent to 50 percent.[81]

One change quickly produced another. Nicaraguans never received many of the benefits given to the Cuban and Haitian entrants in the early 1980s, not to mention the Cubans in the 1960s and 1970s. More important, even the powerful Cuban lobby offered no match for fear of Nicaraguans to come. Thus, the public explanation for denying Nicaraguan students the scholarships offered to Cubans was this: "They may be looking for something they're not entitled to. Why should the public foot the bill?" In reality the

Reagan administration feared that providing even legitimate benefits would quickly produce a swarm of Central Americans, all hoping that the president would do for them what he had momentarily done for the Nicaraguans.[82]

Simultaneously, the Mexican march of the undocumented refugees not only became stronger than ever, it threatened to become an institutionalized part of American life. As Father Harold Bradley of Georgetown University explained it to Congress, "the effect of our military policies" is to propel these people to the United States. Originally they expected a temporary stay; but as the violence continued, they changed course. "I'm giving an example of the 25 year old [El Salvadoran] woman who, 2 years ago, came in with her two children. Last week [June of 1985] she told the Georgetown student tutoring her children the wonderful news that she had paid the same coyote that brought her in, to bring her mother to Houston and put her mother on an Eastern Airlines airplane to Washington, D.C."[83]

What a commentary! Congress argued about who was a refugee, President Reagan gave the nod to Nicaraguans promising to vote Republican, and, all the while, the flow of undocumented refugees marched through Washington's National Airport. More specifically, daughters using seasoned smugglers tearfully welcomed their mothers, as Georgetown students tutored undocumented refugees during the day and in the evening (or the next day) listened to administration officials use Georgetown's luxurious buildings to explain why President Reagan let soldiers like Colonel Oliver North fund the contras.

By 1994 a series of court decisions substantiated that the Central Americans "faced systematic discrimination in the asylum system."[84] Thus, as more than one million undocumented Mexican migrants celebrated the legal status conferred by Congress in the late 1980s, more than one million undocumented refugees waited and worked as the INS plowed throughout the endless backlog of asylum applications. Meanwhile, another half million El Salvadorans received "perpetual" grants of temporary status, as they too used money earned in the United States to pay Mexican coyotes for the safe transport of their undocumented relatives.

Washington policymakers seemed to have reached new heights of nonsense—until, that is, 1994 congressional hearings brought to light an amendment sponsored by New Jersey's Senator Frank Lautenberg.

The Lautenberg Amendment

California had a problem. As of January 1996, almost half of the 75,000 Russian refugees who had settled in Sacramento since 1975 remained on welfare. A profile of the community indicated that newcomers knew one English word, *welfare*, and that Russians of a Pentecostal persuasion sometimes boasted as many as thirteen minor children. While calculations indicated that one such family would need to secure more than $61,000 to surpass its government benefits, the chances of the parents earning that much money appeared quite slim. Neither parent spoke English.[85]

Russian refugees were among those who bothered Senator Simpson when (in 1995) he complained about men and women who, supposedly fearing for their lives, nevertheless waited a year and half before they came to the United States. Simpson wanted to know how these folks qualified, but the senator and his colleagues apparently forgot a huge exception to the refugee rules, the Lautenberg Amendment of 1989.

On May 2 (1989) Senator Frank Lautenberg (of New Jersey) explained why Soviet Jews, Evangelical and Pentecostal Christians, and selected Vietnamese immediately needed an exception to the refugee regulations. The problem was the U.S. Immigration and Naturalization Service. "After years of considering members of these groups to *automatically* qualify as refugees, the INS recently departed from its longstanding practice of presuming these groups have a well founded fear of prosecution" (emphasis added).[86] It was suddenly denying 38 percent of the new Jewish applicants (the previous figure was 7 percent) and as many as 80 percent of the Pentecostal Christians.

To Lautenberg the new policies of the INS seemed both absurd and obscene. "Have conditions facing Soviet Jews, Pentecostals, Baptists, or Vietnamese changed so dramatically as to warrant these new and historically unprecedented denial rates?" Lautenberg answered, "Emphatically not." Seconded by Senator Paul Simon of Illinois, he offered this amendment to the refugee laws: In the future, Soviet Jews, Evangelical Christians, and Vietnamese registered with the United States Orderly Departure Program "are members of groups for whom prosecution, or fear of prosecution, *if alleged, will be presumed*" (emphasis added).[87]

Before Congress voted on this amendment it also heard from two powerful VOLAGS—the United States Catholic Conference and the Lutheran Immigration and Refugee Service. The Catholics expressed concern about "families who have been separated for many years from their loved ones and whose hopes for reunification rested on the admission of their loved ones as refugees." The Protestants, worried about "compassion fatigue," reminded legislators that the INS denial rate "is not deserving of our nation's proud reputation and heritage as an international advocate of human rights and refugee protection."[88]

When the American Jewish Committee, the Hebrew Aid Society, and the Council of Jewish Federations also expressed enthusiastic support for the Lautenberg exception, only the agnostics and atheists needed a spokesperson. The "pure pressure" cited by Senator Simpson proved so effective that, between 1990 and 1995, refugees from the Soviet Union and Vietnam monopolized roughly 70 percent of all refugee slots. For example, in 1990, they accounted for 78,094 of 109,078 refugee admissions, and in 1995 they accounted for 67,600 of 98,520 refugee admissions.[89]

After Lautenberg, nobody asked any questions—at least until the Haitians and Cubans once again threatened to overwhelm Miami.

Same Thing, Only Different

One administration official called it the "traditional start of the rafting season."[90] As in summer nature often softened the Caribbean's hard edge, as Cubans in Miami sailed out to rescue Cubans fleeing from Castro, one administration after another waited to offer immediate asylum to the now traditional flow of Cuban rafters.

The "end" of Communism made 1994 anything but a traditional year. Squeezed first by Washington and then by the collapse of the Soviet Union, the Cuban economy produced so much pain that, in the summer of 1994, 20,000 human beings floated out to sea. In Washington the Clinton Administration promptly expressed serious concern for the safety of the "imperiled rafters," the safety of the overworked Coast Guard, and "the integrity of U.S. borders." After all, with roughly a million Mexicans and El Salvadorans already crossing the Rio Grande, an armada of rafters from the Caribbean could finally exhaust the nation's "compassion quotient."

President Clinton eventually did the politically unthinkable: He said no to Cubans. Instead of allowing rafters to be rescued and processed, he ordered his troops to deposit them in Guantanamo. However, "as the numbers grew beyond Guantanamo's capacity, we secured the agreement of Panama to allow us to open a safe haven there as well."[91] When even that move failed to stem the number of rafters the president countered one unprecedented act—saying no to the traditional flow—with another. He struck a public deal with Fidel Castro in September of 1994 and then, in May of 1995, ordered an undersecretary of state to secure a secret immigration agreement with the government of Fidel Castro.

Alerted to the negotiations, some congressmen first denounced the president and then called for hearings. Thus, two weeks after he signed (on May 2, 1995) the deal with Castro, Undersecretary of State (for political affairs) Peter Tarnoff stood before a wall of red-faced congressmen, all eager to pounce on him as quickly as the Coast Guard pounced on Cubans fleeing to freedom.

Tarnoff produced written answers (to no less than 122 congressional questions) and public testimony that emphasized these facts. Fueled by, among other things, the U.S. blockade, the continuing deterioration of the Cuban economy promised another flood of rafters when the 1995 season began. In addition, the United States had already spent $135 million remodeling Guantanamo, the everyday costs to "run a minimal care type of facility" totaled one million dollars a day, and worst of all, the Cubans in Guantanamo threatened to create an international incident.[92]

Here Tarnoff's testimony received additional, emotional impact from

General John J. Sheehan, Commander in Chief, U.S. Atlantic Command. General Sheehan explained that he controlled "15,000 young males, who are about 18 to 24 years old, or 32 years old, very few women with no exit strategy. In McAlla Field in the summer time it is 120 degrees and we do not have enough hurricane shelters to protect those numbers of people."[93]

Any reasonable person could easily understand the potential for violence outlined by the general. But, to drive home the administration's terrible predicament, the general whispered that some men had already jumped off cliffs, with the intent of swimming to Cuba. Others, intent on getting to Miami, mutilated themselves with tent stakes, walked through mine fields, or used syringes to inject diesel fuel into their veins. Whatever the means, the end remained the same: entrance to a U.S. hospital on the U.S. main-land.[94]

Add to the horror at Guantanamo the prospect of more rafters in 1995 (and of course those waiting in Haiti as well) and you get some idea why Clinton had to negotiate with Castro—and at all costs secretly.

Tarnoff explained that the discussions remained top secret—they were "unpublicized"—for only one reason, "to avoid the very real possibility that rumors about these talks might trigger a massive exodus of new migrants by sea and over land seeking to anticipate any new United States–Cuban mi-gration agreement."[95]

As always Fidel Castro controlled the situation. Let him once again open the spigot and the United States would be overwhelmed. Therefore, Tarnoff explained that he had negotiated a deal that should delight every Cuban in Miami. For their part the Cubans "pledged to take effective action to prevent unsafe and irregular departures." They also agreed to receive and not punish any rafter who returned to Cuba. "For our part we committed to ensuring that legal immigration from Cuba increased to at least 20,000 [refugees] a year, *a higher figure than ever before*" (emphasis added).[96]

Even Jorge Mas Canosa, chair of the Castro-hating Cuban American Na-tional Foundation, agreed with the administration's contention. "What 20,000 people means are a lot of people and let me tell you why. The most amount, the highest amount, of Cubans arriving in the United States in 1 year, during the last 20 years was 3,000 a year. Under the only two admin-istrations that more than 3,000 a year has arrived in the United States was under the Carter Administration with Mariel and under the Clinton admin-istration."[97]

Forget the slight mistake on time frames. Remember instead that despite Bill Clinton's *institutionalization* of a new, huge, guaranteed figure for Cuban refugees, Mas Canosa harshly criticized—"sordid" was too kind a word—the president's secret agreement.[98] Like Jimmy Carter, Bill Clinton was "soft" on communism and a punching bag for Fidel Castro. Presumably Mas Canosa wanted to squeeze Castro until he and his colleagues *slowly* stopped breathing.[99]

Whatever the case, President Clinton chose a compromise that even some moderates found hard to swallow. Congressman Robert Martinez grilled Undersecretary Tarnoff about a passage in his written statement. "What you are saying to the committee is that such an outflow of migrants [i.e., the unregulated rafters] is a threat to the national security of the United States?" Tarnoff took the bait by agreeing, which moved Martinez to ask this question: "Now, how many people cross the border between the United States and Mexico each year?"[100]

With that comment Martinez, noting his tenure as a Marine, artfully brought "front and center" a major contradiction in all U.S. immigration policy. How was a flotilla of 30,000 Cubans on rafts more of a national security threat than "the one million people who cross annually between the United States and Mexico"? When Tarnoff stressed the administration's emphasis on a strengthened border patrol, Martinez first reminded Tarnoff that he had never used soldiers against the Mexicans and then finished with this salvo: "There is a million, or a multitude of reasons versus 30,000 in this case. You say that that is a national security threat. Well, we have one hell of a national security threat going on then, don't we?"[101]

The difference was this. For a hundred years U.S. economic and political interests welcomed the "unauthorized" Mexicans. As Martinez spoke, roughly 600,000 undocumented Chicanos still stooped to maintain an agricultural empire in the American Southwest. Meanwhile, nobody—not even the Cuban American National Foundation—wanted Cubans brokered in a secret deal with Fidel Castro. President Clinton nevertheless opened the refugee door wider than ever because the alternatives included an unregulated flow from Cuba, horror in Guantanamo, and, waiting in the wings, the rafters fleeing the dictatorship in Haiti.[102]

Like President Carter in 1980, President Clinton needed to explain a yes to the Cubans but a no to the Haitians. With the deposed Haitian president Aristede angrily walking the halls of Congress, no one could any longer deny the dictatorial nature of the Haitian government. Thus, in June of 1994— two months before the Cuban rafters even began to flee—Congress held contentious hearings focusing on exceptions to the refugee rules. Both the Lautenberg Amendment and the Cuban exception came under such fire that the chair of the House Subcommittee on International Law, Immigration, and Refugees offered this assessment: "An important concern for me is how we justify treating Cubans differently than we treat Haitians. . . . I just think it is totally inconsistent and is obviously based on the fact that everybody is scared to death of the Cuban-American population, afraid that they will vote against them in the elections, I guess."[103]

After secretly saying yes to another 20,000 Cubans a year, the President needed to somehow square the Haitian circle. He used the precedent set by President Carter. Bill Clinton recreated the catchall category of "Cuban/Haitian Entrants" (the total number for 1995 was 31,819, mostly Cuban entrants[104]) and then argued that all received equal treatment under law. In fact the Cubans retained their traditional prerogatives; thus, while the administration claimed that equality reigned, charts distributed by the INS show that (in 1995) Cubans received over four times as many refugee admissions as the Haitians.[105]

In Port-au-Prince word-of-mouth messages let interested migrants know that America's legal doors remained very hard to open. In Havana U.S. officials quietly processed more Cuban refugees than ever before. And in Washington President Clinton took credit for having the gumption to say no to the Cubans.

This was "great" politics, awful immigration policy. Cubans, Russians, and Vietnamese now dominated the refugee flow, as federal agencies tried to disperse the concentrations of people that Congress invited or, as with the Central Americans, allowed to stay—without the consent of the governed. By 1996 extremes dominated public debate about all aspects of immigration (i.e., legal immigrants, undocumented migrants, and refugees) as Congress and the president continually put politics ahead of principles and votes before meaningful alternatives to the contentious status quo.

Good Questions, No Answers

While the published accounts of Congressional hearings continually contain excellent analyses of particular issues or policies, even the best reports are frequently disregarded. Somehow Congress has investigators ask all the right questions as it simultaneously refuses to accept—or even seriously consider—the answers it receives.

Take a lucid, thought-provoking study submitted in 1985, Susan Forbes' *Adaptation and Integration of Recent Refugees to the United States*. Forbes begins by noting that prior to 1980 "there was little systematic attempt by the government or anyone else to document the experiences of refugees within the context of federal, state or private assistance programs." As nobody really knew what was going on, Forbes, among others, received a request to evaluate the efficacy of federal refugee assistance.

Her report begins with a problem: "While refugees are strikingly heterogeneous in character, Congress has nevertheless treated refugees as if one size fits all." The overriding objective of the assistance program "is effective resettlement of refugees as rapidly as possible." In essence, get them a job and get them off the Federal payroll.[106]

Forbes found that 75 percent of (mostly Indochinese) refugees still lacked a job after a year in the United States. After three years the unemployment rate dropped to roughly 30 percent, while rates of public assistance varied from over 85 percent in California to less than 20 percent in Texas. From the perspective of the federal government—the degree of self sufficiency—the program seemed to be a modest success, although some of those working for forty or more hours labored in jobs that often provided wages at or below the poverty line.[107]

In a concluding section on "Policy Implications" Forbes raised crucial questions. She argued that increased English language proficiency was *negatively* associated with labor force participation.[108] People needed six months to a year to obtain fluency in English. Did Congress want the refugees to learn the language and thus presumably raise the likelihood of cultural as well economic integration? How, after all, could a person love the Constitution if they couldn't read it? What jobs were available to people who spoke little or no English?

Or, did Congress want to continue to press for any job at all costs and so make English language proficiency a hit or miss operation?

Another issue concerned the "forced" dispersal of the Indochinese refugees. The conventional wisdom argued that if you spread the folks about you at least lessened the possibility of the economic and cultural clashes that characterized a city like Miami. But, in sharp contrast to the Cuban (and Haitian) "entrants," the Vietnamese came to a nation with little or no pre-existing ethnic support. They started from scratch. Forbes stressed that "the future of refugee adjustment is, in large part, dependent on the development of these (ethnic community) infrastructures."[109] For example, despite the government's offered employment services, roughly half of all refugees found jobs only through friends and relatives. To achieve success in an "alien" culture, the youngsters about to enter U.S. schools might require strong, everyday support from both the extended family and the ethnic community.[110]

On the issue of welfare and dependency Forbes agreed that more refugees received assistance if they lived in states with generous benefits. Instead of quickly drawing the negative conclusion that welfare served as a disincentive to self-sufficiency, Forbes wrote that the benefits could simply be a safety net for people barely treading water. Even refugees with "transferable skills" earned little more than minimum wage, and household income increased because of multiple wage earners, not increases in pay. So, perhaps it was best to eliminate limitations on the number of hours refugees could work and still receive assistance? Forbes offered no definitive answers, only the request that Congress discard its prejudices about welfare and "carefully assess" the efficacy of a variety of innovative, demonstration projects.[111]

Forbes' final point was the most important of all: One size does not fit all. "Refugee resettlement is a constantly changing process, one that requires substantial flexibility to address new issues."[112] Congress could address those issues or face the consequences of refugees who lived at the margins of society while local communities ranted and raved about the irresponsibility of the federal government and the un-American attitudes of the unwanted refugees.

Ms. Forbes submitted her report in August of 1985. In August of 1996,

Congressman David Obey (of Wisconsin) represented many Americans when he told his colleagues, "I think the Federal government is a damn welsher when it comes to refugees—a huge welsher. I chaired the Foreign Operations Appropriations Subcommittee for ten years. I saw politicians in this place routinely take great credit for bringing large numbers of refugees to this country with the groups that were interested in seeing them come to this country."[113]

The "pure pressure" of the VOLAGS worked. Politics continually trumped the reasoned analysis and common decency of analysts like Ms. Forbes. Thus, Congressman Obey protested, "I strongly believe that the organizations who bring refugees to this country in the first place have an obligation, a more long term obligation than they are now meeting, and I think the Federal government certainly has a much longer-term obligation than it is meeting. I think to simply dump them on local taxpayers is an obscenity."[114]

One response to Congressman Obey came from the federal government's Office of Refugee Resettlement. In its appropriation requests for 1998, the first sentence of the agency's "justification" was, "The program is designed to help refugees and Cuban and Haitian entrants who are admitted to the United States to become self sufficient and socially adjusted as quickly as possible."[115] If this seems farcical, it's also America at the turn of the twenty-first century.

To move forward with any sense of hope, we need to understand the past, assign responsibility, and, because the ethnic strands are here forever, have a policy and an ideal for an actual situation. Nothing less is required if we are to have any chance of peacefully proceeding, as the *United* States, into the next century.

NOTES

1. Hearings to Private Organizations Before the Subcommittee on Immigration and Claims, House, 104th Congress, second session, August 1, 1996 (Washington, DC: GPO), p. 23.

2. Robert Heilbroner, *The Nature and Logic of Capitalism* (New York: Harper, 1982).

3. *Annual Refugee Consultation*, Hearings Before the Subcommittee on Immigration, Senate, 104th Congress, first session, 1995 (Washington, DC: GPO), pp. 2, 14–15.

4. See Barnaby Zall, "The U.S. Refugee Industry: Doing Well by Doing Good," in David Simcox, ed., *U.S. Immigration in the 1980's* (Boulder: Westview, 1988), pp. 258–269. For a list of the major organizations now funded by the federal government, see the statistical pages of the INS Web page. A thorough list was published in March of 1999. See ⟨www.state.gov/www.global/prm/9903⟩.

5. Thomas A. Bass, *Vietnamerica: The War Comes Home* (New York: SOHO, 1996); the quote is on p. 40.

6. Ibid., p. 41.

7. Ibid., p. 91.

8. Ibid., p. 52.

9. *Vietnamese Amerasian Resettlement: Education, Employment and Family Outcome in the United States*, Government Accounting Office, Washington, DC, 3/31/94, GAO/PEMD-94–15, p. 10 of the version downloaded from the Internet.

10. *The Impact of Federal Immigration Policy and INS Activities on Communities*, Hearings Before the Information, Justice, Transportation and Agriculture Subcommittee, House of Representatives, 103rd Congress, first and second sessions, 1994 (Washington, DC: GPO), p. 120.

11. Ibid., p. 122.

12. See Bass, *Vietnamerica*, pp. 157, 189.

13. See ⟨www.famas.org/clinton.htn⟩. The letter is signed by Luisito L. Lopez.

14. See *1996 Statistical Yearbook of the Immigration and Naturalization Service*, U.S. Department of Justice, Immigration and Naturalization Service, (Washington, DC: GPO, October 1997), p. 84. Consistent with the testimony cited during the Senate's 1995 Refugee Consultation, I have added the 20,000 Cubans admitted under special refugee status to the 90,000 cited in the INS charts. See *Annual Refugee Consultation*, p. 6.

15. *Departments of Labor and Health, Education, and Welfare Appropriations for 1978*, Hearings Before a Subcommittee of the Committee on Appropriations, House of Representatives, 95th Congress, second session (Washington, DC: GPO, 1978), p. 409.

16. *The Refugee Act of 1979*, Hearings Before the Committee on the Judiciary, Senate, 96th Congress, first session (Washington, DC: GPO, 1979), see especially pp. 69–71; see also *U.S. Immigration Law and Policy, 1952–1979*, Committee on the Judiciary, Senate, 96th Congress, first session (Washington, DC: GPO, 1979), especially pp. 17–19.

17. Ibid., p. 18.

18. For the comments in 1938 and 1948, see Ronald Fernandez, *Cruising the Caribbean: U.S. Influence and Intervention in the Twentieth Century* (Monroe, ME: Common Courage Press, 1994), pp. 205, 272; for Senator Aiken, see *Executive Sessions of the Foreign Relations Committee (Historical Series)*, vol. 10, 85th Congress, second session (Washington, DC: GPO, 1958), p. 779. These documents were made public in 1980.

19. *Executive Sessions of the Foreign Relations Committee (Historical Series)*, Volume 12, 86th Congress, second session (Washington, DC: GPO, 1960), p. 110. These documents were made public in 1982.

20. President John F. Kennedy Library, Records of the Department of Health, Education and Welfare, Roll 44, document dated January 27, 1961.

21. Fernandez, *Cruising the Caribbean*, esp. chapters 4–7.

22. Kennedy Library, *Records of DHEW*, Roll 44, from page 4 of a document dated February 3, 1961; for the wholesale paroling see *U.S. Immigration Law and Policy*, p. 46.

23. Kennedy Library, National Security Files, Country Files, Cuba, Box 46; the memo is from Q. Hunsaker, and it and its attachments are dated February 7, 1963.

24. Kennedy Library, *Records of DHEW*, Roll 44, pp. 4–6 of Secretary Ribicoff's report.

25. *Departments of Labor and Health, Education and Welfare Appropriations for 1978*, Hearings Before a Subcommittee on Appropriations, House, 95th Congress, first session (Washington, DC: GPO, 1978), pp. 172–205.

26. Kennedy Library, National Security Files, Country Files, Cuba, Box 46; the memo is titled "Cuba: Its Refugees and Its Liberation." It is dated September 6, 1962. The comment appears on p. 4.

27. Ibid.; see document stamped secret, dated April 22, 1963.

28. Ibid.; the memo is stamped secret, dated December 10, 1962.

29. President Lyndon Johnson Library, *Presidential Files of S. Douglas Cater*, Box 95, Federal Task Force Report on Miami, see p. 2; see, too, a long memo at the Kennedy Library, *Records of DHEW*, Roll 44, Position Paper on Miami, dated February 25, 1963.

30. Johnson Library, Administrative History of the Department of Justice, Box 8, Immigration and Naturalization, p. 26 of document titled "Between Blue Pages."

31. Johnson Library, National Security Files, Country Files, Box 30; this is from a memo to McGeorge Bundy dated October 14, 1965; for the president's speech see Office Files—Harry McPherson, Box 8.

32. Johnson Library, Files of S. Douglas Cater, Box 95, p. 2, of the Task Force's Report to the President dated June 28, 1966.

33. Ibid., pp. 5–17.

34. *U.S. Immigration Law and Policy*, pp. 58–59.

35. Ibid., p. 59.

36. *Admission of Refugees into the United States, Part II*, Hearings Before the Subcommittee on Immigration, Citizenship and International Law, House of Representatives, 95th Congress, first and second sessions (Washington, DC: GPO, 1977, 1978), pp. 74–75.

37. Ibid., pp. 13–14, 28.

38. Ibid., pp. 26–27.

39. Ibid., p. 113.

40. Ibid., p. 123.

41. Ibid., p. 175.

42. Ibid., p. 131.

43. Ibid., p. 133.

44. *Department of Labor and Health, Education and Welfare Appropriations for 1979*, Hearings Before a Subcommittee of the Committee of Appropriations, House of Representatives, 95th Congress, second session (Washington, DC: GPO, 1978), p. 407.

45. Ibid., pp. 405–406.

46. Ibid., p. 409.

47. *Refugee Act of 1979*, Hearings Before the Committee on the Judiciary, Senate, 96th Congress, first session (Washington, DC: GPO, 1979), pp. 22–23; for the numbers of refugees, see p. 6.

48. Ibid., p. 22.

49. Ibid., p. 14.

50. Ibid.

51. See, for example, the congressional statement of Lavinia Limon, Director of the Office of Refugee Resettlement, February 6, 1996. On page 1 of the testimony

she indicates that "the refugee program has emphasized early employment through-out its history." The document can be located at ⟨www.hhs.gov/cgi-bin/waisgate⟩.

52. See, e.g., Susan Forbes, "Adaptation and Integration of Recent Refugees to the United States," in *Departments of Labor and Health and Human Services, Education and Related Agencies Appropriations for 1987*, Hearings Before a Subcommittee on Appropriations, House, 99th Congress, second session (Washington, DC: GPO, 1986), especially pp. 653–655.

53. *Refugee Act of 1979*, p. 35.

54. Ibid., p. 32.

55. See *Haitian Asylum Seekers*, Hearing Before the Subcommittee on Interna-tional Law, Immigration and Refugees, Committee on the Judiciary, House, 103rd Congress, second session (Washington, DC: GPO, 1994), p. 137, for Congressman Mazzoli's comments; p. 137, the INS assessment.

56. See the testimony of Deputy INS Commissioner Chris Sale, ibid., especially p. 117; also Congressman Jerrold Nadler of New York, p. 100.

57. President Jimmy Carter Library, Atlanta, Georgia, Domestic Policy Staff—White, Box 22; the Church comment is from a memo to the president dated June 6, 1980, p. 5; the Inouye comment is from a memo dated May 16, 1980; p. 4.

58. Carter Library: document is labeled "Cuba-Haitian Fact Sheet," dated June 20, 1980; figures are from p. 1.

59. Carter Library; this summary is from a Foreign Affairs Memorandum of May 1980; it is attributed to Assistant Secretary of State Brian Atwood; see p. 2.

60. Carter Library, Fact Sheet dated June 20, 1980, p. 1.

61. Carter Library, memo titled "Haitian Refugees," dated April 18, 1980; see p. 3 for the comment cited.

62. See, for example, Fernandez, *Cruising the Caribbean*, pp. 309–350.

63. Carter Library, memo for the president dated June 14, 1980, from Zbigniew Brzezinski et al., p. 2.

64. Carter Library, Foreign Affairs, memorandum attributed to Brian Atwood, May 1980, p. 6.

65. Carter Library, memo of May 13, 1980, p. 1.

66. Carter Library, see, for example, p. 2 of the unsigned, undated memo entitled "Status Options for Cubans and Haitians."

67. Carter Library, copy of a document entitled "Immigration Report," dated July 1980, p. 2.

68. Ibid., p. 2.

69. See *Haitian Asylum Seekers*, p. 147.

70. *Central American Refugees*, Hearings Before the Subcommittee on Census and Population, Committee on Post Office and Civil Service, House, 99th Congress, first session (Washington, DC: GPO, 1985), p. 123.

71. Ibid., pp. 98–99.

72. Ibid., for the El Salvadoran number, see p. 48; for a complete overview by the U.S. Census Bureau, see pp. 7–25; especially pp. 14, 19.

73. Ibid., p. 123.

74. Ibid., p. 50; see, too, Mark Danner, *The Massacre at El Mozote* (New York: Vintage, 1994).

75. Ibid., pp. 52–54.

76. Ibid., p. 72.

77. Ibid., p. 105; see, too, the statement and testimony of Aryeh Neier, vice chairman of Americas Watch, pp. 26–40.

78. See Alejandro Portes and Alex Stepik, "A Repeat Performance? The Nicaraguan Exodus," in *Challenging Fronteras*, edited by Mary Romero, Pierrette Hondagneu-Sotelo, and Vilma Ortiz (New York: Routledge, 1997), pp. 135–153, especially p. 139.

79. *1988 Statistical Yearbook of the Immigration and Naturalization Service*, U.S. Department of Justice, Immigration and Naturalization Service (Washington, DC: GPO, 1988), p. 51.

80. Portes and Stepick, "A Repeat Performance?" p. 140.

81. Ibid.

82. Ibid., p. 141.

83. *Central American Refugees*, p. 114.

84. Roberto Suro, *Strangers Among Us* (New York: Alfred A. Knopf, 1998), p. 100.

85. *Migration News* 3, no. 1 (January 1996): 12.

86. *Congressional Record*, 101st Congress, first session, 1989, 135, pp. S4617–4618.

87. Ibid., p. 4617.

88. Ibid., pp. 4619–4620.

89. *1996 Statistical Yearbook of the Immigration and Naturalization Service*, U.S. Department of Justice, Immigration and Naturalization Service (Washington, DC: GPO, 1997), p. 85.

90. *The Clinton Administration's Reversal of U.S. Immigration Policy Toward Cuba*, Hearing Before a Subcommittee on the Western Hemisphere, House, 104th Congress, first session (Washington, DC: GPO, 1995), p. 20.

91. Ibid., p. 89.

92. Ibid.; for the money, see p. 40; for Tarnoff's answers to the 122 questions, see pp. 114–124.

93. Ibid., p. 41.

94. Ibid.

95. Ibid., p. 14; see, too, Tarnoff's answer to Congressman Martinez, p. 125.

96. Ibid., p. 13.

97. Ibid., p. 71.

98. Ibid., p. 55.

99. Ibid., p. 71.

100. Ibid., pp. 27–28.

101. Ibid., p. 28.

102. Ibid.; see especially Tarnoff's comment, p. 125.

103. *Haitian Asylum Seekers*, p. 32.

104. See *Departments of Labor . . . Appropriations*, Hearings, House of Representatives, 105th Congress, first session (Washington, 1998), p. 1143.

105. See *1996 Statistical Yearbook of the Immigration and Naturalization Service*, p. 85.

106. Forbes, *Adaptation and Integration*, pp. 653–654.

107. Ibid., pp. 658–669.

108. Ibid., p. 665.

109. Ibid., p. 690.

110. Ibid., pp. 690–691.

111. Ibid., pp. 688–689.

112. Ibid., p. 693.

113. Hearing Before the Subcommittee on Immigration and Claims, Committee on the Judiciary, House, 104th Congress, second session (Washington, DC: GPO, 1996), p. 23.

114. Ibid., pp. 23–24.

115. *Departments of Labor, Health and Human Services, Education and Related Agencies Appropriations for 1998*, Hearings Before a Subcommittee of the Committee on Appropriations, House, 105th Congress, first session (Washington, DC: GPO, 1997), pp. 1142.

PART TWO

WHAT SHALL WE DO
WITH OUR AMERICA?

4

How Is Society Possible?

"We do not live to think, but the other way round:
We think in order that we may succeed in surviving."
—José Ortega y Gasset, *Man and People*[1]

RELEVANT ASSUMPTIONS[2]

The market was a shrine to cholesterol, the deli counter an altar on which the throng of recent Russian immigrants happily sacrificed any chance for a long life. Huge hunks of milky white cheese lay next to an assortment of vegetables drowning in oil, crispy fish fried in lard, and such a wide array of sausages that they tastefully provided Mercedes for an army of cardiologists.

In the morning I eat fake eggs, accompanied by low-fat toast, sprayed—not spread—with I'm Sure It's Not Butter. Red meat is my enemy, at least thirty minutes of vigorous exercise my everyday mantra. So, when people talk about culture shock, I say take a trip to Brighton Beach, New York. Go to a Russian deli and enter a culinary world in which new immigrants unashamedly pay homage to their culture of origin.

In front of the deli counter I all knowingly wise cracked about "instant death," only to be overheard by a meaty woman who laughed at my concerns. Sporting a spotless white deli apron, the clerk also wore a smile as she said something in Russian that was as incomprehensible as the food. Embarrassed, I edged past the gauntlet of mouth-watering temptations, only to be sent off with an expression that said this: You Americans are so strange. Worried about your arteries when you ought to be filling them with deli delights and using vodka—the store had a prominent display—to move any problems through the bloodstream.

I breathed easier on the street. But as we walked along the avenues, I never lost a simultaneous sense of isolation and excitement. One newsstand contained three papers, all in Russian. We easily passed four street vendors catering to Eastern Orthodox Christianity; a gift shop displayed dozens of buttons ridiculing Boris Yeltsin; and one woman, with her hair braided in a uniquely attractive fashion, entered a public restaurant that was actually a private club. My son agreed to go in if I persisted but the Russian Mafia ran the restaurant, so, despite its looking like the real thing, locals knew that the criminal owners wanted no actual customers.

For some New Yorkers Brighton Beach is an affront to their melting-pot ideal. For its inhabitants the roughly twelve-block community is an oasis. And for all Americans Brighton Beach is a 1999 manifestation of a four-hundred-year-old fact: A remarkable consequence of immigration to the United States is the persistence of ethnic groups and their distinctive traditions. Huge increases in the sheer number of immigrants have focused attention on new arrivals (averaging almost a million a year during the 1990s[3]) but, whether it's old or new immigrants, the enduring reality is the continued existence and significance of ethnic groups in the fifty states. Think of the Portuguese in Hartford, the Filipinos in San Diego, the African Americans in Harlem. Or the Italians in Boston, the Polish in Chicago, the Hispanos in New Mexico, the Chicanos in Texas, the Hmong in Minneapolis, the Indians and Koreans in Queens, the Chinese in San Francisco, New York, or Washington, D.C.

This book argues that the most intelligent response to the ethnic strands already here is to accept, recognize, and *eagerly explore* the cultural differences among the American people.[4] I stress "eagerly explore" because ethnic differences can be a marvelous source of national strength, personal joy, and positive social change. But, like me at the deli counter, ethnic differences also suggest the impossibility of social life. When I saw those sausages, the only relevant thing for me was cholesterol. As a matter of scientific faith, I *instantly* assumed that, like a bullet aimed at my heart, sausages killed.

Taste, tradition, and pleasure dictated relevance for the big woman behind the deli counter. She laughed at me because she *instantly* assumed—quite rightly by the way—that I was another one of those excessively health-conscious Americans. When would we learn to enjoy ourselves? When would we begin to act like Russians?

The answer is never. Which means that one of our greatest national conundrums is to create a sense of community, despite the instant assumptions that make social, political, and economic life possible for some, impossible for others.

Sam Sue is in his early forties. Growing up in Mississippi in the 1960s, Sue could buy a ticket to the movies but, once inside, it was impossible to find a seat. American society said that color was the only relevant factor required for seating arrangements, yet it made no allowance for a majority of the human race. So, did Sue sit upstairs with the African Americans or downstairs with the whites? Sue ultimately resolved the dilemma by sitting with the whites, always anxious that someone would perhaps ask him to stand—the only alternative when a society sees you and your ancestors as ethnically irrelevant.[5]

One contemporary solution for many Asians is to assimilate, to accept that they are in fact "people of color." Thus, in a newspaper column titled "Wong Words," Bill Wong explains his sense of irrelevance when he attended a 1996 conference of journalists discussing diversity. "The vast majority of the 800 conferees were white people, many of them middle-aged and older. All the main conference speakers were white men and white women. Workshop speakers, like me, were more mixed but not much more."[6]

Wong only felt "slightly uncomfortable" until, at a plenary session entitled "How American Is the Global Village," all the "white" luminaries decided that they "epitomized the new global individual." These were wong words indeed, because "then it hit me. What about most of the world? . . . China and India make up about forty percent of humanity. Add the rest of Asia, toss in Africa and Latin America and you have a sizable majority of the human species. So how can three white people be the epitome of the new global individual when you and I know that there are plenty of Asian, Latin and African 'new global individuals?' "[7]

Wong spoke up. He alerted the audience to his presumed irrelevance and received "quite a bit of applause" when he complained that the instant assumptions of the "white" luminaries mirrored nothing more than an over-inflated sense of self-importance rooted in cultural conceit. Exclude people of color if you will, but know too that until whites change, the Wongs of the world meant to make national conferences as impossible for them as it was for Sam Sue to find a seat in the theater.

This is a national problem: If the relevant assumptions of one group clash with those of another, both everyday and important social encounters will be confusing, embarrassing, contentious, or all three at once. However, unless people like Bill Wong challenge the relevant assumptions of the majority culture, nothing changes. In order to make social life just, is it first necessary to make it impossible?

I believe it is. Societies work because of shared assumptions about self and world. If there is a consensus, interaction proceeds without incident. Everybody knows his or her place in the theater, and everybody tries to imitate the stars of the social show. Thus, in Hawaii, Andrea Kim and her friends used scotch tape to give their eyelids another fold, while youngsters with money endured an operation to make their eyelids double.[8]

Challenge the assumptions with anger and we talk by one another. Or, what is worse, we don't talk at all. Like some of the Indians interviewed for this book, immigrants live in the United States but they are never part of it.

An alternative is to use the insights of sociology to help produce peaceful yet significant social change. Two hundred and seventy million people can achieve a meaningful sense of community, especially if it is rooted in an empathetic understanding of why people think and act as they do.

HOW IS SOCIETY POSSIBLE?[9]

Dominicanyorks. It's a clumsy word that nevertheless stores, like a fancy garment bag full of pockets, a great deal of everyday knowledge. Many Dominicans only migrated to New York to build up the nest egg required for success at home. But, when they succeeded, migrants returning to Santo Domingo discovered that instead of a welcome mat, they received a rash of ridicule and scorn. "Real" Dominicans spoke without an accent acquired in Manhattan, they never wore gold chains, and they never raised children who showed no respect for their elders. Thus, despite fulfilling a lifelong dream of returning home, the Dominicanyork is now—forever—an outsider; he or she lost authenticity in New York, and all the money in the Caribbean can never replace the respect sacrificed on the altar of migration.[10]

The word Dominicanyork also connotes serious competition with the island's traditional elites. Those who stayed do not want to share political and economic power, especially with people who build both English-language schools and exclusive housing complexes *para ausentes* and *para retornados* (for the absent and the returned). The Dominicanyorks argue that their new money provides jobs for local labor, while the traditional elites suggest that the newcomers share dual allegiances. Social scientists may call that the rise of transnational communities,[11] but old-timers complain that those who picked up a taste for Pepsi are never the real thing. In a crunch their bicultural loyalties may place U.S. interests ahead of those of the Dominican Republic—and the native elites who still milk it dry with old-fashioned elegance and violence.

While that's a lot of knowledge squeezed into one word, it's also the social power of any generalization. In any society on earth, people cram an enormous amount of information into words and then learn their meanings with such precision that there is no need for thought. See a Dominicanyork and you supposedly know at once what he or she believes and how he or she will behave.

In reality, any generalization is always subject to one qualification after another. Nearly a million Dominicans migrated. Many experienced so much prejudice, failure and disillusionment in New York that they returned home more committed to the traditional culture than the most rabid nationalist. However, for society to be possible, *for millions of people to get through everyday life without having to think about each and every encounter*, we neglect the nuances and focus instead on the generalizations that, by definition, carry a heavy load of "incompleteness."[12]

Society is possible—I am not arguing just or pleasant—because of the generalizations and the inevitable incompleteness. By neglecting complexities we more easily order the world into a manageable, dependable scheme; when others share our convictions, we walk through life confidant that our perceptions and expectations are both accurate and reliable. Growing up in New York, I was always a "spic." Early on I had no idea what the word meant, only that people didn't like me when I said my last name. In reality, my parents came from Spain (thus the incompleteness), but the generalization allowed many New Yorkers to immediately respond, not to a particular person, but to the influx of 600,000 Puerto Ricans in a span of twelve years (1948–1960). That the generalization used for the newcomers contained so much prejudice is of course a negative commentary on American culture; but the word "spic" nevertheless made it possible for the majority to interact matter-of-factly with the newcomers and with Spaniards like me. We were all "spics" and should be treated as such.

Generalizations are therefore a two-edged sword. They make society possible because, once stored in the brain, they allow us to make immediate sense of the people, things, and events that surround us. Using generalizations, we are even able to successfully interact with a variety of unknown people, in a multitude of social situations. I see a clerk at the store, and as a customer I expect to be helped. In one way if it's a "factory outlet," in another if it's Tiffany's. Or, I am a professor lecturing to students. They often expect to be bored and I expect that, if bored, they will at least sleep quietly.

The down side of generalizations is that, as if forming a veil,[13] they not only hide our individuality, they give it a new form. Sophia Kim—a Korean—was an "F.O.B." when she grew up in a Japanese-American section of Los Angeles. Her classmates often refused to think of her as young or old, rich or poor, smart or dumb, a woman or a man. She was simply "fresh off the boat," a matter supposedly obvious to anyone who heard her foreign accent and looked at her peculiar clothing.[14]

By masking our individuality, generalizations become intended or unintended distortions of the realities that are actually there. In contemporary America catchalls like Asian, Hispanic, or white do help Americans make sense of the world, but they simultaneously add and subtract factors that distort as much as they depict reality.

As Hispanics, Puerto Ricans and Cubans are supposedly alike. However the street name for a Cuban in Puerto Rico is *gusano*, the Spanish word for worm. And the biggest generalization of all—the word *white*—refers to 195 million people who are somehow lumped together under the same "racial" umbrella. Ethnicity, social class, gender, age, language, sexual orientation, political preference, educational level: Who cares? All are scrambled together as white, even a poor, darker-skinned Portuguese and a rich, cream-colored Englishman.

Try, however, not to use the word white (or black) in the United States and you immediately grasp how society is possible but not necessarily just or accurate. Like a school lesson memorized via repetition, the generalizations channel our perceptions along preconceived lines of relevance and, as long as no one seriously challenges the generalizations, society indefinitely reproduces its core beliefs, values, and practices.

If generalizations are as powerful as they seem, how is social change possible? Supposedly prisoners of the generalizations they inherit, where is the room for people to create concepts more in line with the world that actually exists? Or the world they want to exist?

Consider it in terms of a distinction between two types of freedom. Public or external freedoms exist when citizens own the recognized and protected right to openly speak their minds, worship as they wish, assemble where they please, and publish even the trashiest tabloids. Essential to any democratic society these and other public freedoms guarantee not only self-expression but also open discussion of crucial social issues. For example, the first three chapters of this book exist only because the United States maintains a wonderful willingness to open even secret presidential documents to easy inspection by any citizen.

On the other hand, private or internal freedom is a form of personal liberation. It refers to insight into the development of self and world and to the ability to act on those insights. In the 1960s African-American activist Malcolm X argued that one of the worst things whites ever did to blacks was to make blacks hate themselves. The learned desire for straight rather than curly hair, or lighter rather than darker skin, moved African Americans to engage in a form of self-deprecation. But, understand the origins of that learned dislike of self and African Americans could move beyond self-hate to self-consciousness. They could even argue that black is beautiful.[15]

Internal freedom is therefore a form of skepticism that sometimes allows people to deliberately and consciously challenge the generalizations learned as a child and as an adult. In its ideal form internal freedom acts like the wide-open eyes of a first-time tourist standing on the roof of New York's Empire State building. Armed with internal freedom, people transcend their society's taken for granted assumptions and view self and society as if they were strangers.[16]

Internal freedom is possible because, even in societies that experience little social change, people always receive conflicting notions of what is right and wrong, good and bad, acceptable and unacceptable. The dissonance—the mental space—created by colliding cultural information moves us to try to reconcile the irreconcilable.[17]

In general the possibility of internal freedom occurs spontaneously. People don't plan for a cultural collision, it just happens. In New York nuns taught my friends and me that Jewish people killed God. By definition Jews were killers. But, when a friend's sister married a loving, generous Jewish man, my friends and I had a problem. If Jews were terrible, how come this guy was so decent and admirable?

One way to resolve such a spontaneous collision is to argue that this Jewish man is an exception to the killer rule. The dissonance is resolved by forgoing the opportunity for internal freedom, all in the service of a refusal to forthrightly challenge the conventional wisdom.

But, especially in societies that champion public and personal freedom as national ideals, people learn that they can, or even that they should, use the insights of the social sciences to deliberately and "objectively" challenge inherited beliefs, values, and practices. When this happens, internal freedom becomes a passionately desired goal of initiatives as disparate as the women's, gay rights, and black power movements.

Internal freedom is essential for any original answer to the question, "What Shall We Do with Our America?" Thus, the extended discussion of immigration law represents an attempt to understand how so many different ethnic strands got to the United States and who is responsible for the new immigrants, undocumented migrants, and refugees who have changed forever the ethnic makeup of the United States of America.

Trouble is, internal freedom is always a relative achievement. Complete freedom never exists because human beings never create and recreate themselves in a vacuum. On the contrary, all people inherit and learn an array of preexisting assumptions whose power is so challenging that even when we reject them, we are still unalterably determined by them.[18]

That may sound contradictory. How can you be determined by something you reject? Well, reconsider the insights and arguments of Malcolm X. Contending that whites taught blacks to hate themselves, he deliberately contributed to a new use of an old word. Activists in the 1960s stopped using the word *Negro* and substituted the word *black*.[19] While this certainly represented a proud form of self-definition by African Americans, it also kept the "revolutionary" debate firmly within the racist confines of inherited beliefs and practices. African-American activists said "black is beautiful" because whites taught the opposite. They rejected the slurs of a thoroughly prejudiced society but remained immeasurably determined by it because the debate still centered on race and on the identities of white and black.

Even when others were included, they became, like Bill Wong, people of color. White remained the standard against which all groups judged themselves, and few people of color questioned the reasonableness of arbitrarily subsuming a variety of *ethnic groups* under a categorization based on the highly questionable notion of human *races*. One result of this determination by inherited generalizations is the almost universal acceptance of the word *black* as the appropriate label for African Americans. Another is the institutionalization in American universities, not only of Black Studies programs, but a definition of ethnic studies that promises significant social change by focusing on skin color. Among many others, the bulletin of San Francisco State University states that "the Master of Arts in Ethnic Studies is designed to increase a student's knowledge and understanding of the experiences of people of color."[20]

Another approach to internal freedom is to question both the inherited culture and our positive, negative, or confused response to that culture. For example, do races really exist? Has anyone of us actually seen a white person? If white is not the true color of any person's skin, why employ words with such a fragile hold on the skin colors that people actually display? Aren't we saying that seeing is not believing, that we will perceive not what is there, but what we have been taught to perceive?

In a recent nursery school situation an African-American child asked his mom if he was black? The mother said "yes," which produced this response from the three-year-old: "I'm not black, I'm brown." The child was of course right, but the mother (who said she was tan) then had to explain that even though you are brown and I am tan, we will both call ourselves black. And, even though white people are actually different shades of pink, beige, and light brown, we will call them white.[21]

To peacefully yet significantly change American culture we need the wide-open eyes of a stranger. We must transcend both what we have learned and our black and white response to those cultural lessons. Ironically one of the easiest ways to produce such profound change is to see America through the eyes of its most recent immigrants. They are the strangers who often have the freshest insights into the way Americans actually think and act.

For now let's postpone any discussion of the questions asked by the most recent Americans. Let us focus instead on the peculiar power of culture to prevent the internal freedom that is always possible yet normally ellusive.

Cultural Clout

"Dope." During an otherwise pleasant dinner, the word came from no-where. I looked at my wife. She looked at me. Neither of us grasped why our son (then twenty) introduced this presumably irrelevant word. Did he think we were stupid? Was this a uniquely backhand way to confirm any contemporary parent's worst nightmare: Our son used dope? When we asked why the word was used, our son seemed baffled. With food in his mouth he responded, "Didn't you know? It means good. I said dope because I liked the food."

In a sense, we were stupid. Any culture depends on shared universes of meaning,[22] and *dope* never meant *good* for our generation. Ben literally needed to translate his and his friends' inventive use of the English language before we understood the new meaning of an old word.

Besides the notion of good, his usage also signals something else: People make culture.[23] Words and other symbols are the principal means but men and women continually use their minds to shape and reshape social reality. "Ms." is nothing but two letters and a period, yet only Rip Van Winkle missed the revolutionary significance of the word. It has so transformed everyday life that many young couples now paste a list of household responsibilities on their refrigerator doors. As women will no longer wash all the floors, all the time, family society is more or less impossible until and unless couples precisely detail who does what and when.

Ultimately people are in charge. Because we create the societies we inhabit, there is no humanly insurmountable barrier to peaceful yet significant social change. We can answer the question "What Shall We Do with Our America?" in any way we please.

But, there is a rub in any society on earth. People start in second place. First is an inherited culture and then come people, who can recreate the world only on the basis of what they have already learned about it. To sociologists the relationship is dialectical; culture first makes people and only then do people have the opportunity to respond to the arbitrary inheritance of U.S. rather than Korean, Chinese rather than Mexican culture.[24]

What is culture? It's a body of generalizations that theoretically encompass everything we think, everything we do, and everything we have as members of a particular society. *Everything* is a big word indeed, but society is only possible to the extent culture provides long-term, widely shared patterns of living for religious, political, economic, military, educational, and family life.

Start with the world of ideas, what we *think*. Included here are convictions about sex and religion, a faith in science and the value of higher education, a belief in the benefits of globalization and in the manifest destiny of the American people to forcefully spread the seeds of democracy to societies who lack our admirable political ideals. Included too are a host of positive and negative assumptions about ethnic groups. We need not agree with what we were taught, yet few Americans reach adulthood lacking the ability to immediately recite the generalizations that apply to Italians and Puerto Ricans, Chinese and Jewish, Irish, Polish, and African Americans.

What we *do* refers to behavior, conceptualized as a society's set of norms. These include folkways like the etiquette of properly setting a "high class" dining room table, to clearing a Formica topped table at a "restaurant" like McDonald's. Watch, for example, the behavior of fast-food customers after a meal. In general they deposit paper ware in the garbage bins and even neatly stack their plastic trays, one on top of another. Somehow, despite paying for the meal, well-mannered, fast-food customers clean up for the restaurant and give dirty looks to those who do not.

Cultures are so powerful that what we do cannot be separated from what we think. On the contrary, in cultures that enjoy a pervasive consensus, whatever we do is always accompanied by a shared assessment of societal worth. We learn to think that the person who refuses to clean up at

McDonald's is inconsiderate or a slob, and we also learn to think that anyone eating mashed potatoes with his or her hands is a pig. However, it is acceptable to eat ketchup-filled, French-fried potatoes with your hands.

Culture arbitrarily makes the rules, even for what we are supposed to *have*. Magazine ads in the Sunday edition of the *New York Times* often focus on the necessities of upper-class American life. I need to have the Rolex watch so people will think I'm somebody special. I need to wear Versace dresses so all will know I'm fashionable. I need to buy Ralph Lauren jeans so I can think of myself as the reincarnation of the Marlboro man.

What we do and have always goes back to what we think. One cannot be separated from the other. Culture includes knowledge about all three aspects of societal life simultaneously. However, especially in nations as large as the United States or, at another level altogether, India, what anyone actually inherits and learns is a fractional part of the generalization called U.S. or Indian culture. Asked if he felt homesick living in London, a man from Southern India replied, "Not really. I am quite used to being abroad. Before I came to London I was working in New Delhi."[25]

Subculture is a word that admirably suggests the real learning experiences of any particular man or woman. In essence, despite sociological theory, people actually inherit only subdivisions of the cultural whole. In our Catholic stronghold of Brooklyn—called Bay Ridge—nuns consistently emphasized that while Jews killed Christ, Protestants deserved an even hotter place in hell. Protestants, after all, had a chance to be Catholics. Because they arrogantly rejected the world's only "perfect religion," Protestants needed to be shunned. The only thing waiting for them was a fiery, eternal comeuppance.

Did we believe this? Absolutely. That is culture's awesome power. The catechism taught that nuns and priests were the actual representatives of God on earth; they acted as temporary stand-ins for Jesus. We rarely disagreed with the lessons we were taught. Equally important, since our subdivision of the United States contained so many Catholics—and we needed to maintain serious social distance from the Protestants—where would we learn to challenge the accepted wisdom of our sacred elders?

Any of us can easily chart the religious, political, family, and geographical subcultures that we arbitrarily inherited. Urban or rural, Fargo, North Dakota, or San Diego, California—that's our America. It is for sure only a part of the whole, yet, that part always contains critical universes of meaning shared throughout the fifty states and its thousands of Bay Ridges. Thus, on the Fourth of July my friends and I illegally bought special firecrackers about six to eight inches long. We laid them in the street, lit the fuses, and watched the explosives race down the street with a loud, whistling noise. Everyone enjoyed the spectacle and none of us then grasped the terrible social lesson. The firecrackers were called "nigger chasers."

The idea of subculture gets us closer to home, to the cultural world any one of us actually experienced. But, to forever drill cultural knowledge into our brains, teachers always use one of humanity's greatest gifts: words. Thumb through a dictionary and words appear to be both precise and fixed. Here are the definitions; learn them and you can communicate.

That's true, yet only in the sense that an English teacher teaches the English language. Words are actually exceptionally efficient storehouses of cultural knowledge, and indoctrination into a culture is most successful when we never see what words hide. Like Pavlov's dog or B. F. Skinner's pigeons, people continually use words as clear and immediate signposts to proper behavior and fail to question or analyze the information buried, in a circle of cement, below ground.

Cement is a fair metaphor because, once internalized, the cultural information stored in words *never* disappears. Conjure up a song you learned as a child. It may be twenty years since you repeated the words, but the lyrics are nevertheless subject to instant recall. Words that store cultural knowledge function in the same way. They lie there until needed, always ready for cultural use.

Consider the words "chink" and "sayonara." The first is a slur against Chinese people, the second (especially when it's "sayonara, baby") a phrase used sometimes to smilingly employ violence. While each word contains information that can easily be brought to the surface, if socialization is successful we act on cue and never stop to question internalized beliefs and attitudes. In a period of intense pressure on immigrants in general, and Asians in particular, Luyen Phan Nguyen received a fatal beating from "white" Americans in Florida in 1992. Fellow adolescents taunted him at a party, chased him into street, and yelled "chink" and "sayonara" as they beat him to death. Unfortunately, Nguyen was a Vietnamese welcomed into the United States under the refugee programs sponsored by one U.S. president after another.[26]

In explaining this murder a variety of variables were certainly involved, everything from the personality of the assailants to the widespread animosity against Asians who allegedly take American jobs. My point is that the words "chink" and "sayonara" served as terribly efficient vehicles to trigger the use of deeply internalized cultural information. The contemporary battle over political correctness is not a meaningless fight over one word versus another, but at the level of unstated assumptions, a disquieting demand to rethink our cultural inheritance.

Words like chairperson (instead of chairman) or firefighter (instead of fireman) do initially sound awkward. They should. Because use of the new words is a forceful request to think, not only differently, but to think at all. If we use the old words we make society possible by matter-of-factly reinforcing the universe of meaning encompassed by particular generalizations.

But, use a new word or phrase—for example, the recent request to use "South Asians" in addition to "Asians"[27]—and its awkwardness demands that we analyze the assumptions buried at the level of that long "forgotten" song.

This analysis is normally resisted because, at the level of social structure, a desire for substantial social change threatens the economic and political interests of people from all social classes. Simultaneously, at the level of what we think, using new words to demand change threatens to make daily life everything from contentious to downright impossible. Finally, even those who sincerely empathize with social activists are still stuck with the cultural information that will never disappear. Memories of the "nigger chasers" are forever a part of who I am as a person. The trick is to somehow forget what cannot be forgotten. Or, more accurately, the trick is to steadfastly ignore what some words bring to mind and use instead our dormant power to recreate even the most troublesome cultural inheritance.

All re-creations of culture must be rooted in an unalterable fact of social life: Any shared generalization about people always contains not one or two but *four* interrelated assumptions. Concurrently, using the word "japs" says something about you as a member of a social group, something about others (e.g., "white" Americans), something about expected behavior, and something about life's possibilities. In the 1920s college placement officers reported that "as far as I know there have been no calls to this office for Japanese, either the first or second generation, in the lines of teaching, engineering, manufacturing and business." While later generations did begin to break down the walls created by a hundred years of prejudice, for many years after World War II "no financial firm in San Francisco would hire a Japanese college graduate."[28]

Words shape lives, at the level of culture and at the level of your existence or mine. So, to more accurately understand our cultural opponent, let's spotlight not 270 million people but one. How does culture get into the head of any particular person? And, once it's there, how can any one of us overcome what cannot be forgotten?

Senses of Self[29]

Religions often provide believers with a tangible form of everyday assistance. Hindus embrace Ganesh, a broken-tusked, elephantine god mounted—spectacularly!—on a rat. Ganesh removes obstacles to the fulfillment of desires because, "like an elephant he can crash through the jungle, uprooting every impediment in his path, while like the rat he can burrow his way through the tightest of defenses."[30]

Catholics teach believers that each person has a guardian angel. In my experience nuns never pictured the angel; it was always a man, but beyond its gender, believers imagined what they wanted, secure in the knowledge that the angel literally sat beside you each moment of the day. He acted as a protector and, like Ganesh, he removed obstacles, but only if they should be eliminated. Nuns stressed that you could ask the guardian angel to get you a bike, knowing that if the present never appeared the invisible angel had done his best, only to be overruled by God himself.

People do need help. But if the obstacle is internalized beliefs, values, and practices, only women and men can remove the mental and institutional barriers created by socialization. It's I vs. them, it's any one of us trying to personally grapple with the perpetual influence of others any moment of any day.

Start with self-images. Briefly, any self-image is what you think of you. Your beliefs could be true or false, exaggerated or understated; the essential point is that, if asked, virtually all of us could easily fill in twenty or fifty of these blanks: I am _____: a man, an American, a Spaniard, a Latino, a father, a husband, a brother. Each is a self-image, and each inextricably includes the perpetual presence and influence of others.

Short must be compared to tall. Fat to thin. Black to white. Asian to African to European. No human being can ever—for even a second—see himself or herself apart from others. However, in societies that stress individuality, "I" is a word that often produces self-deception. People learn that only they control their own destiny when, in truth, others are most in charge when we deny their inevitable and continual influence.

George Herbert Mead explained this by using everyday English. "Me" was the attitudes of others which one assumed; it was what I voluntarily or involuntarily heard others say about me. "I" was the reaction of the individual to the attitudes of others. I could agree or disagree, be indifferent or indecisive but, once I heard somebody say something about me, I had to react to the information that was now in my head.

Take a personal example. My mother used to tell *me* that I had a small brain and that if I studied too much I would wear it out. This was, shall we say, not conducive to self-esteem, yet I had no alternative but to listen to what she told me. In my case *I* accepted her assessment and thought of myself as stupid well into my adolescence. I partially "won" this battle when I got a Ph.D. I thought she would give me some credit for brains; she reacted with no emotion at all, and I finally realized that if I won the Nobel Prize, my mother would think of "me" as stupid. I couldn't change her; I had to change my response to what she told me, knowing that I could never erase what were mental scars.

That's on a personal level. But I also hear others talk about me in social or cultural terms. Man or woman; upper, middle, or lower class; Irish, Italian, or Native American; young or senior citizen; white trash or person of color. Each of these is a social identity that also always involves the influence of others.

To assess the attitudes of others Mead argued that we all used the same process: We think about it. But, for Mead, thinking means internalized conversation; whether in relation to personal or social images of self, thought is nothing more than using words and other symbols to talk to myself about myself and the world in which I and others live.

The gift of thought is anything but free. In fact, just like our inability to remake culture until we first inherit one ready-made, thinking as internalized conversation cannot occur until others *first* make us the subject of *their* thoughts and actions. From this perspective, self-consciousness not only always includes others, it *starts* with others. We can only reach conclusions about ourselves *after* others provide the accurate or inaccurate, sane or bizarre, prejudiced or objective information.

Mead conceptualized this with two lasting concepts: the *generalized* and *significant* others who teach us about self, world, and our place in it.

Mead defined the generalized other as the organized communities—the social groups—that tell us who we are and what we are in terms of the inherited culture. As with any of the generalizations that make society possible, when "they" teach me something about myself—for example, I am white—I also simultaneously learn something about others, about appropriate behavior for whites (and blacks) and about life's possibilities.

One important clue to understanding the power of the generalized other is to analyze our everyday use of the word "they." For instance, when our oldest son was ten, he pestered us to buy a bike that, once we bought it, he refused to ride! Why? The bike had "faggy" handlebars. Neither of us then knew that bike handlebars had an allegedly negative sexual orientation, so we asked who told him about the bike's terrible problems. He could not come up with a specific name. "They" said it; and Adam refused to ride the bike because "they" ridiculed him into submission.

Three things about this story. It once again underlines that people make culture; for all its maliciousness, the idea of "faggy" handlebars was both creative and (I think) utterly unique. Second, what we have relates back to what we think, not only about a bike but also about ourselves. The handlebars were "faggy" and so was Adam. Finally, the power of the generalized other appears all the more notable when we recall that Adam could not identify who "they" were. He did, however, behave as "they" demanded.

Telegraphed every time we use the word *they*, the generalized other represents the power of groups. To focus on the individual, Mead talked about "significant others." These included anyone who furnished what *you* perceive to be important beliefs about self and world. In societies with weak extended families, parents are generally the most obvious significant others. However, importance is always in the eye of the beholder, and a significant other could be dead or alive, related or a stranger.

"Jesus freaks" passionately embrace their interpretation of a figure who lived more than 2,000 years ago. And there is also no need for many members of the contemporary "White Identity" movement to meet either the dead David Koresh or the living Randy Weaver. True or false, stories of the federal assaults on Waco or Ruby Ridge become the mental benchmarks that help move "patriots" to use a figure like Koresh as a significant other. He graphically symbolizes what must be eliminated and what must be protected: the federal government and the rights of God's chosen people, white Americans.[31]

Any of us can easily catalogue the generalized and significant others who furnished our initial and continuing perceptions of self and world. Mead's insights are therefore pregnant with revolutionary potential because, as an adult, I can see what they told me, assess its truth or falsity, and then decide with some degree of objectivity my future beliefs about self and society.

Peaceful yet significant social change is of course the principal purpose of this chapter; we can't recreate society until we struggle to understand how it works and we can't grasp the *personal* significance of ethnicity, race, and immigration until we apprehend the three sides of the self.

First, any of us has a *summary* image of self. This is your "bottom line" on you at a particular point in time. Some of us might need fifty words or less to describe our summary self; some of us might want to write a treatise; and some of us could be short and sweet. "I don't have the vaguest idea who I am." That too is a summary self; you are lost.

To determine a summary self-image we need data, that is, the assumed attitudes of our generalized and significant others. These come in two forms, personal identities (e.g., I am patient or impatient, outgoing or shy) and social identities (rich or poor, man or woman, gay or straight, Hindu or Jewish, black, white, or other).

A summary self is therefore an assessment that represents a point-in-time conclusion based both on personal and social identities and on your or my particular response to those identities. Is there a way to assess the contribution of particular identities to the summary self? With so many personal and societal images to choose from, how do we determine importance? Is it personal? Random? Or is this too determined by culture?

The actual importance of any particular image to your summary self rests on its *everyday relevance* to you or to the larger society. When I, for example, took my mother at her word—"I am stupid"—I then used that one image as a crucial part of my adolescent summary assessment and made it unnecessarily relevant in many social situations. If I failed to grasp a point in school, that was to be expected; I was after all, dumb. If teachers asked about the future I often gave no response because I lacked any confidence in my own abilities.

I and my mother made that personal image all important. But, just as often, society makes particular identities so all pervasively relevant that it is hard to reach a summary conclusion without according special significance to identities arbitrarily chosen by the inherited culture.

In the United States man and woman and black and white are arguably the most important social identities any of us receive. This is so because these self-images are, like the threads in the finest Egyptian cotton, inextricably interconnected to literally hundreds of social situations. It is, for example, impossible to use a restroom without gender being relevant, and even today waiters and waitresses still automatically ask the man to taste the wine before the woman gets a drop. Or, in a friend's situation, visitors compliment the woman of the house for her beautiful plants when, in truth, the man does all the work.

The eminent African-American historian John Hope Franklin offers three 1997 examples of the imposed relevance of white and black. As chair of the President's Commission on Race, the eighty-two-year-old Franklin stayed in New York's St. Moritz Hotel; he was standing in the lobby, waiting for a colleague, when a white woman said, "Here, take this trash and put it in the trash basket." In his own club in Atlanta, "white women" ask him to hang up their coat because they assume he's a servant. In an Oklahoma hotel, Franklin recently had this encounter; he was chatting with a friend when a white man came up and said, "Here, boy, go and get my car."[32]

When societies make particular identities relevant across a wide variety of social situations, *the interconnections assure that the attitudes of others are continually reinforced*. I can, of course, disagree with the assessments of others. But to the extent men like Dr. Franklin (and, in the preface, Dr. Rasheed Hamsa) experience such encounters as everyday phenomena, black is an all-important component of my summary self whether I accept or reject the beliefs and attitudes of others.

While ethnicity is also, potentially, an important component of any summary self-image, one crucial long-term consequence of the 1924 immigration laws was to make ethnicity *irrelevant* to many millions of Americans. The distant memory of great-grandparents does not make for strong ethnic ties. Thus, as 23 million newcomers and their relatives attach great significance to their ethnic origins, many "old blood" immigrants "have come to understand themselves and their interests as white." In a society that is allegedly more and more colorblind, studies show that many young Americans "have attached new meanings to being white and have used those meanings as the basis for forging an identity (i.e., a summary self) centered around race."[33]

Sorting out the consequences of these changes is crucial for any answer to the question of what we shall do with our America. At all costs we want to avoid a future that, instead of a national consensus, produces a polarization rooted at one end in the central relevance of race and the irrelevance of ethnicity. For example, instead of white, why not ask the descendants of earlier immigrants to center themselves on a neglected ethnicity, American. We could then together create a meaning of *American* that is broad enough to provide everyone with both self-esteem and shelter from horrors like the bombing in Oklahoma City.

That is our task. The social sciences can help by reminding us that, because social identities as important as white and black are always interconnected to hundreds of social situations, the *ripple effects* of significant social change will consistently manifest themselves for the foreseeable future. Focus on American instead of white, and you must rethink not only your summary self, but also your behavior in countless everyday situations. Moreover, if you rethink these situations, others must follow suit or everyday life becomes utterly impossible.

Why would people be willing to live with "wong word" encounters as a staple of everyday life? One motive is self-interest. The polarization around white is already occurring, and the allegedly divisive ethnic strands are not only here, they are increasing at the rate of roughly a million legal newcomers a year. Consider agendas like California's Proposition 187 or the smoldering rage of the militia movements and you realize that violent social conflict is a real possibility. From this perspective, we reluctantly embrace serious challenges to our everyday assumptions because it is the peaceful lesser of two evils.

Another motive is as American as apple pie: idealism. If nothing else, the Constitution proves that people make culture. You can start with a blank sheet of paper and end up with a superb blueprint for political life. Let's root our search for a national consensus about ethnicity, race, and immigration in the revolutionary beliefs of the Declaration of Independence. Let's challenge even our deepest assumptions about self and world so that the United States finally achieves a spectacular ideal: All people are created equal, "endowed by their Creator with certain unalienable Rights, that among these are Life, Liberty and the Pursuit of Happiness."

The challenge is Jefferson's. The choice is ours.

NOTES

1. Jose Ortega y Gasset, *Man and People* (New York: Norton, 1963), p. 23.

2. Alfred Schutz, *Reflections on the Problem of Relevance* (New Haven: Yale University Press, 1970).

3. *1996 Statistical Yearbook of the Immigration and Naturalization Service*, U.S. Department of Justice, Immigration and Naturalization Service (Washington, DC: GPO, 1996), p. 30.

4. See David Hollinger, *Postethnic America* (New York: Basic Books, 1995).

5. Sam Sue, "Growing Up in Mississippi," in *Asian Americans*, edited by Joann Faung Jean Lee (New York: New Press, 1992), pp. 3–10, esp. p. 3.

6. Bill Wong, *Wong Words*, May 27, 1996, ⟨www.phoenixteahouse.com/wong.html⟩, p. 1.

7. Ibid., p. 5.

8. Andrea Kim, "Born and Raised in Hawaii But Not Hawaiian," in Lee, ed., *Asian Americans*, pp. 24–31, esp. p. 24.

9. See Georg Simmel, "How Is Society Possible?" in *Essay on Sociology, Philosophy, and Aesthetics* (New York: Harper, 1959), pp. 337–356.

10. Luis Guarnizo, "Los Dominicanyorks: The Making of a Binational Society," in *Challenging Fronteras*, edited by Mary Romero, Pierrette Hondagneu-Sotelo, and Vilma Ortiz (New York: Routledge, 1997), pp. 161–174, esp. pp. 164–165.

11. Alejandro Portes, "Global Villagers: The Rise of Transnational Communities," *American Prospect*, no. 25 (March-April 1996): 74–77.

12. Simmel, "How Is Society Possible?" p. 343.

13. Ibid., p. 344.

14. Sanford Ungar, *Fresh Blood: The New American Immigrants* (Urbana: University of Illinois Press, 1998), p. 291.

15. *The Autobiography of Malcolm X*, with the assistance of Alex Haley (New York: Grove Press, 1964); see, too, William Grier and Price Cobbs, *Black Rage* (New York: Basic Books, 1968).

16. Ronald Fernandez, *The Promise of Sociology* (New York: Praeger, 1975), p. 24.

17. Simmel, "How Is Society Possible?" pp. 345–350.

18. Karl Mannheim, *Ideology and Utopia* (New York: Meridian, 1963).

19. For example, Stokely Carmichael and Charles Hamilton, *Black Power* (New York: Vintage Books, 1967).

20. See Ethnic Studies, San Francisco State University, ⟨www.sfsu.edu/~bulletin/noindex/9496/programs/pgms-e/eths.ht⟩.

21. Beverly Daniel Tatum, *Why Are All the Black Kids Sitting Together in the Cafeteria?* (New York: Basic Books, 1997).

22. Peter Berger and Thomas Luckmann, *The Social Construction of Reality* (New York: Doubleday, 1996), p. 61.

23. Ibid., especially part 1; see, too, Ortega y Gasset, *Man and People*.

24. Berger and Luckmann, *Social Construction*, especially Part Two.

25. Gita Mehta, *Snakes and Ladders* (New York: Anchor Books, 1997), p. 27.

26. Angelo N. Ancheta, *Race, Rights and the Asian American Experience* (New Brunswick, NJ: Rutgers University Press, 1998), p. 11.

27. Lavina Dhingra Shankar and Rajini Srikanth, eds., *A Part, Yet Apart: South Asians in Asian America* (Philadelphia: Temple University Press, 1998).

28. Robert Jiobu, "Ethnic Hegemony and the Japanese of California," *American Sociological Review* 53 (June 1988): 353–367, esp. 363; see, too, Won Moo Hurh and Kwang Chung Kim, "The 'Success' Image of Asian Americans: Its Validity and Its Practical and Theoretical Implications," *Ethnic and Racial Studies* 12, no. 4 (October 1989): 512–538, esp. 527–528. For an overview of the Japanese-American experience, see Paul R. Spickard, *Japanese-Americans* (New York: Twayne, 1996).

29. These pages are deeply rooted in the insights of George Herbert Mead; see, especially, *Mind, Self and Society* (Chicago: University of Chicago Press, 1963).

30. Shashi Tharoor, *India: From Midnight to the Millennium* (New York: Harper, 1997), p. 62.

31. For example, Joel Dyer, *Harvest of Rage: Why Oklahoma City Is Only the Beginning* (New York: Westview Press, 1997); also Jess Walter, *Every Knee Shall Bow* (New York: Harper, 1995).

32. See the November 17, 1997, edition of *U.S.A. Today*; the interview with Professor Franklin appears on page 8A.

33. Charles Gallagher, "White Racial Formation: Into the Twenty-First Century,"
in *Critical White Studies*, edited by Richard Delgado and Jean Stefancic (Philadelphia:
Temple University Press, 1997), pp. 6–12, especially p. 7.

5

Changing Colors

"For most of us, race is simply accepted as a given, and on faith, no more subject to questioning than the reality of our existence."
—Ellis Cose, *Color Blind*[1]

QUESTIONING THE UNQUESTIONABLE

I'm beige. People call me white, but I've looked in the mirror a number of times and my eyes always tell me the same thing: I'm beige, which, according to my edition of *Webster's*, means that I'm a shade of yellowish brown.

Now I don't have any problems with that. Brown is a nice color. Moreover, if I do say so myself, a yellowish tint is a wonderful addition to my complexion. It makes me a colorful person.

But U.S. culture still labels me and more than 195 million other citizens white. Meanwhile more than 32 million African Americans are called black, and immigrants who come from nations such as India, the Philippines, and Pakistan are labeled "other." Asians find no home in the racial straitjackets of U.S. culture so, like a Chinese person on an Alabama bus in the 1950s, these Americans are today left standing. Asians are Americans without a color.

Newcomers are often simultaneously amazed, angered, and confused. From the president to the local councilperson, concerned politicians often exhort them to assimilate, yet our black and white thinking systematically excludes, not only Japanese and Pakistanis, but the largest group of newcomers by far: Mexican Americans. Many Mexicans are wheat colored, but since the United States never sees that skin shade, Mexicans are also forced to choose between black, white, and other.[2]

One 1990 selection was "none of the above." Indeed, despite a U.S. Census check list that included no less than fourteen separate racial categories, over 18 million respondents said "no way." They wrote in what they wanted, the Census Bureau recoded about 40 percent against their will, and the rest—mostly of "Spanish origin"—now live with Peter Pan in a racial never-never land.[3]

Meanwhile, migrants from the Caribbean also resist and question the U.S. dichotomy. Jamaicans and Barbadians identify as nationals of independent nations; they share a culture and generally refuse to use skin tone as the principal axis of personal and social identity. For example, one widely accepted definition of any contemporary Caribbean person totally disregards color: "We are part African, part European, part Asian, and totally Caribbean."[4]

In a mischievous mood, many Caribbean natives would agree with the facetious reasoning of Francois Duvalier. When in the 1960s a U.S. reporter asked the dark-skinned dictator of Haiti what percentage of his population was white, Duvalier answered "95 percent." The reporter laughed, yet Duvalier quickly proved his point by reversing U.S. thinking. In the United States new mothers perform miracles: A white woman can give birth to a black child, but a black woman can never give birth to a white child. So, if a drop of African blood made you black in Peoria, a drop of European blood made you white in Port-au-Prince. Either way, the racial designation existed only in the cultural eye and mind of the beholder.[5]

While President Clinton also agrees that the United States has a problem, his 1998 dialogue about race forcefully endorsed the assumptions that make the United States—despite all the ballyhoo about the declining significance of race[6]—a society more fixated than ever on skin color. Just speak American English and you realize that we continually subsume important social identities like ethnicity, gender, and social class under the banner of race and then use white and black as the "trump" social identities for 270 million people. That's bluntly racist when it has positive or negative personal and institutional consequences for the Americans so labeled. But, on a level too often hidden from view, the identities white and black also condemn us to repeat the past because they perpetually root our thinking in the provably false concept of race.

As if on a merry-go-round that never stops, even those of us who want to get off still go round, ad nauseum. What's the option in a culture whose everyday vocabulary dichotomizes countless interconnected social situations into black and white experiences? (Recall that despite being a well-dressed professional, John Hope Franklin, head of the President's Commission on Race, is still asked by white people to hang up coats in his own club.[7])

Mr. President, the deepest root of our national problem is not racism but the concept of race. In a biological sense races do not exist; if we dialogue about race without recognizing—first and foremost—that we have embraced a pernicious fiction, the result will be more nonsense purporting to be fact. Newspapers and journals spent a year arguing about *The Bell Curve*. The book claims to show racial differences in intelligence; but if races are a fiction, the book collapses because it has no cornerstone. Or, what about Thomas Sowell's well-reviewed *Race and Culture?* In the opening pages Sowell writes "neither race nor its related concepts can be used in any scientifically precise sense to refer to the people inhabiting this planet today." Sowell nevertheless roots his book in this admittedly loose concept; a priori, his observations are as precise as the concept that is their foundation.[8]

What Shall We Do with Our America? My request is that we examine the legitimacy of the idea of human races. It may be one sure way to finally erase a part of the pain, confusion, and nonsense that punctuates our daily discourse. After all, if only one race exists, all the contemporary talk of "mixed" or "biracial" children is a dialogue in a scientific vacuum. Equally important, the known genetic dangers in a choice of a mate inhere most ominously when we breed in too small and homogeneous a group. Close family members pose the greatest danger of all. The white who shuns a black says, "Marry your own kind but never your own family!" Your first cousin Melissa is dangerous; but an unrelated neighbor who looks like Melissa could be perfect.[9]

THE CONCEPT OF RACE

In early 1999 the world boasts a population of more than six billion people. Superficially we seem to be quite different, but if genes are the issue, all six billion of us are, in fact, very similar. "It must be remembered that 75% of known genes in humans do not vary at all but are monomorphic throughout the species." Human beings are *identical* for three-quarters of the total genetic endowment of the species; indeed, while this next fact may bother those of us with an ego, men and women are more genetically identical than chimpanzees. By one calculation, if a catastrophe struck the earth and the only survivors remained in Africa, women and men would still retain fully 93 percent of the total variation of the former population of the species. Admittedly, certain traits—skin color, for example—would have different average expressions, but the human race would still draw from a very similar gene pool.[10]

Our similarities could be a wonderful basis for a global sense of solidarity. Realizing that we are all literally brothers and sisters under the skin, we could relish the differences and smilingly thank god for the human variety that, like orchids in a rain forest, is a delight to behold.

Instead, we use depthless differences like skin color to simultaneously divide and define ourselves. Consider for instance that the "human blueprint" boasts somewhere between 50,000 and 100,000 gene pairs. Thanks to molecular biologists we also know that fifty different genes may affect skin color, "although perhaps only half a dozen will be shown to have really substantial effects."[11] If we figure on the high side and divide fifty pairs by 50,000, the totally unreasonable result is that one thousandth (.001) of all known human genes are the principal basis for most divisions of people into so-called human races.

This is especially dangerous because molecular biologists also provide a great deal of information about the formation of skin color. Start with the pigment melanin. It can color us as light as a Swede or as dark as the Bougainville Islanders of the South Pacific. Color "starts" in tyrosine, an amino acid made in large quantities in the cells, the melanocytes that make up melanin. What happens is that the amino acids are converted into a "master enzyme" called tyrosinase and, "perhaps the most remarkable discovery made by molecular biologists," all six billion of us have "quite enough of this enzyme in our melanocytes to make us very black."[12]

I'm beige because something prevented my stockpile of tyrosinase from operating at full capacity. Biologists are still trying to sort out what actually happens, but those of us with lighter skin produce inhibitors that inactivate the master enzyme. It's still there, yet it adds none of the tints that make some of us tan, others wheat colored, others brown, and still others ebony.[13]

Historically, European writers building ladders of racial hierarchy put light-skinned people on top, dark-skinned people on the bottom. This quickly produced a sure sense of superiority rooted in the concept of race. Thus, in 1900, U.S. political leaders easily justified "good colonialism" in Cuba and Puerto Rico because the island's populations were "largely mongrels," a mixed group of evolution's rejects. As Congressman Scudder told his colleagues, islanders resisted our sanitary improvements because they had no choice; "the Cubans liked smells and they had a fondness for dirt."[14]

Today's absurdity is the notion that darker skin makes us "sun people." Born with a coat of ebony, blacks are smarter, "more attuned to life's rhythms" and even have genetically inspired personalities: Blacks are warm and outgoing.

This "modern" nonsense is still rooted in the same intellectual quicksand: The notion of human races. Skin color did not determine human behavior in 1900, nor will it do so in the year 2000. Skin color is nothing more than an adaptation to a *particular environment*. Theoretically a darker color protects us from the power of the sun and a lighter tone certainly has consequences in places like Hawaii, where "whites" have the highest documented rate of skin cancer in the United States. Moreover, if we continue to deplete the ozone layer at the present rate, darker-skinned people should have a particular advantage in that particular environment. But, make a racial mountain out of a molehill built on one-thousandth of the gene pool, and we will continue to drown in the balderdash that produced "races" in the first place.[15]

Focusing on the differences they could see—hair, skin, eyes, noses, skulls—race builders used the 25 percent of our genes that produce human variation to creatively manufacture any number of races. As the accompanying chart suggests, officials in the U.S. Census Bureau often outdid themselves. Mexicans, a race in 1930, are no longer a race in 1940. Hindu, a race and a religion in 1930, is now only a religion. Meanwhile, new racial discoveries of the 1990s included Pacific Islanders, Samoans, and Guamanians.[16]

U.S. Census Classifications of Race and Color

1890	1910	1930	1950	1970	1990
White	White	White	White	White	White
Black	Black	Negro	Negro	Negro or Black	Black or Negro
Mulatto	Mulatto	Mexican	Amer. Indian	Amer. Indian	Amer. Indian
Quadroon	Chinese	Indian	Japanese	Japanese	Eskimo
Octoroon	Japanese	Chinese	Chinese	Chinese	Asian or Pacific Islander
Chinese	Indian	Japanese	Filipino	Filipino	Chinese
Japanese	Other	Filipino	Other	Hawaiian	Filipino
Indian		Hindu		Korean	Hawaiian
		Korean		Other	Korean
		Other			Vietnamese
					Japanese
					Asian Indian
					Samoan
					Guamanian
					Other

One difference in 1999 is the work of dedicated scientists. Their accumulated evidence demonstrates that the majority of genetic polymorphisms (i.e., the different forms of a gene that lead to variations between people) occur *within* rather than *between* designated populations. Get me a transfusion from another beige person and I could have real problems; but choose an ebony person with the same blood type and we reaffirm human indivisibility with the gift of life. Moreover, even genetic differences that supposedly define various groups are *not* homogeneous for the designated group. In the U.S. "blacks" are commonly linked to sickle cell anemia but "the highest recorded frequency of the sickle cell gene in West African populations (never mind the rest of the continent!) is 15–25% and it is more commonly 10–15 percent or less." Therefore, even in a population supposedly characterized by the gene, most people lack it.[17]

The most important point of all comes from *The History and Geography of Human Races*. After an exhaustive search of the entire world, Cavalli-Sforza and his colleagues emphasize that not only are the same polymorphisms (e.g., blood type) found in most populations but also, because the geographic differentiation of humans is so recent, "there has been too little time for the accumulation of a substantial divergence." Put differently, the populations that belong to the major "races" of everyday life do *not* generally cluster together. In one analysis of ABO frequencies the clusters of blood relatives included one African, three Asian, and one European population. In relation to type O, the geneticists underline that between 70 and 80 percent of light-skinned Scots, dark-skinned Central Africans, and brown-skinned Aborigines are type O.[18]

The traits we see don't stick to what we can't see. In 1931 a researcher accidentally spilled PTC (phenylthiocarbamide) on the laboratory floor. Some colleagues immediately complained about a bitter taste in their mouths; others were ready for lunch. Subsequent research allowed anthropologists to divide the world into those who sense PTC and those who do not. In Asia the tasters range from 15 percent to 40 percent, while there are twice as many nontasters in Japan as in China and three times as many as in Malaysia. This is therefore both an example of wide variation *within* a "racial" grouping and of close similarity *between* Asian and American tasters and nontasters.[19]

PTC tastefully challenges the notion that what you see is what you get. If human races actually existed, biologists and geneticists correctly argue that the pattern in the variations—such as between skin color, hair type, blood type, and even PTC—should hang together. This concordance would allow scientists to divide people into *natural* units that could legitimately be labeled races. But, since the pattern of variation in one characteristic (e.g., blood type) generally appears unrelated to that in others (e.g., skin color), those who wish to subdivide always hit the same brick wall: What traits should we use to divide people? Where do we draw the line between one group and another?

Any answer to these questions is as subjective as the person making the classification. For example, in trying to understand "the history of genetic fissions in the expansion to the whole world of anatomically modern humans," Cavalli-Sforza and his colleagues did create "clusters" of populations and order them into a hierarchy. But, the ordering into human layers has nothing to do with notions of superiority and inferiority; it exists only as a way of understanding genetic transmissions from one place to another. Equally important, "at no level can clusters be identified with races, since every level of clustering would determine a different partition *and there is no biological reason to prefer a particular one*" (emphasis added).[20]

Clusters are scientific tools that aid understanding. Races are battleaxes that divide and conquer. They are rooted, not in hard evidence, but in the imagination and prejudices of their makers. The word *Caucasian*, for example, derives from a classification made by Johann Friedrich Blumenbach. In 1775 he divided human beings into five races and used Caucasian for whites because of what he called a "poetical motivation." Blumenbach remembered that the Ark of Noah was stranded in the Caucasus on Mount Ararat, so he decided to call white people Caucasians. In a different mood he could have called this race Ararats, but he chose Caucasian because the region supposedly contained the world's most beautiful people. Caucasians "have in general the kind of appearance, which, according to our opinion of symmetry, we consider the most handsome and appealing."[21]

Talk about cultural determinism! Blumenbach blithely picked the "best" race based on a story in the Christian bible and his own Western perceptions of beauty. Two hundred and twenty-three years later, many if not most Americans still use his poetic invention in everything from daily discourse to university texts.

On the one hand the word Caucasian is a graphic example of the power of inherited generalizations to help us sleepwalk through history. Forget science. We'll continue to rely on a man who liked the mountains where Noah left his ark and we left our power to reason.

On the other hand the word Caucasian underlines the arbitrary basis of all racial classifications. Why light skin? What makes this phenotypic trait so much more important than blood type or height or size of the jaw? Eskimos, for example, reportedly have larger jaws than many other groups of people. Would we then say that because of their jaw size they are smarter or dumber than other groups? That sounds ridiculous. But, if it's ridiculous for jaws, then it's also nonsense for color. You cannot *reasonably* pick out one trait and say, as Blumenbach did in 1775, that this trait is the basis for "racial" classifications.

Equally important, where do you draw the line? My beige color is simply a spot on the human continuum. Is tan the precise break between one race and another? Pink? Chocolate brown? Mocha? Ebony? Most Americans solve the dilemma by seeing only two colors, and we then teach our children that seeing is not believing. In a 1996 study of nursery school children, observers found that a three-year-old's "evaluation of the racial status of another child was sophisticated and showed awareness not only of how to use racial epithets but also of the negative stigma attached to black skin." This upset the teachers, who confronted the parents, who denied any responsibility. Ultimately all concerned stopped their search for the source of the child's prejudice; "It doesn't really matter where she learned it from. What we need to accomplish is unlearning it."[22]

I agree, wholeheartedly. But when the teachers gave the children a number of "multicultural toys" they and the sociological observers stayed on the racial merry-go-round. Whether in Polish or African, Indian or Mexican costumes, the toys would still be labeled white and black, and observers reporting the children's reactions would still discuss change in terms of racial groupings.

Races don't exist, and white is the color of a shirt I wear to work. It is not the color of virtually any human being on the face of the earth. However, even many social scientists who accept that racial categories are "at best imprecise and at worst completely arbitrary," nevertheless agree to continue to use race in both everyday and scholarly discourse.

In *Racial Formation in the United States*, Omi and Winant quickly accept the power of culture: "It is rather difficult to jettison widely held beliefs, beliefs which moreover are central to everyone's identity and understanding of the social world. So, the attempt to banish the concept as an archaism is at best counterintuitive." Indeed, "despite its [the concept of race] uncertainties and contradictions," the authors argue that "we should think of race as an element of social structure rather than as an irregularity within it; we should see race as a dimension of human representation rather than an illusion."[23]

But it is an illusion! Among others, geneticists and molecular biologists prove—with especially convincing evidence—that the concept of race is as solid as watered-down Jell-O. Omi and Winant nevertheless use its "contradictions" to create a few of their own. For example, textbooks in sociology always sing the praises of the scientific method; students are taught that facts matter, that truth is in the hard evidence. But, because culture is decidedly difficult to change, we will embrace the nonsense that, I could not agree more, "is central to everyone's identity and understanding of the social world."

Think, for example, of the successful efforts to eliminate a variety of hateful words from everyday use: darkies, nigger, colored, Negro. Activists would fight these generalizations tooth and nail, but when it comes to the concept that is the ideological basis for these slurs—the concept of race—activists often accept the status quo. They fight the obvious manifestations of prejudice but leave its foundation stone untouched! As Manning Marable writes in a December 1998 article in *The Nation*, "We are mobilizing people in part around a concept that is morally repugnant and shouldn't exist. Yet even though race is socially constructed, it nonetheless sets the parameters of how most Americans think about politics and power."[24]

Let's be clear about the profound consequences of continuing to use the word *race*—and its black-and-white version of reality.

We have agreed that a core concept of American civilization is rooted in scientific nonsense. It's "at best" imprecise, but we nevertheless agree to see ourselves in the grossly distorted images provided by racial mirrors.

We have agreed that seeing is not believing. I'm white even though I'm really beige.

We have agreed that, after the identities "man" and "woman," black and white will remain a crucial axis of personal and social identity—of summary self-image—for at least 227 million Americans (i.e., the 195 million whites and the 32 million blacks).

We have agreed that Chinese and Mexicans, Japanese and Filipinos, Koreans and Indians will continue to be "almost Americans."[25] Excluded from the racial categories that continually trump ethnicity, we have agreed that many millions of Americans will remain "others" or, what is even more alarming, that they will assimilate themselves and their children into a culture rooted in the illusion of race.

We have agreed to allow whites to create an all-powerful sense of nationwide solidarity between people who, except for their alleged whiteness, often have very little in common. Think, for example, of the enormous differences between a poor, illegal Polish immigrant living in Chicago, a third-generation Portuguese-American living in Hartford, a Russian evangelical immigrant in Brooklyn, a second-generation Cuban patriot in Miami, a fifth-generation Texas farmer, and a "fresh off the boat" Irishman hiding out in Boston.[26]

In the most cavalier fashion, the social identity *white* puts these very different people under the same racial umbrella and that undermines social change because it emphasizes what the beige and pink majority have in common with America's political, economic, educational, and media elites. "It de-emphasizes liberatory potential and emphasizes instead the way all white people 'benefit' from oppression of blacks."[27]

As undocumented immigrants Poles, Irish, and Mexicans could work together. Living in the shadows of American life they share many of the same experiences, especially exploitation by bosses who also say they are against more U.S. immigrants.

But, once Poles and Irish identify as white, the Mexicans are pushed to the side because, among other things, to identify with "people of color" is to risk being as marginal as they are in U.S. economic, political, and educational institutions. Like crazy glue, whites stick together even when it's not in their best interest.

Finally use of the social identity *white* only widens the gap between whites and 70 million other Americans. Just the absolutes matter, so blacks generally think of whites as polar opposites; openly accepting the scheme devised by whites, blacks often try to squeeze "others" into the hateful paradigms of U.S. culture. For example, one African-American writer uses the word *black* because it is more inclusive than African American. Her point is that "there are Black people in the United States who are not African American—Afro-Caribbeans, for example—yet are targeted by racism, and are identified as black."[28]

That Jamaicans or Trinidadians are called black and subjected to prejudice in the United States is undeniable. But, in sharp contrast to many African Americans, Jamaicans regularly refuse to embrace the black/white absolutes of U.S. culture. At our university West Indian youngsters are often alienated from whites who call them black, and sometimes even more alienated from the blacks who want—and sometimes angrily demand—that the West Indians accept their status as blacks.

The sin of the West Indian (or the Pakistani or the Filipino) is to refuse to think like an American. And my response is "Go for it!" Consider, for example, the battle being waged by the parents of so-called multiracial children. Like Japanese or Indian or Mexican Americans, the multiracial child does not fit into the black/white absolutes. But, in asking for a multiracial box, the advocates of the new category are demonstrating that, like the vast majority of whites and blacks, they accept race and its accompanying dichotomization of 270 million people as continuing realities of U.S. life. The advocates of a multiracial identity want to refine, not overthrow the dual racial basis of U.S. thinking.[29]

We do have a choice. We can confront the culture, proudly endorse our ability to recreate it, and walk into the future with this pledge in hand. *We will consciously make social life impossible until and unless the words white and black lose their place as core social identities in hundreds of interconnected social situations.*

As cultural generalizations, these words perpetuate the fiction called race; and, as crucial concepts of U.S. culture, the words black and white act as two of the biggest obstacles to serious social change in this and the next century. How, after all, can we welcome the "ethnic strands" that are here and the "ethnic strands" to come, when our core concepts disregard a majority of the world's inhabitants? Why would an ethnically centered Indian or Mexican want to embrace a culture in which, as its geneticists call race a scientific fiction, its political and economic leaders nevertheless make skin color far more important than the ethnic axis of any person's existence?

WE NEED TO MAKE WHITE SEEM STRANGE[30]

Walk into a white room, and what's the first thing many people say? "You need some color, a little red here, a little green there. But, don't leave it white. White is so boring."

Webster's dictionary agrees. It defines white as "free from color"; it is the omnipresent neutral against which "real" colors are judged. Thus, "white light is just light" until someone adds a red, yellow, or blue hue. A sheet of white paper is blank until we use black ink to make the page come to life.[31]

In the United States white is the "invisible" color that nevertheless acts as the Amy Vanderbilt of racial etiquette. Whether in Florida or Washington, Maine or Arizona, white silently serves as an uncontested neutral because its cultural function is to designate a group of people that allegedly represent the human ordinary. As a polar opposite, blacks stand out because, on that sheet of blank paper, whites write in whatever meaning of black they see fit.[32]

Following the Egyptians, the creators of U.S. culture could have said that black stands for fertility; dark as the silt of the Nile, black is beautiful because it perpetually furnishes the nutrients required for growth. Or, as in the Early Middle Ages, Americans could have built a culture which saw blacks as allies in the struggle against the infidels. Thus, Prester John, the legendary king of a Christian kingdom in Ethiopia, actually guarded the gates of paradise. Presumably Prester John smilingly welcomed all comers because, as God's creation, all people got a reserved seat in their heavenly home.[33]

Colors remain the same; what changes is our interpretation in and through time. We need, therefore, to spotlight the color white because "the invisibility of its assets is part and parcel of the sense that whiteness is nothing in particular."[34] In reality the color white is a background source of enormous power and privilege. For instance, instead of the fertility celebrated by the Egyptians, in contemporary America, "white is light, black is its absence," white is clean, black is dirty, white is good, black is bad, white is superior, black is inferior.[35]

If this seems too strong a series of comparisons, consider these examples from *The Rage of a Privileged Class*. Ellis Cose discusses a number of instances in which two men, trained to present themselves in an identical manner, were nevertheless treated very differently. The white guy got instant service at an electronics counter; the black guy was ignored. In a record store the white guy was allowed to browse freely; the black guy was followed. While passersby never saw the black guy locked out of his car, the white guy was "showered" with offers of help.[36]

Like the black jelly beans at the bottom of the Texaco Corporation's jar, these examples of everyday prejudice are a staple of U.S. life.[37] The task for those of us interested in significant change is to make people challenge their preconscious assumptions in a manner that offers *this* generation of children a real chance to end the cycle of hate.

Let's start with a question and an answer. Who are white people? Answer: "*White people are who white people say are white*" (emphasis added).[38] This is a provable point if we recall the chart of U.S. Census Bureau racial classifications. For a hundred years officials have added and subtracted groups as they see fit. The changes sometimes seem bewildering, but they nevertheless underline the "profoundly controlling effect" of making white the right color, black the wrong color, and everything in between a hellhole for the misfits.

Richard Dyer stresses that the strength of white power rests on two and only two racial categories. "If there are only two colors that really count, then which you belong to becomes a matter of the greatest significance."[39] Conversely, eliminate the categories and you have eliminated the power of the dominant culture to produce *profound pain* for so many American children.[40]

In *Life on the Color Line*, Gregory Howard Williams explains how, overnight, white people changed their mind about his humanity. No one, including his father, mentioned the family's African-American roots. Williams thought he was white until, after his father lost his business, the family moved back to the "colored" section of Muncie, Indiana. Struck by the poverty and the host of "black people," Gregory and his brother suddenly received this instruction from their now-black father. "This is the Projects, boys. Colored families live on this side of Madison, and crackers on the other. Stay outta there. If the crackers learn you're colored, they'll beat the hell out of you. You gotta be careful here, too. Coloreds don't like half-breeds either."[41]

Half-breeds! Williams writes, "An electrical charge surged through my body. Never before had I thought of myself as a half-breed. TV Westerns taught me half-breeds were the meanest people alive. They led wild bunches of Indians on rampages, killed defenseless settlers, and slaughtered innocent women and children. Nobody liked half-breeds."[42]

And with good reason. Half-breeds dared to defy the white/black dichotomy created by white people and, however reluctantly, accepted by most black people. Neither this nor that, Williams received the scorn of whites because his mother mixed her white blood with that of a black man. He received the scorn of blacks because, among other things, he glaringly reminded his neighbors what happened to blacks when they mixed with whites: They turned into "bestial mongrel mulattos, the dregs of human society."[43]

How does a child become a mongrel? How does a boy become a beast? That is the profoundly controlling effect of the dichotomy. White people are who white people say are white. Williams and his brother fit into neither of the two dominant categories. Treated like the Indians they led on TV Westerns, mongrels deserved the scorn of all races.

Williams discusses a childhood in the 1950s. But as Lise Funderberg shows in *Black, White, Other* (published in 1994), the dichotomy still dominates when contemporary Americans try to understand who they are. Danielle Williams explains that "I sort of have this new term: I would say that I am a 'black-slash-biracial woman.' . . . I am *two* things you know . . . that's why I like the word mulatto. Because mulatto only means black and white. When you say biracial, it's a mixture of any two, and for me, being mulatto is so special that I want an official word, just as white people have white and black people have black, and Japanese and whatever. When I say mulatto or whatever, I want people to say, I know what that is."[44]

Later Ms. Williams calls herself the "marginalized, tragic mulatto."[45] However, whatever self-image she chooses, all those cited underline the continually controlling effect—into the very late 1990s—of the dichotomy walled in by the concept of race. Biracial, for example, *simultaneously* accepts the legitimacy of human races and the two, and only two, color categories. Biracial may be a new census selection, but it offers no real resistance to the dichotomy championed by those who, like Admiral Richard E. Byrd, always want to find the pole.

Another theoretical term of resistance is "people of color," but, for all its generosity, this social identity "reiterates the notion that some people have color, and others, whites, do not."[46] We need to scream it from the rooftops:

WHITE IS A COLOR, a cultural generalization of such power that we can only erase it by first recognizing its colorful significance and then calling that significance into question across a large number of interconnected social situations. Make white seem strange, so that no child is ever again boxed in by the concept of race and the profoundly controlling consequences of refusing to see that, like a kangaroo court, white is anything but a neutral color.[47]

INVITATION TO A BANQUET

Despite a plethora of serious problems, there is cause for optimism, real reason to believe that significant change is possible. Among others, Ellis Cose's eloquent analysis of the rage of a privileged class underlines an important fact: Many African Americans are angrier than ever. Intelligent, well-educated, well-dressed, and speaking Standard English, African-American lawyers, doctors, professors, and executives understandably assumed that these other characteristics would matter more than their skin color. But, since whites are systematically trained to exclude those characteristics, they see black and act white. Thus, a professionally dressed black woman running through an airport to catch the Avis bus is both followed and questioned because white police officers assume that she is carrying drugs. The assumptions—this black woman is only well dressed because she is a drug courier—are never stated; instead, the officers instantly act on the internalized beliefs that guide their behavior.

A wide variety of social interactions are already impossible—or at least contentious—because whites refuse to confirm the new assumptions of African Americans. In addition, nationwide groups like the American Anthropological Association have requested that the race category be removed from future U.S. censuses; cutting to the quick, the anthropologists forcefully asked that we all stop using a word with no scientific validity. Finally, a number of scholars—for example, Richard Dyer with *White*, F. James Davis with *Who is Black?*, Jan Nederveen Pieterse with *White on Black*—produced books that already call into question not only the concept of race, but the bedrock assumptions on which the color dichotomy is based. As Dyer notes, white people are called white because the word translates into a pervasive yet invisible sense of personal and group superiority. White means power and prejudice; it has little to do with the actual color of people's skin.[48]

Another cause for optimism is a waiting army of potentially 40 million Americans. As of early 1999, the Census Bureau says that the United States contains 195 million whites, 34 million blacks, and almost 40 million "others," such as "Hispanics of any race" and "Asian and Pacific Islanders." The Internet is already full of sophisticated homepages—for example, Little India and Azteca—that focus not only on ethnic pride, but on an attempt to understand the place and predicaments of "others" in U.S. life. As Achal Medra recently editorialized, Indian Americans are "proud to be confused." They are "the hornet's nest of a series of contradictions" and perfectly willing to live between past and future until a satisfying resolution appears.[49]

Along with Indian Americans, Japanese, Chinese, Korean, Vietnamese, Mexican, and Filipino Americans should be wide open to any conversation that creates a race-free consensus for all Americans. Indeed, if that consensus is partially rooted in an eager exploration of cultural differences, the army of "others" may actually ask to enlist.

Also available for mobilization are a huge number of well-intentioned, open-minded "white" Americans. But, and this is a big *but*, to bring these folks on board any train destined for serious social change, activists must avoid replacing one dichotomy (white/black) with another—victim/ victimizer. Spilt the world into good and bad and we forget an elemental fact about the power of culture: It is the dichotomy that is awful, *not necessarily the people who use it.*

Like me with the experience of "nigger chasers" or Gregory Williams accepting the label "bestial mongrel mulatto," we are all initially prisoners of the cultures we inherit. People therefore deserve, not the cultural world they got, but the one they are willing to consciously tolerate. The task for activists is to root the search for change in a profound sense of empathy. If white is as invisible as many scholars suggest, then its effects must be brought to light in a way that enables people to change culture and themselves without being told that they are also responsible for a world they did not create.

Start with empathy and the facts. The ominous alternative is a society of victims and victimizers, a world where even the most privileged talk by rather than to one another.

This is, of course, easier said than done. But the seeds of change nevertheless exist and, most important of all, only people make culture. We *are* in charge. As a step in the direction of change, let's scrap (more on this in chapter 6) two century-old metaphors for American life. As countless ethnic communities prove, the "melting pot" has never absorbed millions of Americans; and assimilation to a culture that systematically excludes so many "others" is appealing to only one group of newcomers: masochists.

Cultural pluralism is also an appealing idea. But, as the Jamaican writer Rex Nettleford notes, "my own distrust" of multiculturalism is that it moves people "to live side by side but not together."[50] Somehow, we need to create a sense of community that allows us to accept, recognize, and eagerly explore our ethnic and other differences, yet come together as a society of people genuinely committed to a shared set of (at a minimum) political ideals.

My own suggestion for a new metaphor is stolen from the Indian writer Shashi Thadoor. Discussing his vision of India, he describes it as a "thali, a set of sumptuous dishes in different bowls. Each tastes different, and does not necessarily mix with the next, but they belong together on the same plate, and they complement each other in making the meal a satisfying repast."[51]

Ironically, many United States–based multinational corporations already sponsor "thalis" in December of each year. In East Hartford, Connecticut, United Technologies (its divisions include Pratt and Whitney Aircraft, Carrier Air Conditioners, Otis Elevators) celebrates the cultural and global diversity of its workforce by hosting a banquet at which employees bring dishes from all over the world. Nothing clashes, because the idea is to draw from any many plates as you wish and to literally taste another's world while you simultaneously respect and explore it. (However appealing this idea is, it is much harder for poorer Americans to easily embrace the idea of a banquet. They can't sit at the table. See chapter 7).

This is a classic case of the glass that is half full or half empty. We are the music makers, and if we are disposed to think of our ethnic differences as a Christmas "thali" we can indeed unite Western and Eastern cultures, the world of the "old" immigrants and that of the "new."

However, we can't *all* sit down at the banquet table until we eliminate the color dichotomy that, like segregated restaurants in the 1950s, erects a wall of white and black between 270 million human beings. There is, in short, no comprehensive answer to the question of what we shall do with our America unless we first resolve to recognize the only race that actually exists, the human race.

AFRICAN AMERICANS: A UNIQUE ETHNICITY

To dramatically challenge the past and present, we must call African Americans what they actually are—an ethnic group with a four-hundred-year history of terrible exploitation and victimization in the United States. Skeptics might argue that this is an unnecessary change or, even worse, more political correctness; what makes the term "African American" better than "black"? Isn't it just another generalization, another category that hides or excludes variables like social class, gender and level of education?

Let's start with an indisputable fact: Social life is impossible without generalizations, which are by definition incomplete. This is an inherent problem of social life. However, like adding salt to an open wound, the words black and white trace their deepest roots to the fiction of race; their level of incompleteness is so great—i.e., *white* puts over 195 million people under the same label!—that they explode rather than simply distort reality and simultaneously define us by what divides us, the alleged colors of our skin.

Substituting African American for black and a variety of other words for white is the best way to instantly initiate a process of significant yet peaceful social change. Words, after all, trigger thought and behavior, and we proceed on the basis of those already internalized assumptions until someone asks us to challenge them.

New words are that challenge. They can be a gentle push or a slap in the face but, either way, the new words indicate that one partner to a social interaction refuses to abide by the society's traditional beliefs and practices.

In the United States, the awful beauty of the words black and white is that they are tightly woven into the fabric of virtually every aspect of American life. We have so "successfully" dichotomized U.S. life that *not* to use the words black and white requires deliberate thought. Try, for example to discuss any issue that relates to European and African Americans and not use the black/white dichotomy; it is so hard to do that we would all have to think before we spoke. *In those roughly half a billion daily pauses lies the possibility of serious social change.*

Attitude will be crucial. To erase the dichotomy is to challenge not only a set of ubiquitous preconscious assumptions but at the dichotomy's deepest level, the summary self-images of the people who run the United States. For example, in studies of ratings of very similarly qualified supervisors, psychologists discovered that Irish- or Polish- or German-American evaluators consistently described high-ability African Americans as less intelligent than they. This occurred because a "white" person does not expect to see a "black" person as a supervisor; the situation is, one, still out of the ordinary and, two, threatening to the way, for example, British, Greek, Italian, Russian, German, or Spanish Americans see the world. As an assumption of U.S. life they have been taught that they run the society. Thus, the African American cannot be more intelligent than they; his or her success must be due to factors like luck or the social engineering excesses of a misguided central government.[52]

The everyday consequences of simultaneously challenging both assumptions and self-images are clear: Hundreds of social interactions would be at best anxiety provoking and at worst impossible. Journalists would be asked never again to use bold headlines about "black women" attending a Million Women March, and in the many conversations that make up everyday life millions of people would be asked to stop in mid-sentence and replace white or black with our chosen substitutes. Little would be taken for granted and much be open for discussion.

Why would 270 million people want to consciously make social life impossible? How will the advocates of change manage an attitude that is non-threatening? What are the word substitutes you offer? Wouldn't, for example, the generalization "African American" make it harder for government programs to assist those who have been victimized and exploited by the ideological and institutionalized racism of U.S. society?

Let's start with motivation. In a biological sense races don't exist, yet the black/white dichotomy revolves around biological characteristics. Assuming therefore that many millions of Americans sincerely want to root their thinking in truth, an analysis of race as fiction is a possible backdoor into millions of otherwise culturally closed minds. Indeed, instead of a "hot button" issue like affirmative action, political, religious, and educational leaders could begin a national discussion—spilling over into classrooms and churches, synagogues and conferences, cafeterias and car pools—of the cold genetic facts.

The president could even indicate, "My fellow Americans, this is the deepest root of our struggle with hate: Races don't exist. So, as a president who wants to leave a profound mark on American life, here is my request: Let's walk into the next millennium on the basis of a shared and corrected past. Let's remove the cornerstone of the black/white dichotomy and begin to teach a simple fact: "There is only one race, the human race.' "

Besides a desire for truth, a second motivation is arguably more important: national interest and self-interest. Since 1965 more than 23 million people have legally migrated to the United States. As of October 1997, another 3.5 million are on waiting lists to enter but there is no cause for concern: Roughly two-thirds of the immigrants on the waiting list are already here illegally. Meanwhile, no matter what Congress does with the immigration laws, the flow of new Americans will not stop for the foreseeable future. On the contrary, as Mexico and the Caribbean increase their level of modernization, the United States can expect what analysts call a "migration hump." As societies modernize, they displace large numbers of traditional workers. Thus, as mechanization of agriculture accelerates, increased migration from, among others, Mexico, the Dominican Republic, El Salvador, and Jamaica will continue through the first decade of the twenty-first century.[53]

The vast majority of the new immigrants do not fit into the white/black dichotomy. Politicians can tell them to assimilate, but that is impossible when core concepts of the civilization accord them no recognition or, even worse, the U.S. government threatens to further confuse what is already confused. Consider, for example, the racial typology proposed by the Census Bureau and approved by the president for the year 2000:

White

Black or African American

Hispanic or Latino

Asian

Native Hawaiian or Pacific Islander

Native American or Alaska Native

The Census Bureau mercilessly confuses racial, panethnic, and ethnic identities. The result is cultural confusion that has its roots in the same problem: The main dividing line is the white/black dichotomy. A principal problem is that Latinos, Asians, Pacific Islanders, Native Americans, and now two new races, Alaska Native and Native Hawaiian, remain a national afterthought. In black and white the Census Bureau stresses that there are 195 million white Americans, 32 million black Americans, and the leftovers.

If we mean to include the fastest-growing sector of our population into the mainstream of a changed American life, we need to eliminate the black/white dichotomy. Otherwise we will perpetuate a system that systematically alienates new immigrants and leaves more than 195 million people with no choice but to remain white. For example, several studies show that third- and fourth-generation Americans have no more than a symbolic identification with their Italian, Irish, or German roots.[54] Instead of giving them an ethnic identity that matters—for example, American—we squeeze them into the white category. In the Census Bureau typology approved by the president, the white category is the only one with no ethnic identity attached. It is therefore another ten-year guarantee that more than 195 million people will be asked to see black and act white.

A third motivation to make social life impossible is a desire for justice. In recent years the national debate has focused on affirmative action; we have become bogged down in arguments about competency or reverse discrimination and forgotten the most important issue of all: Whatever their shortcomings, programs like affirmative action are necessary because *this is a society even more separated by caste than by class*. In *American Apartheid*, Massey and Denton underline the extraordinary segregation that persists throughout the United States. In Chicago and Atlanta, St. Louis and Washington, D.C., the concentration of African Americans living with African Americans approaches 90 percent. The United States has greater degrees of spatial segregation than South Africa, yet we find many Americans confidently asserting that the employment and educational problems encountered by African Americans are based on class, not caste.[55]

However, as William Julius Wilson convincingly demonstrates in *When Work Disappears*, the negative prejudices rooted in the white/black dichotomy remain a crucial variable in explaining the inability of African Americans—especially African-American men—to find work. In Wilson's words, "Employers make assumptions about the inner-city black workers *in general* and reach decisions based on those assumptions before they have had a chance to review systematically the qualifications of an individual applicant" (emphasis added).[56]

New language will never instantly erase four hundred years of inherited and learned hate. Significant social change is the work of generations. But the new words can, over time, forever interrupt the cycle of hate. Indeed, used with empathy, the new words can move people to voluntarily challenge and change the assumptions (e.g., they're ignorant; they don't work; jobs exist, globalization has changed nothing) that make the ideal of equal opportunity a still distant dream.

What are those words? As a panethnic label, most U.S. citizens could use European American. Or, a person who felt strongly about his or her ethnic heritage could more specifically identify as Italian or Irish or Polish American. Finally, those of us without a strong attachment to our ethnic roots could simply identify as Americans.

The next chapter presents a detailed discussion of the new ethnic labels. Here the concern is *first* to stop thinking in terms of a biological fiction.

Thus, to those who say that European American is an awkward or a gross generalization, there is the obvious question: Why it is appropriate to use Latino, Hispanic, Asian, or Native American? Under the panethnic identity Asian, the Census Bureau confidently places more than twenty separate ethnic groups. Native American is a label that subsumes more than three hundred tribes, and Latino is a word that easily includes more than twenty-five separate nations and cultures.

European American does sound strange or awkward. But that is the point. We need to challenge our assumptions and the new words are that deliberately cumbersome invitation. The generalizations—the words—we use not only hide the individuality of another person, they give it a new form, based on new assumptions and different behavior. The label European American would be used because it is grounded in assumptions like these: Races don't exist. The black/white dichotomy nourishes beliefs and practices based on antipathy. And the black/white dichotomy systematically excludes groups who are already a greater percentage of the American people than African Americans.

From the perspective of African Americans the ethnic—the colorless— label has two distinct advantages. First, it would once again focus national attention on African Americans. Their unique history was center stage during the civil rights era but, however ironically, the success of leaders like Martin Luther King and Malcolm X helped move other groups to share and often dominate the national stage. Women, gays, Latinos, the handicapped, the aged, and the aging all also received widespread attention. The end result is that despite a conventional wisdom that places racial problems at the center of civil rights complaints, the truth is that by the mid 1990s only 25 percent of the claims made to the Equal Employment Opportunity Commission revolved around race. Together, gender, age, disability, and religious discrimination complaints were twice as common as complaints made by African Americans.[57]

Refusing to speak in black and white will move more than 270 million people to expressly focus on African Americans. This specific attention would deal—in those half-a-billion daily encounters—with issues that range from preconscious assumptions about expected behavior to a dismal fact of U.S. life. The proportion of metropolitan African Americans living in poverty is fast approaching 50 percent; and, while the rate of poverty for African Americans outside the cities is decreasing, it is increasing for those who live in places like Hartford, Chicago, and Washington, D.C.

To solve social problems this specific attention is crucial in and of itself. But, one of the ripple effects of eliminating the grandest generalization of all, the label *white*, is that we validate the ethnic differences, which paradoxically could allow us to recognize ethnic, class, educational, and religious similarities. As used in U.S. culture, white and black are absolutes that exclude all other variables. While a focus on ethnicity can be just as exclusive—

think of Nazi Germany or contemporary Rwanda—it can also be a vehicle for recognizing what unites different social groups. For example, African American and other activists would no longer use the words black and white to filter their perceptions. Activists would instead see specific groups of people (e.g., Puerto Ricans or Amerasians[58] in New York, Filipinos or Chicanos in California) who may also be victimized and exploited by the economic or political system. The focus on the ethnic differences could then lead to a recognition of social similarities, if we follow the advice of Michael Lerner: Refuse to discuss who is most oppressed and focus instead on alliances with groups who may in fact be "less oppressed on material grounds or grounds of rights denial."[59]

Take the word *Jew*. When I grew up in New York it referred to a particular group of people. While you might add Hasidic Jew in certain parts of Brooklyn, either way the reference was always to an ethnic or religious group. But, when I moved to Connecticut, Jew turned into a verb! Bargaining for a car, a house, or an appliance you "jewed" someone down. The often explicit indication was that Jewish people behaved like Shakespeare's Shylock, so, "Jew them down" and you got them before they got you.

In early 2000 Jew is still used as a verb all over Connecticut. It is an almost unnoticed manifestation of deep-seated anti-Semitism; and, as such, it is a bridge to the alliances that can be formed if, instead of seeing black and white, we ask questions like these. Why is the Talmud or the Midrash not part of a course in Western Civilization? Why is it so hard to think of Jewish studies as an integral part of a course of study in other cultures? Why do Jewish activists often receive this response from the advocates of multiculturalism: "What? You are not a separate entity? You're part of the white mass and you've already had your time." Which, as Michael Lerner stressed, "is ludicrous because the Jewish canon has been systematically excluded from the Western canon all the way through Western history."[60]

Alliances between similarly mistreated groups would serve two crucial purposes. They would provide unprecedented power to, for example, now united African, Filipino, Mexican, and Jewish citizens of the United States. But, even more important, those alliances could work to produce serious social change much more quickly. Psychologists argue that one way to break down the barriers created by prejudice is to get people from groups to work together. Focusing on a common goal, people let down the guard created by cultural generalizations and, especially if group efforts are successful, women and men are disposed to discard the mental baggage that comes with socialization in a dichotomized society.

Attitude will be crucial. We all normally resist challenging, much less changing, our taken for granted assumptions; yet, to take the road I am suggesting is to deliberately produce half a billion challenges a day. Activists must root any strategies for change in empathy. We must put ourselves in the other person's head and at all costs resist any display of arrogance or self-righteousness. To eliminate the white/black dichotomy is to request changes at the deepest roots of U.S. culture. Combine that request with arrogance and 195 million mostly European Americans will resolve their dissonance by blaming the messenger instead of hearing the message.

The message? Races don't exist. Unless we wish to continue teaching that seeing is not believing, let's begin the process of using the new words that can, at long last, bury the dichotomy that poisons American life.

NOTES

1. Ellis Cose, *Color Blind: Seeing Beyond Race in a Race-Obsessed World* (New York: Harper, 1997).

2. See, for example, Tomas Almaguer, *Racial Fault Lines* (Berkeley: University of California Press, 1994).

3. *Review of Federal Measures of Race and Ethnicity*, Hearings before the Subcommittee on Census, Statistics, and Postal Personnel, House, 103rd Congress, first session (Washington, DC: GPO, 1993), p. 55.

4. Rex Nettleford, *Inward Stretch, Outward Reach* (London: Macmillan Press, 1993), p. xiii.

5. F. James Davis, *Who Is Black?* (University Park: Pennsylvania State University Press, 1991); also Cose, *Color Blind*, p. 4.

6. William Julius Wilson, *The Declining Significance of Race* (Chicago: University of Chicago Press, 1979); for a change in Professor Wilson's assessment of race's significance, see *When Work Disappears* (New York: Vintage, 1997).

7. See *USA Today*, November 17, 1997, p. 8A.

8. Thomas Sowell, *Race and Culture* (New York: Basic Books, 1994).

9. Mark Nathan Cohen, *Culture of Intolerance* (New Haven: Yale University Press, 1998), p. 24; for the biracial debate, see Lise Funderberg, *Black, White, Other* (New York: William Morrow, 1994).

10. Michael Alan Park, *Biological Anthropology* (San Francisco: Mayfield, 1996), p. 301.

11. Christopher Wills, "The Skin We're In," in *Critical White Studies*, edited by Richard Delgado and Jean Stefanic (Philadelphia: Temple University Press, 1997), p. 13.

12. Ibid.; see, too, Jacques Barzun, *Race, A Study in Superstition* (New York: Harper, 1965). The first edition of this book appeared in 1936.

13. Ibid.

14. *Congressional Record*, House, 56th Congress, 2nd session, March 1, 1901, pp. 3371–3372; this is quoted in Ronald Fernandez, *Cruising the Caribbean* (Monroe, ME: Common Courage Press, 1994), p. 22. For a superb analysis and understanding of the development of human societies, see Jared Diamond, *Guns, Germs and Steel* (New York: W. W. Norton, 1999).

15. Cohen, *Culture of Intolerance*, esp. pp. 25, 39.

16. This chart is an abridged version of the one that appears in Sharon Lee, "Racial Classifications in the U.S. Census: 1890–1990," *Ethnic and Racial Studies* 16, no. 1 (January 1993): 75–94.

17. On this see Cohen, *Culture of Intolerance*, p. 44.

18. L. Luca Cavalli-Sforza, Paolo Menozzi, and Alberto Piazza, *The History and Geography of Human Genes* (Princeton: Princeton University Press, 1994), esp. pp. 18–20. See, too, R. C. Lewontin, Steven Rose, and Leon J. Kamin, *Not in Our Genes: Biology, Ideology and Human Nature* (New York: Pantheon, 1984). Also Marvin Harris, *Our Kind* (New York: Harper, 1989), p. 107.

19. Ibid., pp. 107–108.

20. Cavalli-Sforza et al., *Human Genes*, p. 19.

21. Jan Nederveen Pietersen, *White On Black: Images of Africa and Blacks in Western Popular Culture* (New Haven: Yale University Press, 1992), p. 46; see, too, Stephen Jay Gould, *The Mismeasure of Man*, rev. ed. (New York: Norton, 1996).

22. Debra Van Ausdale and Joe R. Feagin, "Using Racial and Ethnic Concepts: The Critical Case of Very Young Children," *American Sociological Review* 61 (October 1996): 779–793, esp. p. 782.

23. Michael Omi and Howard Winant, *Racial Formation in the United States*, 2nd ed. (New York: Routledge, 1994), p. 55.

24. Manning Marabel, "Beyond Color-Blindness," *The Nation* 267, no. 20 (December 14, 1998): 30.

25. See, for example, Patricia Justiniani McReynolds, *Almost Americans* (Santa Fe: Red Crane Books, 1997).

26. These ideas are drawn principally from Lee, "Racial Classifications," see especially p. 85.

27. Michael Lerner and Cornel West, *Jews and Blacks* (New York: Plume, 1996), p. 70.

28. Beverly Daniel Tatum, *Why Are All the Black Kids Sitting Together in the Cafeteria?* (New York: Basic Books, 1997), p. 15.

29. A splendid examination of this issue is James McBride, *The Color of Water* (New York: Riverhead Books, 1997).

30. This section is heavily indebted to Richard Dyer's *White* (London: Routledge, 1997).

31. Ibid., p. 47.

32. Ibid.

33. Pietersen, *White on Black*, pp. 24–25.

34. Dyer, *White*, p. 9.

35. See, for example, Maureen T. Reedy, *Crossing the Color Line: Race, Parenting and Culture* (New Brunswick, NJ: Rutgers University Press, 1997).

36. Ellis Cose, *The Rage of a Privileged Class* (New York: Harper, 1993), p. 4.

37. For the institutionalized prejudices of another major corporation, Shoney's Restaurants, see Steve Watkins, *The Black O: Racism and Redemption in an American Corporate Empire* (Athens: University of Georgia Press, 1997).

38. Dyer, *White*, p. 48.

39. Ibid., p. 52.

40. See, too, Grace Elizabeth Hale, *The Making of Whiteness: The Culture of Segregation in the South* (New York: Pantheon, 1998), especially chapter 2.

41. Gregory Howard Williams, *Life on the Color Line* (New York: Dutton, 1995), p. 38.

42. Ibid.

43. Ibid., p. 91.

44. Lise Funderburg, *Black, White, Other* (New York: William Morrow, 1994), p. 48.

45. Ibid., p. 49.

46. Dyer, *White*, p. 11.

47. For a splendid book about a particular community, see Russ Rymer, *American Beach: A Saga of Race, Wealth and Memory* (New York: HarperCollins, 1998).

48. Ibid., p. 50.

49. See Achal Mehra, "Proud to be Confused," *Little India*, September 13, 1997, ⟨www.littleindia.com⟩.

50. Nettleford, *Inward Stretch*, p. xiii.

51. Shashi Thadoor, *India: From Midnight to the Millennium* (New York: Harper, 1997), p. 76.

52. Tatum, *Why Are All the Black Kids*, pp. 119–121.

53. Philip Martin, ed., *Migration News* 3, no. 11 (November 1995): 12–13; for an analysis of Dominicans and their conceptions of both color and migration, see Michelle Wucker, *Why the Cocks Fight: Dominicans, Haitians and the Struggle for Hispaniola* (New York: Hill and Wang, 1999).

54. Richard Alba, *Ethnic Identity: The Transformation of White America* (New Haven: Yale University Press, 1990); also Mary Waters, *Ethnic Options: Choosing Identities in America* (Berkeley: University of California Press, 1990).

55. Douglas Massey and Nancy Denton, *American Apartheid* (Cambridge: Harvard University Press, 1993).

56. William Julius Wilson, *When Work Disappears: The World of the New Urban Poor* (New York: Vintage, 1996).

57. Farai Childeya, *Don't Believe the Hype: Fighting Cultural Misinformation About African Americans* (New York: Penguin, 1995), p. 104.

58. Thomas Bass, *Vietamerica: The War Comes Home* (New York: Soho Press, 1996).

59. Michael Lerner and Cornel West, *Jews and Blacks* (New York: Plume Books, 1996), p. 239.

60. Ibid., p. 153.

6

Ethnic Extremes

"Imagine the white Maine kid growing up in an all-white community, going to a virtually all-white university or college, getting a job in an all-white establishment, and someday leaving the state to learn that most of the rest of the world is composed of people of color . . . the culture shock could be severe."
—Editorial, *Maine Sunday Telegram*, October 4, 1998

TWENTY-TWO CARAT GOLD

We were lost. My guide had said to drive down the main drag of Jackson Heights and "You couldn't miss it." I did. Stopping at a local gas station, I asked the two attendants walled in by a glass barricade if they knew the location of the Indian community. After the men turned their eyes to the sky—another tourist!—they told me to make a right on Roosevelt Avenue, drive past the Korean enclave, and Indians grouped themselves right next to the El Salvadoran and Guatemalan immigrants.

As if an official greeter, one gentleman sported billowy slacks under a robe that reached to his knees. The silk "suit" was colored sky blue and topped off by a pair of rubber sport sandals made (I would guess) in China. With a smile this entrepreneur passed out flyers for the "Success Computer Training Institute." You could earn $2,000 a month "while you learned"; the institute happily prepared work visas for its graduates, and it offered everything from courses in "client server programming" to a focus on "Java with advance functions and certification."

Skeptics might laugh at the man's claims but, even if he failed, many NRI's (non-resident Indians) use their entrepreneurial and computer skills to earn far more than $2,000 a month. In truth, Indian families enjoyed incomes as high as those of any native or immigrant group in the United States. For example, with his wife, Bharat Desai founded Syntel in 1980. "To customers we wanted to be their application management partner of choice; to employees we wanted to provide superior career opportunities; and to shareholders, we wanted to provide superior long-term returns." Today Syntel (based in Michigan) employs close to 1,750 people, it is one of the nation's "hot growth companies," and Desai proudly boasts, "We have already created 15 millionaires in the company . . . we believe in the next five years we will create 100 millionaires."[1]

I hope so. Because somebody has to buy the gold necklaces that filled the display windows of one jewelry store after another. Without exaggeration, Fort Knox Avenue was an appropriate name for the Indian thoroughfare. The gold necklaces looked huge; worn around the throat they could easily hang below the cleavage line and, presumably, make it hard to lift one's head. We hesitated to explore prices but, when I later asked an Indian student if the necklaces were fourteen-carat gold, she looked at me, eyebrows raised, with an air of surprise, bordering on disdain. "No Indian buys less than twenty-two-carat gold."

A bit of research indicated that mothers started buying the necklaces for daughters as soon as finances allowed. "In Indian culture, the woman of the house—the embodiment of the family's honor—treasures her gold jewelry both as her soundest asset and as the symbol of her status."[2] At social gatherings, especially weddings, the necklaces often make an appearance, but it is allegedly the height of bad taste to wear more gold than the bride and her family. That is "conspicuous consumption" parading about as rudeness; even if you own the necklaces, you nevertheless keep them at home, a sure sign of genuine social status because you feel no need to throw around your weight in gold.

Like Fernandez among Latinos, Patel is arguably the most common Indian family name in the United States. More than 12 percent of Indians are called Patel.[3] One especially large family business—Patel Brothers—controls a network of supermarkets located throughout the United States. Aretsia, California; Sterling Heights, Missouri; Decatur, Georgia; and Jackson Heights, Queens, are among the locations that contain a handsome Patel Brothers store.

Filled with a wider variety of (for example) nuts than I had ever seen in my life, the Queens market also contained shelves full of diverse flours, vegetables shipped from India, and an array of chilies sure to excite anyone with a taste for fire.

I bought a bag of chilies, thinking I would leave with something really Indian, only to discover that "if you look at the art of cooking—the distinctive feature of Indian cooking is thought to be the food being hot and the liberal use of chilies. But chilies were unknown in India until the Portuguese brought them. And yet, when we think about Indian food being hot, we don't think of it as a Western product."[4]

In an article entitled "Culture and Identity," Nobel Prize winner Amartya Sen illustrated a wonderful second meaning of "NRI": never relinquished Indian culture. In this sense NRI refers to a willingness to consistently ask hard questions even if no immediate answers exist. Sen notes that "India has more Hindus than any other country in the world, more sects than any other country, more languages (fully 35 are spoken by more than a million people) than any other country, and more religions than any other country." Indeed, after Indonesia and Pakistan, India is the third largest Muslim country in the world, and if the Portuguese brought chilies, Indians created Buddhism. It "caught on" elsewhere, but Buddhism's deepest roots are in the subcontinent.[5]

Sen argues that any Indian "is the coexistence of various identities." The nation's extraordinary diversity made that a certainty so, for the NRIs looking for a perfect label, for the NRIs who move forward looking in a rearview mirror pointed at Bombay or New Delhi,[6] Sen artfully suggests this disposition toward life in the United States. "Whatever we understand and enjoy in human progress instantly becomes ours, wherever it might have its origin."[7] No Indian could or should forget the past, but Indians could nevertheless happily coexist by opening themselves to the differences that defined them both at home and abroad.

Some NRIs apparently refuse to accept Sen's advice. A September 1998 editorial in *Little India* asks readers to imitate the sense of solidarity allegedly characteristic of "West Asian countries, fondly referred to here as the Middle East." The editor said, "It is quite remarkable how a Lebanese, an Iraqi and even an Iranian would find themselves breaking bread out of a common bond." Meanwhile, "popular memory among Indian groups here is buzzing with stories of our divisiveness."

American visitors in Jackson Heights saw a group of all-alike Indians. NRIs, however, knew that rich Indians funded disputes, engaged in "petty struggles" in local community groups, and joined "last but certainly not least, the petty and real struggles in the business community where we perceive our own countrymen as near rivals over the others."[8]

Unity was the clarion call. Stop wasting time fighting with one another, and among other things, let's discover some way to make the Americans remember that 1.2 million Indians now live in the United States. In an article titled "Neither Black nor White," Vineeta Vijayaraghavan complains, "The contemporary race debate seems to have no place at all for minorities such as Indian Americans."[9] In Los Angeles, home to the O. J. Simpson trial, a third of the city boasted Asian or Hispanic origins, yet the debate about juries occurred in black and white. Indians needed to make their political clout felt because politicians "pandering" to racist fears might try to *exclude* the very Indians they simultaneously failed to *include* in the national debate.

Remember, readers were told, 75 percent of all Indian immigrants come to the United States under family reunification provisions of the U.S. immigration laws. As those statues could easily be changed, minorities had to unite.[10]

Minorities! An immigrant group with the highest family income in America nevertheless called itself a minority. While this was a form of assimilation never desired by worried U.S. politicians, use of the minority label does reflect a fact of U.S. life: Even those immigrants who succeed can nevertheless feel alienated. As with African Americans, this sense of alienation was the expressed rage of a privileged class who wanted to be part of America—if they were allowed to do so and if they could retain what local newspapers called "Indian spiritual and cultural values."

The matrimonial section of *India in New York* spoke to those values in a manner that would make even Pat Robertson or Jerry Falwell think twice about a parent's Godgiven power over children. One ad said, "Parents invite correspondence from Punjabi professionals in the U.S or India." The "charming daughter," convent educated, was thirty-three years old; she had an MBA, she was well traveled, and she managed the family business.

Another ad came from "Telugu Brahmin" parents who invited proposals for their twenty-six-year-old son. He was a physician in his first year of residency, he was very fair and good looking—and only "Telugu Brahmin" need apply for his hand in marriage.[11]

This was indeed India in New York! It was also one good indication of the profound conflicts and yearnings experienced by Indians who succeed in the United States but still live, spiritually, in India.

Consider, for example, this cartoon from a 1996 article entitled "NRI Mid-Life Crisis." Two Indian men are seated on a park bench. Kids are playing in the background, surrounded by trees and a montage of skyscrapers. Then, one Indian says to the other, "Frankly, since 1970 I'm still debating whether to live in this country or go home."[12]

That Indian may never reconcile his contradictory longings. But his predicament and ours will be eased if, instead of excluding him from national debates, we insure that he and all other Indians are always welcome and respected members of U.S. society.

MARK McGWIRE AND ALEXIS DE TOCQUEVILLE

We were late. The game began at 8 A.M.—sharp!—and the main manager said to be there at 7:30. Chalk lines needed to be precise, somebody had to secure the bases to the ground, somebody else had to retrieve the equipment, and the girls needed to warm up in the ten or so minutes allotted to each softball team.

The park was literally a "field of dreams." In Brooklyn we had played on sandlots, fenced in by traffic and supervised by the P.A.L., the Police Athletic

League. In the upscale Portland, Maine, suburb of Cape Elizabeth, a wall of trees provided the background for a field of manicured (by parent volunteers) grass, a "press box" with a loudspeaker system, bleachers, a soon to be opened refreshment stand, and—my envy was palpable—two cement dugouts. No one chewed tobacco, but the girls nevertheless strutted about, punching their gloves or yelling encouragement—"attaway"—to their teammates just coming in from the field.

Our pitcher stood six feet tall. At thirteen she understandably terrified the opposition—and her father as well. He was head coach, she was the team's star, and, like many a standout, she preferred to do things her own way. After one bit of instruction that bordered on pestering, she simply exclaimed, "Shut up," and the coach turned his attention to team players more open to instruction.

Each game lasted two hours, no less and certainly no more. As the volunteer umpire explained, he would be calling balls and strikes, until six that evening, for five different games. Whether girls or boys, teams got two hours to play only as many innings as 120 minutes allowed. In our case, the rules permitted stealing, but the young catchers often lacked the power to reach second base. Predictably, every time somebody got to first, the runner also got to third and sometimes home. The umpire explained that it was a judgment call; you wanted the game to be authentic so you allowed the stealing, which prolonged the innings and eventually made watching a chore.

Parents didn't seem to mind. Mothers dutifully cheered on the girls and the all-male coaching staff while men in the middle of middle age watched the offspring from their second or third families. As divorce was as common in Portland as in Peoria or Pittsburgh, in the summer of 1998, the "mix and match" families now seemed as all-American as the sport they played.

An hour into the game, I went across the road, walked through the park, elbowed my way across a blacktopped lot full of shiny sport-utility vehicles, and wound up at a series of fields containing as many parents as five- to nine-year-old girls. Like a smiling crowd at Disneyland, a legion of moms and dads provided an enthusiastic audience for kids swinging bats that seemed taller than they. Yet again there was an umpire, and as this one called balls and strikes I suggested to friends that he offered the only perceivable ethnic difference on any of the fields. How come this guy had a slighter darker skin and what appeared to be an Italian, Greek, or Spanish face?

No one knew for sure, but one person guessed that he was Portuguese, welcomed to the field because he had two daughters on the team—and a nationwide reputation as a specialist in treating a particularly virulent form of cancer.

Whatever the man's actual ethnic origins, studies of suburban communities like Cape Elizabeth suggest that he and the other men, women, and children on those fields actually had nothing more than a symbolic attachment to one or *more* ethnic groups. Like the families of divorce, fourth- or fifth-generation Americans are mix and match, a composite of heritages from which women and men apparently choose whatever ethnic roots then suit their fancy. Thus, at one extreme, cultural or physical appearance forever chains the Indians and Koreans of Queens to their ethnic origins; meanwhile, at the other extreme, the multiethnic millions who live in communities like Cape Elizabeth (or West Hartford, Connecticut) can choose any roots they wish—or no roots at all.[13]

Oddly, the one identity people seldom embrace is American. Yet the parents on those fields lovingly displayed two all-American cultural traits clearly evident to Alexis de Tocqueville in the 1830s. Comparing one nation to another, the French aristocrat wrote, "The English often perform great things singly, whereas the Americans form associations for the smallest undertakings. It is evident that the former people consider association as a powerful means of action but the latter seem to regard it as the only means they have of acting."[14]

That's certainly true in Cape Elizabeth. "Feelings and opinions were recruited" and the "heart enlarged" by men and women who, on their own time, mowed the lawns and organized the practices, the games, the all-star teams, and the playoffs that spilled over into the next season of the next sport. Soccer, for example, followed baseball. With different men coaches, the girls traveled Southern Maine to play games for the "associations" organized by their continually supportive parents. Each soccer family paid the $90 players fee, bought all the appropriate equipment, drove the kids to practice, came to their soccer games (sometimes two in a day), and cheered on both the children and the coaches, who loved the sport and treated the kids with both affection and respect.

These Americans stood tall as the democratic descendants of the volunteers who amazed de Tocqueville more than 160 years ago. Yet, even though they did identify as Americans, the "Diversity Day" editorial from the *Maine Sunday Telegram* taught that the racial identity "white" continually trumped even the ethnic identity American. Equally important, the "individualism" still championed by American culture moves us to believe that we can somehow live alone, school systems away from the Somalis and Kuwaitis who recently immigrated to the city of Portland and a world away from the Indians and Koreans who walk the streets of Jackson Heights.

De Tocqueville argued that in the United States a dangerous sense of individualism "proceeds from erroneous judgement more than depraved feelings; it originates as much in deficiencies of mind as in perversity of heart."[15] Americans, said de Tocqueville, actually "acquired the habit of always considering themselves as standing alone"; in churches and schools Americans learned that only they controlled their own destiny. So, as if Clint Eastwood playing Dirty Harry, not only does democracy in America "make every man forget his ancestors, but it hides his descendants and separates his contemporaries from him. It throws him back forever upon himself alone and threatens in the end to confine him entirely within the solitude of his own heart."[16]

That is not a pretty prospect. Nor is it an accurate portrayal of the way either America or any society actually works. The volunteerism so wonderfully displayed in a Portland suburb is deeply rooted in the cultural creations of our distant American ancestors. The illusion of standing only on our own two feet is at least two hundred years old; we simply echo our ancestors whenever *Fortune* or *Time* magazine trumpets the achievements of Bill Gates, the richest *self-made* man in the country. Or, from a more selfish angle, whenever Americans proudly identify with Frank Sinatra defiantly singing "I did it my way."[17]

Individualism is dangerous for at least three reasons. First, by separating us from our contemporaries, the illusion of standing alone develops at best a very limited sense of community. In the extreme, we willingly draw apart with family and friends, "leaving society at large to itself."[18]

Second, and this is particularly ironic in communities where parents are so lovingly devoted to their children, by hiding our descendants a commitment to individualism offers no way out of the myth of the self-made American. Children echo what their parents preach even as they play a game that depends on the coordination of eight other people, not to mention the scores of volunteers who act as everything from chauffeurs to gardeners.

Finally, individualism is dangerous because (see chapter 4) self-consciousness not only always includes others, it starts with others. The kids in any homogenized suburban community reach conclusions about themselves only after others provide the accurate or inaccurate, sane or bizarre, illusory or truthful information.

The problem for the nation is that if Jackson Heights represents one pole on the ethnicity continuum, upscale suburbs like Cape Elizabeth represent the other. Both poles exude ethnicity, but many of the most privileged and powerful Americans are preparing their children for a game that no longer exists. Or, what is worse, for a game in which both sides leap out of the dugouts, ready for a melee that also draws fans from the stands.

Recall George Herbert Mead's notion of the generalized other. It is the organized community that teaches children who and what they are in cultural terms. In trying to explain exactly how children internalized a culture, Mead used the example of a baseball game. When youngsters *instantly* understood how they interconnected to more than nine other people on a field, they could "play ball" with no need for further instruction.

Baseball was Mead's metaphor for society; once people understood their position on the field and its interrelation to others, they acted on what they inherited and played according to their successfully internalized expectations and rules. Thus, in suburbs as homogenized as Cape Elizabeth, the children learned—at the level of assumptions taken for granted—that the players all looked the same, that nobody dressed or spoke differently, that ethnicity had meaning on "diversity day," and despite girl's softball and soccer, that "white" men still managed the world.

Those lessons can be unlearned, and they are partially contradicted in any family where men and women equally share authority. But, it would be much easier for the 270 million of us if we developed a consensual ethos that defines us by what unites us. The motivation can be a combination of idealism and self-interest, but the need is urgent because one ominous alternative is the culture shock predicted by the *Maine Sunday Herald* and experienced by my guides to Cape Elizabeth. Driving through Hartford, one eleven-year-old youngster from Portland's suburbs spotted an African American wearing leather gloves and exclaimed, "Look, mommy, there's OJ."

The child was serious. The responsibility is ours. We all watched the extremes develop but, instead of rethinking the past, we are still determined by it. The two dominant metaphors that supposedly describe our alternatives—the melting pot and cultural pluralism—are as questionable today as they were in the decade that preceded the national origins legislation of 1924.

PREACHERS PRESENT ARMS[19]

The sign looked like this:

SPEAK THE AMERICAN LANGUAGE

IF you don't know it—learn it
IF you don't like it—move out.[20]

In 1917 this sign greeted all visitors to Abilene, Kansas. Mentioned in a book about the mobilization of "preachers" for the Great War, the sign helped mark the midpoint of a national campaign against an insidious enemy: hyphenated Americans. Theodore Roosevelt, once again charging up San Juan Hill, let out a battle cry directed to "one hundred percent Americans" as he warned "of the extreme danger to this country of permitting the up growth here of any system of group citizenship." To the former president, "This country is a crucible, a melting-pot, in which many different race strains are being fused into one. *If some of the material remains as an unfused lump, it is worthless in itself, and it is also a detriment to the rest of the mixture*" (emphasis added).[21]

Strong language, matched by strong action. In Philadelphia (on January 19, 1916), Americans like S. Stanwood Menken, Mrs. Cabot Ward, Mr. and Mrs. Edward T. Stotesbury, and Mr. and Mrs. Vincent Astor attended a dinner sponsored by the "National Conference on Immigration and Americanization." In gowns and tuxedos, diners devised plans to spread this message throughout the United States: "We can no longer endure as a polyglot boardinghouse." All residents needed to put the American flag above all others and, to avoid "scattering our fire," Americanizers needed to move the battlefront to the factories and homes that harbored "hyphens" of all shades and types.[22]

Under the auspices of "the Board of Commerce," Detroit waved the flag in a variety of ingenious ways. "Practically every factory and shop in Detroit displayed large posters furnished by the National Americanization Committee and showing, in three colors, Uncle Sam welcoming the immigrant and directing him to the public school, the road to the English language and to American citizenship."

If workers somehow missed the posters, they always looked in their paychecks, which, along with cash, now contained "small night school notices." In some factories "interpreters were especially deputized to approach every man separately and find out whether he will attend night school." Finally, some factories simply lined up their workers at noon "and gave a talk on the relation of night-school work to their chances of getting and keeping a job."[23]

Taking the war against the hyphen into the nation's polyglot boardinghouses, Joseph Mayper discussed "Americanizing immigrant homes." He started in a community (the exact location is not mentioned) where "garbage reduction plants provided employment" for the newcomers. Working day and night shifts, different immigrants occupied the same bed at different times. One result was "foul odors" and "constant indulgence in alcohol."

So, during seventy-five visits a week in the spring of 1916, nurses—who actually functioned "as Americanizing domestic educators"—did double duty. They "instructed mothers in matters of cleanliness, ventilation, personal hygiene, and sanitation of the home." Then, despite the garbage reduction plants in the background, young girls enlisted in a "Little Mother's League" where they learned the lessons their mothers never learned. Finally, "through the courtesy of one of the garbage plants," some wasteland became both a ballfield and a garden. Plants blossomed near the city's waste and, for their troubles, immigrants received a "boat ride to a nearby resort." There, literally waving an American flag and (presumably) munching German-origin hot dogs and French-fried potatoes, immigrants listened as "short addresses in their own language were made by a few of the more Americanized men."[24]

Action produced reaction. In the July 1916 *Atlantic Monthly* Randolph Bourne reminded readers, "We act as if we wanted Americanization to take place only on our own terms and not by the consent of the governed." As Bourne read history, the early colonists never came to "be assimilated into an American melting-pot. They did not come to adopt the culture of the American Indian and they had the smallest intention of giving themselves without reservation to the new country."[25]

This reading of history helped produce the only serious challenge to the melting-pot ideal. The pragmatist philosopher Horace Kallen said to think of America as a symphony orchestra. As each instrument has its special timbre and tonality that, together, produce beautiful music, "so in society each ethnic group may be the natural instrument, its temper and culture may be its theme and melody and the harmony and dissonances and discords of them may make the symphony of civilization."[26]

Kallen called his approach "cultural pluralism," and, well into the 1960s he lectured[27] about the "orchestration" that various ethnic groups could achieve if America ever provided "conditions under which each might attain the cultural perfection that is *proper to its kind*" (emphasis in original).[28] As a profoundly committed democrat, Kallen called his ideal a "democracy of nationalities," but he never explained how, if ethnic groups lived side by side, they could also produce the harmony required to live together. For example, would one or many "maestros" lead the orchestra? Or, would the harmony develop spontaneously?

An equally glaring omission was the role of excluded or banned groups. It was never explained whether African Americans, Native Americans, and the (then banished) Asian Americans would even be allowed onstage, much less made prominent members of the orchestra.

Kallen simply stressed that, whereas a musical symphony is written before it is played, "in the symphony of civilization the playing is in the writing."[29] The pragmatist genuinely trusted the will of the people, but he had glaring doubts about the Americanizers. "Do the dominant classes want such a society? Or will vanity blind them and fear constrain, turning the promise of freedom into the fact of tyranny, and once more vindicating the ancient habit of men and aborting the hope of the world?"[30]

A contemporary answer to these questions appeared in the form of the national origins legislation of 1924. America closed its doors for forty-one years and tried to achieve a melting pot that still had no room for, among others, 20 million African Americans, 10 million Mexicans, 1 million Puerto Ricans, and an unspecified number of Filipinos and Jamaicans. Meanwhile, once the nation's doors were reopened in 1965, more than 20 million ethnically centered newcomers arrived. Simultaneously, we created a nationwide series of homogenized suburbs, filled with people who are often just as worried about immigrants as the Americanizers of World War I.

As a bridge to a united future, we could seek new ways to understand a New World. But the power of inherited culture is so great that, eighty-two years after this "polyglot" debate first took place, we continue to use metaphors—the melting pot and cultural pluralism—whose origins lie in terrible prejudice and a weak, race-blind reaction to that prejudice. Indeed, despite a variety of pronounced differences between yesterday and today, we are still trying to resolve the "old American problem" of the one and the many by rushing to the poles of simplification that offered little hope in 1916 and offers no hope in the twenty-first century.[31]

To have any chance of creating generalizations that unite us all, we need to grasp the changes that create, along with problems, a tremendous opportunity for peaceful yet significant social change. The following section therefore highlights six principal differences between the worlds of Theodore Roosevelt and William Jefferson Clinton. My aim is to root any answer to the question, What Shall We Do with Our America? in the complex world that is actually there.

ETHNIC OPTIONS[32]

His name is Juan Sanchez. Born in Puerto Rico, he is brown skinned, he sports a handsome mustache, he speaks with a heavy accent, and he started out American. After enlisting in the army, Juan fought in Nicaragua, returned to Puerto Rico, and then decided to study in the United States. He is, like many Puerto Ricans, quite proud of his U.S. citizenship but, in the fall of 1998, Juan is nevertheless reconsidering his self-identification as American.

One experience started this process. Working in a restaurant, one manager said, "Hey, taco bell, come here." Juan, a man of muscles, saw red. He confronted the manager, angrily asking if *he* had ever served in Desert Storm. Instead of punching the fellow, Juan used the experience as a benchmark for change.

He knew, of course, that like Luyen Phan Nguyen, the Vietnamese youngster beaten as a "chink" (see chapter 4), the restaurant manager confused one ethnicity with another and then ridiculed Chicanos as he simultaneously disregarded Puerto Ricans.

Juan agreed that the guy was a prejudiced, ignorant, jerk. But the "taco bell" remark still hurt so much that it moved him to question his commitment to America first, Puerto Rico second. Juan now feared that despite his continued willingness to die for his country, most Americans perceived him, like the whiskered, heavily accented Chihuahua in the Taco Bell commercials, as a cartoon character.

Juan's experience underlines that ethnicity is a *process* rather than a once-and-for-all identification.[33] Ethnic questions and choices are the order of the day in contemporary America, yet Juan and other newcomers are nevertheless constrained by a variety of obvious markers, such as name, accent, and skin color. Juan begins the process of ethnic identification centered in a heritage that is both *tangible* and *ever present*. His wife, his relatives, his friends, his neighborhood: They are all Puerto Rican and, in everything from food to language to customs, all the "Ricans" practice and celebrate an ethnicity that is *lived* as well as *remembered*.

The first difference between 1916 and today is that an arguably substantial majority of the American people no longer experience their immigrant roots as a lived or vividly remembered aspect of everyday life. Percentages vary with the author and the study, but since Congress shut the door in 1924, large numbers of "old blood immigrants" neither encounter nor recall with detail their ethnic past. Even Senator Edward Kennedy's efforts to help restore the balance with "diversity immigrants" (see chapter 1) cannot erase a reality that, in sharp contrast to 1916, contains a majority of people who identify with their ethnic origins only "if they *want* to."[34]

For Juan ethnicity is, by definition, a crucial component of his summary self-image. For many other Americans, ethnicity is important only if they decide to try to recall roots that lie six feet deep, buried with great and great-great grandparents. Thus, any efforts at a national consensus must be rooted in a definition of American that allows wide room for those who are unalterably ethnic, for those who *choose* to be ethnic, and for those who could care less.

A second difference between 1916 and today is the multiethnic heritage of the American majority. Teddy Roosevelt worried about an American population with roughly 10 percent of its people of German birth or ancestry. Heritage-wise, these folks were "one hundred percent Germans"; would they fight for the United States or for the "Fatherland" that was still a lived and remembered part of their everyday existence?

As a second-generation immigrant, my own roots are 100 percent Spanish, yet that makes me an exception to the contemporary ethnic rule. In one 1990 study of New York's Capital Region, fully two-thirds of the "native born whites claim an ethnically mixed ancestry."[35] Mary Waters' work in Silicon Valley also discovered third-, fourth-, and fifth-generation Americans who are as ethnically diverse as the most fervent of today's campus activists.

This could be a wonderful opportunity. Millions of Americans are born multicultural, and they are choosing the extent to which ethnicity is a salient part of summary self-image. Americans are making culture as I write and you read, but instead of using the majority's mingled ancestry to create a sense of empathy with the advocates of multiculturalism, many fourth- and fifth-generation Americans are making choices that once again define us by what divides us.

The inherited privilege to select an ethnicity is the third characteristic that separates one century from another. Millions of multiethnic Americans make changeable choices based on the receipt of often confusing or contradictory information.

Theoretically front and center is the truth about any person's heritage;

then comes your accurate or inaccurate perception of that truth; also important is the self-identification you choose to make; and a final factor is the reaction of others to that choice.[36] As one young Californian put it, "I remember when we got to do ethnic things in class, and they would always say raise your hand, how many kids are Irish, how many Italian, and the teacher never asked about Slovenian. I was always glumped in other, and they never asked."[37]

In the United States skin color is the variable that arguably imposes the greatest constraints on the choices made by any person. Talk to a census interviewer, say you are German and Irish but self-identify as Irish, and no one accuses you of trying to "pass" as non-German. But, say you are German and African American and, as always, race trumps ethnicity. The interviewer will not allow the African American to "pass" as German.[38]

Of course, a person could still self-identify as German and in the process emphasize the dialectical relationship between the truth about ethnic heritage, your perception of it, your point-in-time self-identification, and the reaction of others.

In the ethnically poor communities that, like so many dots on a map, pop up in the United States, school often replaces family and neighborhood as a first source of contact with ethnic roots. Teachers ask students to draw a family tree, the kids go home, ask mom and dad what's up, and the family then discovers roots that until then had remained buried, neglected, or forgotten. As one person put it, "My family had not done a lot. I mean they knew who their ancestors were basically, but they never sat down and really figured it out, so we did it then. We still have that [i.e., the sixth-grade family tree]."[39]

Other catalysts include a relative who lives in the home, one who comes to visit, or one who sends information the individual might not want. A Jamaican woman living in Hartford thinks that she may have European roots in both England and Scotland. She could care less, but her aged aunt researched and completed a family tree. "Aunty" is willing it to the family and, despite her reluctance, "Cynthia" (this is a pseudonym) will now discover the truth about her ethnic heritage.

In deciding whether to affirm one or all of their ancestries—for example, a number of the people I interviewed identified as "mutts"—individuals rely on a fascinating mix of variables, including proximity, family practice, and personal preferences influenced by community preferences. One person interviewed has "fifty-fifty" Italian and Irish roots. But as Italian was the only influence that dominated the home, she self-identifies as Italian and simply disregards her Irish mother and her mother's family. Meanwhile, another person lived with a mother born in France and with a host of recognizable relatives who still lived there. But, despite "murky knowledge" of Irish roots, the person chose Irish and disregarded French. "I lived in the mission district and that was Irish. . . . The nuns at school were Irish. In 3rd grade the little nun would really give it to you if you didn't have any green on . . . the green, even the dogs wear green. I am Irish."[40]

Once made, choices by the multiethnic can be remade. Fluidity is so normal that census interviewers are told to check one self-identification on a first visit, and, talking to the same person, the interviewer is told to catalog a different ethnic identity the second time around. Waters argues "that some proportion of whites whose ancestors came more than two generations ago change their mind about ethnic label about as readily as they change their minds about presidential candidates or social issues."[41]

This degree of open-mindedness is a sure sign that significant social change is possible. Third-, fourth-, and fifth-generation Americans are, instead of being locked into an ethnic identification, busily using their inherited privilege to reinvent themselves.

Like the combination that unlocks a safe, this could be the peaceful opening to a different tomorrow. But, rather than trying to see self and society as if they were strangers, the available evidence argues that old immigrant Americans root their new conclusions about ethnicity in a set of *pre-selected* reference groups. The result is that people draw their shifting conclusions about heritage on the basis of beliefs and values that ever so safely guide them through waters well within the territorial limits of U.S. culture.

Sociologists define a reference group as any collectivity used for the purposes of self-evaluation and attitude formation.[42] The essential idea is that I refer back to the group for a judgment about self, and I also refer back to the group for the "proper" disposition toward particular issues and events. Thus, a Chicano judging an issue like immigration from Mexico uses the INS as a negative reference group because this federal agency says that Mexican labor migrants are illegal rather than undocumented U.S. workers.

White and European are two very positive reference groups for many old immigrant Americans. Indeed, the marriage of one to the other is so solid that even the best analysts rarely discuss ethnicity without also mentioning skin colors. Richard Alba writes about "ethnic identity, the transformation of white America"; Mary Waters begins a chapter with this question: "What does claiming an ethnic label mean for a white, middle-class American?"[43] In 1996, Roger Waldinger and Michael Lichter compared and contrasted Los Angeles "white ethnics" with the city's "non-European origin population."[44]

Why use the panethnic identity "non-European" for Asians and Chicanos yet identify Germans, Irish, and Italians by the racial label "white"? American English is still so subservient to the black/white dichotomy that even superb social scientists follow their subjects by *reaffirming the concept of race as they simultaneously confuse it with ethnicity.* Thus, we either change the language and the assumptions on which social identities are based or, still on the merry-go-round, we will continue to chronicle choices that react to expressions of ethnicity by rooting themselves in the battleaxe concept of race.

As early as the 1980 census analysts discovered "unhyphenated whites." Roughly 10 percent of the American people, these ethnically poor respondents failed to remember any ancestral heritage; if prodded, they might call themselves American, but without necessarily seeing it as an ethnic label. Overall, unhyphenated whites appeared to be politically conservative, but beyond that weak generalization, the significance of using white as a primary, positive reference group remained unclear.[45]

By the late 1990s many whites had openly established a sharp social focus. One study of college students argued that "after generations of assimilation, only whiteness was left as an identity with any real social or political import." Yet, instead of choosing elements of the American heritage like the Declaration of Independence or the Emancipation Proclamation, whites fabricated an identity rooted in "resentment, anger and frustration." Arguing that, as if Davey Crockett at the Alamo, whites lived under siege by Chicanos, African Americans, and Asians, white students wanted to believe that America was colorblind as they simultaneously defined themselves in terms of color. Some blamed minority groups for the polarization but, whatever the ultimate explanation, many European Americans used their inherited right to choose an ethnicity by embracing a whiteness that focused on issues like reverse discrimination and proud support for an undefined set of Western European beliefs and values.[46]

While some Americans exercised their inherited privilege to choose by selecting white, others picked one ethnicity among the three or four they inherited and then used (for example) Irish or Italian to loosely identify with proudly *shared* European roots. Richard Alba calls this the ethnic transformation of America. His point is that the millions of European Americans who do choose an ethnic identity literally redefine the national experience by making immigrant roots as important as the overthrow of King George. Valley Forge and Ellis Island become equal partners in defining a supposedly "prototypical American experience against which non-European minority groups, some of long-standing on the American continent and others of recent vintage, are *pressured to measure themselves*" (emphasis added).[47]

By focusing on Europe's "old blood" immigrants as a positive reference group, German or English Americans transform the historical significance of ethnicity by locating themselves and their families "against the panorama of American history." In 1915 Teddy Roosevelt demanded 100 percent Americanism; scrap your past, embrace the flag, and learn the English language or leave on the next boat.

In 1999 a European American can proudly and easily choose to be Polish or Portuguese because these labels allegedly imply an identification with the best brand of Americanism. For Alba's subjects, that brand now inextricably includes the old blood immigrants who, along with founding fathers like

George Washington and James Madison, turned thirteen colonies into fifty states, all heavily indebted to shared roots in the same place—Europe.[48]

One obvious problem with this redefinition of the national significance of European ethnicity is that, like Senator Sam Ervin during the 1965 immigration debates (see chapter 1), it completely disregards the central contribution of many millions of African Americans. In addition, the Chinese who worked to build the railroads or the Chicanos who stooped and squatted to create an agricultural empire in the Southwest are assigned, despite even older roots in the United States, an invisible or secondary place against the panorama of U.S. history.

This alerts us to the fourth difference between the beginning and the end of the twentieth century. In 1918 the Americanization movement preached assimilation to newcomers who challenged, not the worthiness of U.S. society, but the demand that German or Italian immigrants relinquish commitments to their culture of origin. In 1999 Eurocentrism is not only the enemy, it is blamed for a form of second-class citizenship that is supposedly every bit as odious as the conflict between capital and labor, bourgeoisie and proletariat.

Marx condemned capitalism because it doomed people to everlasting poverty; today's multiculturalists flay U.S. culture because its Eurocentric focus produces a different type of perpetual poverty: People learn to deprecate or even hate themselves and their ancestral roots.[49]

Too often dismissed as only "identity politics," the essential argument of the multicultural movement is actually grounded, quite firmly, in political idealism and sociological truth. If our God-given equality entitles every American to an "identical basket" of rights and immunities, that same equality should ensure that the "unique identity" of all people receives recognition and respect. But, when one culture contemptuously dominates another, or when one culture demands that another assimilate, the results include the loss of God-given equality and the receipt of a learned sense of inferiority.[50]

Critics might respond by saying, "poor baby," but the potentially profound consequences of a negative summary self-image reflect an accurate understanding of the human condition. Recall chapter 4. We can't think about ourselves until others first think of us. We are, at least as children, the prisoners of the first people who teach us about self, ethnicity, and its place on the ballfields of U.S. life.

Everyday language in contemporary Los Angeles maintains a crucial distinction "between Anglos and all others." "White ethnicity" is organized around the dominant group of Anglos[51] who, by cultural definition, teach Chicanos that they are racial "others," hired to illegally do the "dirty, demanding and dangerous" work shunned by the Anglos.

To the extent any Chicano embraces a second- or third-class summary image of self, the consequences can be as damning as a confrontation with a brick wall. I may, potentially, stop at the mental barrier created by the

"Anglos" because I accept that American life legitimately imposes obstacles to me and to those who share my ethnicity.

Enter the multicultural movement. In fostering or demanding "ethnic studies," the laudable aim is to respect the equal identity rights of all by forever eliminating illustrations that teach hate and fear. In an 1896 drawing in the French magazine *Le Rire*, an African native hovers over a woman who has fainted from fear. The caption reads, "Like a succubus, Africa weighs on the repose of Europe."[52] However, instead of the demon assuming its normal female form, this African devil is a male, about to rape the prostrate maiden called Europe. In the background are caricatures of African colonies, with each displaying the problems caused by those ungrateful, uncivilized Africans.

Meanwhile, an advocate of multiculturalism might note that the real rapists wore European uniforms, adorned by metals won on the battlefields that produced the European colonization of the African continent. Indeed, while the illustration dates from 1896, the consequences of Europe's political and cultural behavior rippled across Rwanda in the 1990s. It was, after all, the Belgians who institutionalized the segregation—with identification cards, no less!—of Hutus and Tutsis in the 1930s. Europe, in the person of Belgium, should share *some* responsibility for the horror in Rwanda, but multiculturalists would correctly note that contemporary media accounts of the genocide rarely point a finger at the North. Instead, it is the African beast that cannot be tamed.[53]

The examples suggest a real dilemma for all inhabitants of the United States. As millions of *multicultural* Americans choose an ethnic identity that celebrates European roots, others denounce the continent as the original source of all evil. The result is yet another dichotomy: a nation of victims and victimizers, the exploited and the exploiters.

However understandable, dividing the world into good and evil perverts "two valuable impulses in contemporary America: The impulse to protect historically disadvantaged populations from the effects of past and continuing discrimination, and the impulse to affirm the variety of cultures that now flourish within the United States."[54]

We must, at all costs, make a sharp and continual distinction between cultural and political identities. Labels like African American refer to groups with outstanding economic, educational, *and* cultural grievances against mainstream America. Means of resolving these grievances could include anything from affirmative action to a form of support as vigorous as that offered to Cuban refugees. But, ground the nation's incredible cultural diversity in an analysis of the exploitation and victimization of particular ethnic groups and you create an America in which people will understandably refuse to come to the banquet, much less sample its sumptuous cultural dishes.

Our aim must be to create a philosophical framework that endorses cultural differences as it also endorses those who choose to reject or affiliate only marginally with their culture of origin. To ground diversity in political labels is to risk demonizing the majority; that is not only an error, it creates a climate in which too few people ever display the empathy that is an essential first step for cultural harmony and social change.

This brings us to the fifth difference between America in 1916 and America in 1999 and beyond. A conspicuous addition to contemporary ethnic discourse is the adoption of panethnic labels. Produced by, among other factors, a sense of ethnic solidarity stemming from the civil rights movement and a reaction to the immigration of more than 20 million newcomers, close to ten panethnic labels are now in everyday use. Think, for example, of Hispanic and Latino or Asian, European, African, Native and Latin American.

Like any cultural generalization, these new words exist as a means to make sense of the social world. People see something they can't explain and create new words supposedly to describe the new realities. In 1978, the federal Office of Management and Budget issued "Statistical Directive 15." While only a demographer's heart beat faster, this directive nevertheless created "five basic racial and ethnic categories for Federal statistics."[55]

The intent was admirable; produce numbers that allowed the federal government to correctly allocate resources to, among others, disadvantaged groups. But the new labels—Asian or Pacific Islander, Hispanic, black, white, American Indian or Alaska Native—once again *mercilessly* confused racial and ethnic categories, and one new label produced another. Refusing to identify with Spain, many Mexican Americans instantly rejected the label Hispanic. As "Latino" supposedly became the new panethnic label of choice, at meetings of the Connecticut Hispanic Chamber of Commerce members called themselves Latino to one another and Hispanic to the world![56]

The new generalizations underline the multiple layers of contemporary ethnicity and the "continual creation and recreation of culture."[57] For example, with a name like Fernandez, I am often called Hispanic, Latin American, or Latino but once I announce total ancestry from Spain, I become a European American who may or may not be eligible for simultaneous Latino status.

It's confusing to everyone. Let's try to make some sense of the panethnic labels. By definition they are, even for cultural generalizations, woefully incomplete. Consider the term Asian American. This allegedly includes Chinese, Japanese, Vietnamese, Korean, Cambodian, Filipino, Indian, Pakistani, Bangladeshi, Hmong, Amerasians, and Laotians—to name only groups with significant U.S. populations.

Neglected in the magical homogenization process are a variety of historical animosities between ethnic groups (e.g., between Japanese and Chinese, Pakistani and Indian) and, in a city like Los Angeles, enormous variation in relation to factors like education and place of birth. In 1970, 57 percent of Asians in Los Angeles said they were born in the United States. The figure for 1996 is 31 percent and dropping.[58] How much do well-educated Koreans and Japanese born and raised in California have in common with Ameraisans born in Vietnam and educated neither in Saigon nor in Los Angeles?

Despite their incompleteness the panethnic labels do serve a useful purpose for some of the groups that use them. For example, prior to World War II, Japanese immigrants responded to the terrible prejudice against Chinese by "insisting that their Japanese workers wear American work clothes and even eat American food."[59] But, once many of the Asian immigrants assimilated—that is, learned English—the unanticipated consequences of learning the language included the new ability to communicate effectively across the many different ethnic groups. American English therefore built the bridge that allowed Japanese, Chinese, and Koreans to recognize similar interests all pointing to the need for a united expression of political clout.[60]

To be sure, the label "Asian American" reflects temporary alliances that are instruments for change, not necessarily expressions of any shared culture. But, when too many Asians succeeded in the nation's universities, the drive to set quotas against Asians produced a powerful nationwide movement grounded in Asian solidarity. As Dana Takagi stressed, all the different ethnic groups united to counter the effort to transform the "model minority" into a group of "academic nerds" or, even worse, a homogeneous pile of "narrow-minded, overly technical science majors."[61] From an Asian-American perspective, the United States either embraced its own call for merit as the basis for university admissions or it proved itself as hypocritical as the California regents who "bought" admissions for their friends and family members.[62]

Chinese and Japanese often use panethnic labels as a way to resist or promote social change. By contrast, many European Americans use the labels to conveniently and instantly squeeze millions of people into presumably similar "racial" and language groupings. As to "Anglo" eyes, Asians "all look the same," they are neatly lumped together. Indeed, even the widest cultural differences are sometimes overlooked in the service of supporting prejudices that can still be seen whenever television stations play an old "Charlie Chan" movie.

Hispanics, for example, allegedly share both a language and geographical proximity, but Brazilians speak Portuguese, most people in Guyana communicate in English, and those in the dependency of Guiana still speak French. Millions of Indians in Mexico and Guatemala also speak their own native languages. However useful for the purposes of federal statistics, the word *Hispanic* captures a reality that is arguably as incomplete as any of the panethnic labels.

One solution for old immigrant Americans is to stop using the all-inclusive "racial," geographical, and language generalizations. Focus only on the specific ethnic groups, make that specific focus a nationwide goal, and recognize that since U.S. culture *now* lumps the ethnic groups together, activists will continue to create new terms until and unless there is a transformation of the majority culture.

Latino, for instance, is arguably "a label looking for a group."[63] In group meetings, Ecuadorians and Mexicans, Puerto Ricans and Peruvians often realize that they actually share very little, yet despite its weaknesses, the term Latino creates a real sense of solidarity because it announces a refusal to be labeled by the majority culture. People using the term *Latino* believe that they share a status as cultural outsiders. All other things being equal, they will continue to organize around this admittedly confusing term because, as with Asian Americans, it may produce the clout needed to win battles over issues that range from language to dual citizenship, from affirmative action to the appropriate national holiday.

One panethnic label to applaud is European American. Clearly it contains all the language and geographical incompleteness of Hispanic or Asian American. But, *within the context of U.S. history*, the term *European American* nevertheless focuses on ethnicity instead of race. It moves us away from the black and white dichotomy and toward a world in which skin color is an unimportant part of any person's humanity.

That would be a monumental achievement. Use European American based on a new consensus about its meaning. Today it apparently connotes an ethnic transformation that applauds European roots as it simultaneously asks Asians or Hispanics to measure their immigrant passage against the European ideal. But, in a humane manifestation of people's ability to make and remake culture, European American could represent one catchall category that, as it proudly takes credit for achievements like the Magna Carta, also accepts responsibility for the historical and contemporary consequences of five hundred years of European colonialism.

The alternative is one continent symbolically at war with the other, each championing its achievements, each citing the others' cruelties (for example, Sendero Luminoso and the Fujimori dictatorship in Peru), none reaching for the brass ring that could begin to unite us all—the ethnic-label American.

"Too much" assimilation is the sixth and final difference between the beginning and the end of the twentieth century. As in 1900 or 1910 many of today's newcomers concentrate in the central cities. Immigrants still flock to the metropolis, but instead of offering opportunities to all nonskilled residents, cities like Chicago, Hartford, and Newark often ask newcomers to absorb beliefs and values that channel them not into the mainstream, but into the exhausted tributaries of urban America. In Hartford, it's called the North End; in Chicago, it's the South Side.[64]

When my father arrived in 1916 he spoke Spanish and had neither an education nor marketable skills. However, he quickly found work in a factory and stayed there for almost fifty years. Today the factory has moved abroad and a machine efficiently performs my father's job. People need not apply.

As Americans we like to think in terms of ladders. You get on the bottom rung and through hard work and perseverance, you—or at least your children—climb the ladder that leads to success. In reality the United States has long had two ladders. You don't generally get on the one that leads to "real money" unless you first have one or two university degrees. But, as with my father, even that lower-class ladder provided a "living wage" and a good degree of social security.

In 1999 many large and small American cities look as inviting as Western ghost towns. Throughout the Northeast display windows that once contained an assortment of goods now contain schoolroom drawings or signs toasting long-dead businesses. Meanwhile empty factories point to the jobs that disappeared or, even more contemptuously, to the "factory show rooms" that sell goods produced abroad for folks who work in the city but live in the suburbs. In Los Angeles the high wage auto, steel, rubber, and aircraft jobs once held by African Americans have, like the smoke over Watts, vanished. In his recent study of Chicago, William Julius Wilson asks a terrible question: What happens when work disappears?[65]

One obvious answer is that people lose hope. Another is that men and women, old and young, create a "counterculture" whose beliefs and values further circumscribe their already limited possibilities. In the suburbs people with money worry about crime or random attacks by "those people." Meanwhile those people rarely leave their own neighborhoods, much less the city. As one seventeen-year-old adolescent told Wilson, "The kids around here, all they see, OK, they see these drug addicts, and then what else do they see? Oh, they see thugs, you know, they see gangbangers . . . who is their role model? They have none but the thugs."[66]

That's life for those who inherit cities without work. But what happens when recent immigrants also inhabit these neighborhoods? One alternative is to accept the lowest-paying opportunities that exist (e.g., Chinese in New York's new garment sweatshops) and, over time, create ethnic niches that offer few opportunities to the African Americans stranded in urban ghettos.

Another alternative, especially for Haitians in cities like Miami, is to assimilate to the role models offered by gangbangers. Encountering both hostility and color prejudice from the majority culture, Haitians "enter into ready contact" with the ghetto's subculture. Indeed, "its influence is all the more powerful because it comes from people of the same national origin, 'people like us' who can effectively define the proper stance and attitudes of the newcomers."[67]

Similar patterns exist among some West Indians in New York and among Puerto Ricans in Chicago. The problem is that the melting-pot metaphor suggests *one* America, willing if not happy to embrace newcomers. In truth, the United States contains a variety of subcultures and, especially in major cities, alternatives that detour newcomers into the most underdeveloped areas in contemporary America.[68]

Cities are only part of the role model problem. In rural as well as urban

America, newcomers create subcultures that deliberately distance them and their successors from "mainstream" American life. Thus, Chicanos in a small coastal community of central California ridiculed as "wannabes" those who succeeded in school. The ideal for these Mexican outsiders included no participation in school, no hard classes, and no education if you can help it.[69]

One antidote to the counterculture is a strong ethnic community. In New Orleans the Vietnamese forged strong institutions revolving around the Catholic Church. The children live under "a Vietnamese microscope" of such power that "if a child flunks out or drops out of school, or if a boy falls into a gang or a girl becomes pregnant" they rain down shame on the family and the community. Conversely, like the suburban bumperstickers boasting that my child is a "student of the month," in New Orleans a Vietnamese child who makes good grades or wins an award is honored by the ethnic community. Even in America, it remains the reference group that provides the child's major sense of personal and social esteem.[70]

The irony is that these children succeed by *not* assimilating. Ethnicity linked to a strong family and a supportive community provides the shield that protects these kids from the subcultures that, however understandably, nevertheless act as self-perpetuating schools, graduating students slated for economically dead-end lives.

Any answer to the question, "What Shall We Do with Our America?" must recognize that at the end of the twentieth century the United States faces a terrible Catch 22. Ethnicity may be one of America's best and cheapest weapons to fight both economic globalization and the forgotten war on poverty. Meanwhile, to the extent newcomers use ethnicity to create employment niches that exclude outsiders, they condemn the poorest African Americans to fewer and fewer opportunities. The conventional wisdom suggests a huge proliferation of low-skilled jobs in the central cities; the reality is slight growth and, to the extent that ethnic monopolies occur, the exclusion of African Americans from the low-skilled jobs that, without so many newcomers, could be theirs.[71]

Ethnicity may help the poorest of Americans to come to the one-race cultural banquet. But, are all ethnic heritages equal? Or is it valid to argue that some are superior to others? For example, if life in the inner cities is as miserable as analysts suggest, how explain the apparent success of Koreans in Los Angeles and New York? They own both stores and a strong work ethnic. Why can't the Puerto Ricans, Haitians, and Hmong act like the Koreans and stop moaning about insurmountable economic and subcultural barriers?

It's not that simple. Especially because, as Thomas Sowell notes in *Migrations and Cultures*, "The immigrant population from a given country living in another country is often highly *atypical* of the population from which they came" (emphasis added).[72]

Immigrants are different. Lump them together, and, like the generalization *Hispanic*, you miss far more than you perceive.

MAKING IT IN AMERICA[73]

People adapt to everything, to the best and the worst, the cruelest and the bizarre. "To one thing only do people not adapt themselves": To not being sure what they believe about the nature of things.[74]

Because we like simple solutions to complex problems, we fix on one variable—say, the supposed culture of a particular ethnic group—and define success or failure in cultural terms. In *Money* Andrew Hacker offers a long list comparing "median household income" to "region of ancestry." The presumption is that the latter "causes" the former. Yet, as a mischievous way of introducing uncertainty, Hacker writes, "that we rarely hear media pundits pondering aloud why the Irish lag so far behind the Greeks in median income ($37,212 to $31,845) and why all four Scandinavian nationalities fall in the bottom half of the European roster."[75]

Are Swedes lazy? Are Greeks, almost banned in the 1924 National Origins legislation, trying to make up for lost time? Are the Irish tired? Or, is the villain affirmative action? Eliminate the privileges offered to African Americans and the Irish would make as much as the Greeks. But, if that's so, why do the Greeks make so much more than the Irish?

In the service of simplification, people key on ancestry. Indeed, instead of using Korean or Mexican culture to mark the *beginning* of an inquiry, "culture is taken at face value and treated as self explaining."[76] The unfortunate result is the charts that, while accurately listing family income, also suggest the superiority of some cultures and the inferiority of others.

But, just because immigrants are generally atypical of their country of origin, any attempt to impute superiority or inferiority to culture is defeated by the facts. For example, while Korea is a Buddhist nation, a large, albeit unspecified number of Korean immigrants are Christian. In addition, many of the first wave came from North Korea (they fled South during the war) and happily migrated when the South Korean government encouraged and assisted migration in the early 1960s. As North Koreans, even the well-educated experienced insuperable roadblocks to mobility in their own country; the United States did indeed look like the land of opportunity.[77]

Finally, mobility in South Korea is often closely linked to region of origin. Come from Kyongsang and your chances of educational, political, or business success are enhanced. Come from the "enemy" region of Cholla—stereotypes portray the people as treacherous—and you often find that the doors leading to success remain closed. While no studies (as of late 1998) precisely identify the number of Korean immigrants coming from one region or the other, the undeniably diverse origins of the migration pose a real conundrum for those imputing superiority to Korean culture.

Which culture are we talking about? The Christians coming from North Korea? The treacherous, well-educated Buddhists from Cholla? The well-connected, well-educated Christians from industrial cities like Seoul?[78]

Begin with culture, and legitimately note that the strong work ethic shared by Koreans of many persuasions undoubtedly plays a significant role in successes achieved. But, as U.S. farmers told Congress one generation after another, a key attribute of the Mexican is his or her ability to work hard under the hottest California sun. If we add family values, only a blind person would deny the love and loyalties of a Mexican who, after a week's work in the sun, still manages a trip to Western Union, money for the family firmly in hand.

Thomas Sowell talks about "historic head starts."[79] Whether in the country of origin and/or the destination of a migration, specific realities often mock the American ideal of equality of opportunity. At least three variables allow some folks to start one, two, or even three laps ahead of the others. To make better sense of the importance of a particular culture, we need to consider the advantages or disadvantages faced by particular migrants.

First, what is the *reception policy of the U.S. government?*[80] Does Washington welcome two-thirds of the faculty of the University of Havana, disregard federal refugee law, and immediately establish—at the presidential level—a form of almost unprecedented monetary and spiritual support?

Or, at the other extreme, does Washington close its eyes to farmers busily recruiting poorly educated Chicanos and then, especially under President Clinton, enforce federal law with more force than ever before?

A second variable is the *educational and occupational experiences of the U.S. immigrant community.* Is it, like the Amerasians, composed of youngsters with little education and no marketable skills? Or, like many of the Koreans, who own and manage stores in Harlem or Watts, do the people have a college education and business experience? In-Jin Yoon emphasizes that "about 30% of the Koreans aged 25 and older who were admitted between 1970 and 1980 had received four years of college education."[81] Christian or Buddhist, from the North or the South, these Koreans boasted a higher percentage of college graduates than natives of the United States.

A last, general variable is *labor market reception.* In *Caught in the Middle,* Pyong Gap Min explains that most Korean immigrants never intended to open stores in the United States. They migrated because of prejudices at home, and they settled in New York or Los Angeles fully expecting to obtain white-collar and professional positions in their fields of training. However, when poor English language skills and U.S. prejudices against Asians moved them into "low-level, blue collar occupations," they "reluctantly turned to small businesses as an alternative to these undesirable jobs."[82]

To their celebrated credit, well-educated Koreans took advantage of opportunities in America's central cities. They and their families work extraordinarily long hours for wages that can never compensate for the time spent earning a college degree. But, in assessing the early successes of so many Korean shop owners, remember too the link to Korea. Storeowners sold wigs, handbags, jewelry, and toys made in Korea, wholesaled by United States–based Korean suppliers; and, if the storeowner needed credit, he or she was often offered generous terms by suppliers, assisted by the mother country.[83]

Whether measured in economic or cultural terms, immigrant success or failure in the United States depends on a variety of variables. Immigrant culture certainly counts, but ever to forget the number of factors involved is to grossly oversimplify reality and, in the process, make it much harder for Americans to understand not only the head starts of Koreans and Indians, but the handicaps of Amerasians or El Salvadorans.

ROOM TO MANEUVER

Cognitive dissonance theory argues that people hate contradiction. Create conflict about important beliefs or core self-images, and people will resolve the dissonance with the truth, with lies, or with a creative combination of fact and fiction. The unwavering goal is social psychological security, a personal sense of sure footing in a slippery world.[84]

New immigrants are especially prone to conflicts and contradictions. In one instance a Colombian woman tried to answer the Census questionnaire but she failed to grasp the government's separation of race and ethnicity. "Whoever did this made a lot of mistakes. Whoever did the census form wasn't educated enough about race." For example, how could a dark-skinned person who spoke Spanish check the race category? It made no sense to a Latin American person. Confronted with a contradiction between what she and the Census Bureau thought, Soledad resolved the dissonance by referring back to Columbia for a negative assessment of U.S. thinking.[85]

Soledad had a choice. It included exclusionary costs never paid by third- and fourth-generation European Americans, but Soledad nevertheless exercised her "ethnic options." She made a choice every bit as significant as the one made by the imprecise number of Latin Americans who run from the label Hispanic. Many choose Latino while others, in a pointed rebuke to dissonance theory, stoically live with no notion of their place in U.S. society. "Who am I?" is an "unresolved given"; hopefully some sense of place will ultimately arise, but in the meantime, many Latin American immigrants resign themselves to confusion, based on America's ignorance about race.[86]

The good news is that Latinos and other immigrants are often just as confused as many of the rest of us. They too are searching, and they too sometimes reach the most extraordinary conclusions. For example, Kathy Marquez's "ethnic identification is remarkably inconsistent." In her first interview, she answered "American"; in her second (a year later) she identified as Spanish. However, if she were talking to other Mexican Americans she would like to be called "an American of Mexican descent"; to the Anglos in Los Angeles she is a "Chicana"; and when she travels in Mexico, she asks to be identified as a Spaniard.[87]

Others with Mexican roots may not display Kathy's dizzying sense of ethnic self, but they do show significant variations in their expressed identifications. Widely shared labels include Mexican, Mexican American, Chicano, and Hispano.[88] Each affirms the reality of selected rather than ascribed ethnicity, and each also suggests an uncertainty that offers wide room to maneuver into a humane and optimistic consensus about a new-millenium meaning of race and ethnicity.

If Latinos or 1.5 immigrants like Shashi Singh (as in preface) lock themselves into a permanent sense of self, they foreclose our possibilities as well as their own. Thankfully, as new immigrants are also struggling to make sense of the United States, our opportunity to remake culture is both real and tangible. Grab the gold ring and widespread uncertainty offers us a chance to reshape culture in any manner we see fit.

Besides uncertainty, another cause for optimism is the meaning now commonly attached to the word *American*. Instead of focusing on traits like our informality or our love affair with punctuality, citizens who embrace the label American understand the word in relation to loyalty, patriotism, and political ideals. American means a love of the Constitution and a commitment to the public freedoms it both endorses and guarantees.[89]

This meaning of *American* is a wonderful first step toward a consensus that adds to the political base, a superstructure focusing on race, ethnicity, and social class. For example, we could argue that:

An American is someone with a spiritual goal welded to the commitment of a pioneer.

The commitment signals a willingness to eliminate what now—for no good reason—profoundly divides us.

The goal is a nationwide sense of community, founded in a twenty-first-century reaffirmation of the Declaration of Independence.

All people are born equal, none deserves to inherit either poverty or a culture poisonously divided into whites, blacks, and forty million others.

We can maneuver ourselves into this or other definitions of what it means to be an American. But before any attempt at specificity (see chapter 9), let's first deal with an issue raised by Randolph Bourne in 1916. Discussing the dangers posed by immigration, Bourne wrote, "It is not the Jew who sticks proudly to the faith of his father . . . who is dangerous to America, but the Jew who has lost the Jewish fire and become a mere elementary grasping animal."[90]

Bourne feared those who stood somewhere between the past and future. Whether Polish, Jewish, Mexican, or Korean, those who lost their original cultural moorings "become the flotsam and jetsam of American life, the downward undertow of our civilization with its leering cheapness and falseness of taste . . . this is the cultural wreckage of our time."[91]

On this issue Bourne was wrong. Accept his view and you cavalierly dismiss an experience that unalterably characterizes not only immigrants, but many of the rest of us as well. For example, especially for first- and second-generation immigrants the realities of American life include the feeling "that I am not wholly of either place. And that's exactly the diasporic experience, far enough away to experience the sense of exile and loss, close enough to understand the enigma of an always postponed arrival."[92]

This is both inevitable and accurate. With one culture at home and another on the street, how can a recent immigrant possibly arrive—once and for all—anywhere? But, instead of dismissing the person who is between two (or more) cultures, let's recognize that the immigrant's location is, first, normal, second, an opportunity, and, third, a welcome meeting place for all Americans. Indeed, if we do seriously challenge the beliefs and assumptions that now divide us, the national rule will be 270 million people between the culture that was and the culture that will be.

This is an American Dream we should all embrace, because it offers an antidote to the identities that poisonously divide us. Further, as the other side of Randolph Bourne reminded his contemporaries, "In the light of our changing ideal of Americanism, we must perpetuate the paradox that our American culture lies in the future. It will be what we all together make out of this *incomparable opportunity* of attacking the future with a new key" (emphasis added).[93] One horrible response to Bourne's eloquence was the National Origins legislation of 1924.

We need not repeat history. We can instead vow to learn from it.

NOTES

1. Mukul Pandya, "Counting All Their Chips," *Little India*, August 1998, p. 2, ⟨www.littleindia.com⟩.

2. Shashi Tharoor, *India: From Midnight to the Millennium* (New York: Harper, 1997), p. 160.

3. Lavinia Melwani, "What's in a Name?" *Little India*, June 1998, p. 8, ⟨www.littleindia.com⟩.

4. Amartya Sen, "Culture and Identity," *Little India*, August 1998, p. 4, ⟨www.littleindia.com⟩.

5. Ibid., pp. 1–2.

6. For example, Shaski Khorana, "NRI Mid-Life Crisis," *Little India*, April 1996, pp. 1–2, ⟨www.littleindia.com⟩.

7. Sen, "Culture and Identity," p. 5 G.

8. Shekhar Deshpande, "Independence from Independence Day," *Little India*, September 1998, p. 1, ⟨www.littleindia.com⟩.

9. Vineeta Vijayaraghavan, "Neither Black Nor White," *Little India*, November 1995, p. 1, ⟨www.littleindia.com⟩.

10. Ibid.

11. *India in New*, July 24, 1998, p. 36.

12. Khorana, "NRI Mid-Life Crisis," p. 1.

13. Mary Waters, *Ethnic Options* (Berkeley: University of California Press, 1990); Richard Alba, *Ethnic Identity* (New Haven: Yale University Press, 1990); Herbert Gans, "Symbolic Ethnicity: The Future of Ethnic Groups and Cultures in America," *Ethnic and Racial Studies* 2 (January 1979): 1–20.

14. Alexis de Tocqueville, *Democracy in America*, vol. 1 (New York: Vintage Books, 1945), p. 115.

15. Ibid., vol. 1, pp. 104–105.

16. Ibid., p. 106.

17. For example, Irwin Wylle, *The Self-Made Man in America* (New York: Macmillan, 1954).

18. De Tocqueville, *Democracy in America*, p. 104.

19. Ray H. Abrams, *Preachers Present Arms* (New York: Round Table Press, 1933).

20. Ibid., p. 116.

21. Theodore Roosevelt, "Americanization Day," *Immigrants in America Review* 1, no. 3 (September 1915): 33–39, esp. pp. 36–37.

22. On the dinner, see *The Immigrants in America Review* 1, no. 4 (January 1916): 38–39; for the specific suggestions, see Miss Frances Kellor, Executive Officer, Americanization Society, "Americanization As a Means of Preparedness," *Proceedings of the Congress for National Security*, under the auspices of the National Security League, Washington, DC, January 20–22, 1916, pp. 202–208.

23. Esther Everett Lape, "The English First Movement in Detroit," *Immigrants in America Review* 1, no. 3 (September 1915): 46–50, esp. p. 46.

24. Joseph Mayper, "Americanizing Immigrant Homes," *Immigrants in America Review* 2, no. 2 (July 1916): 54–60, esp. p. 60.

25. Randolph Bourne, "Transnational America," in *War and the Intellectuals*, edited by Carl Resek (New York: Harper, 1964), pp. 107–123, esp. pp. 108–109.

26. See "Democracy and the Melting Pot," in Horace Kallen, *Culture and Democracy in the United States* (New York: Arno Press and The New York Times, 1970), pp. 124–125.

27. As a graduate student I was privileged to have Horace Kallen as a teacher at the New School For Social Research.

28. Kallen, *Culture and Democracy*, p. 121.

29. Ibid., p. 125.

30. Ibid.

31. David Hollinger, *Postethnic America* (New York: Basic Books, 1995), p. 162.

32. Mary Waters, *Ethnic Options*; this section owes a great debt to Waters's insights and observations.

33. See Mary Waters, *The Process and Content of Ethnic Identification: A Study of White Ethnics in Suburbia* (Ph.D. dissertation, University of California at Berkeley, 1986), p. 38; also William Yancey, Eugene Ericksen, and Richard Juliani, "Emergent Ethnicity: A Review and Reformulation," *American Sociological Review* 41, no. 3 (June 1976): 391–403.

34. Waters, *Ethnic Options*, p. 7.

35. Alba, *Ethnic Identity*, p. 44.

36. Stanley Lieberson, "Unhyphenated Whites in the United States," *Ethnic and Racial Studies* 8 (January 1985): 159–180.

37. See Waters, *Process and Content*, p. 77.

38. Ibid., p. 57.

39. Ibid., p. 76.

40. Personal interview; also ibid., p. 87.

41. Waters, *Ethnic Options*, p. 39.

42. See, for example, Robert Merton, *Social Theory and Social Structure* (New York: Free Press, 1957).

43. Waters, *Ethnic Options*, p. 147; the full title of Richard Alba's wonderful book is *Ethnic Identity: The Transformation of White America*.

44. Roger Waldinger and Michael Lichter, "Anglos: Beyond Ethnicity," in Roger Waldinger and Mehdi Bozorgmehr, eds., *Ethnic Los Angeles* (New York: Russell Sage, 1996), pp. 413–441, esp. p. 429.

45. Lieberson, "Unhyphenated Whites," esp. pp. 159, 173.

46. Charles A. Gallagher, "White Racial Formation: Into the Twenty-First Century," in Richard Delgado and Jean Stefanic, *Critical White Studies* (Philadelphia: Temple, 1997), esp. pp. 8–10.

47. Alba, *Ethnic Identity*, pp. 315–317.

48. Ibid., p. 319.

49. See, for example, Charles Taylor, *Multiculturalism* (Princeton: Princeton University Press, 1994).

50. Ibid., pp. 38–39.

51. Waldinger and Lichter, "Anglos," pp. 414–415.

52. Jan Nederveen Pieterse, *White on Black* (New Haven: Yale University Press, 1992).

53. Ibid., p. 122. See the example of "cannibal humor" from 1987.

54. Hollinger, *Postethnic America*, p. 49.

55. Review of Federal Measurements of Race and Ethnicity, Hearings Before the Subcommittee on Census, Statistics and Postal Personnel, House, 103rd Congress, first session (Washington, DC: GPO, 1993), pp. 42–43.

56. See, for example, Harold Augenbraum and Ilan Stavans, eds., *Growing Up Latino* (Boston: Houghton Mifflin, 1993); the comment on the Hispanic Chamber of Commerce is based on my own experiences with this group.

57. See Yen Le Espiritu, *Asian American Panethnicity* (Philadelphia: Temple University Press, 1992), p. 5.

58. Lucie Cheng and Philip Q. Yang, "Asians: The 'Model Minority' Deconstructed," in *Ethnic Los Angeles*, pp. 305–343, esp. p. 309.

59. Le Espiritu, *Panethnicity*, p. 21.

60. Ibid., p. 25.

61. Dana Y. Takagi, *The Retreat from Race* (New Brunswick, NJ: Rutgers University Press, 1992), p. 58.

62. Ellis Cose, *Color Blind* (New York: Harper Collins, 1997), p. 133.

63. Samuel Betances, *African Americans and Hispanics/Latinos: Eliminating Barriers to Coalition Building*, Ethnic Diversity Roundtable, Chicago Urban Policy Institute, April 15, 1994, p. 3.

64. For example, Stephen Steinberg, *The Ethnic Myth* (Boston: Beacon Press, 1989), esp. pp. 42–43.

65. For Los Angeles, see David M. Grant, Melvin Oliver, and Angela James, "African Americans: Social and Economic Bifurcation," in *Ethnic Los Angeles*, pp. 379–411, esp. 388–389; also William Julius Wilson, *When Work Disappears* (New York: Vintage, 1997).

66. Wilson, *When Work Disappears*, pp. 56–57.

67. Alejandro Portes and Min Zhou, "Should Immigrants Assimilate?" *Public Interest* 116 (Summer 1994): 21.

68. Alejandro Portes and Ruben G. Rumbaut, *Immigrant America* (Berkeley: University of California Press, 1996), p. 247.

69. Ibid., esp. pp. 245–247.

70. Ibid., pp. 243–244.

71. Roger Waldinger, *Still the Promised City: African Americans and New Immigrants in Post-Industrial America* (Cambridge: Harvard University Press, 1996), pp. 7, 17.

72. Thomas Sowell, *Migrations and Culture* (New York: Harper, 1996), p. 4.

73. Portes and Rimbaut, *Immigrant America*; this is the title of their chapter 3.

74. José Ortega y Gasset, *Man and Crisis* (New York: Norton, 1958), p. 108.

75. Andrew Hacker, *Money* (New York: Scribner's, 1997), pp. 158–159.

76. Stephen Steinberg, *Turning Back* (Boston: Beacon Press, 1995), p. 13.

77. In-Jin Yoon, *On My Own* (Chicago: University of Chicago Press, 1997), pp. 73–80.

78. Ibid., p. 76.

79. Thomas Sowell, *Preferential Policies* (New York: William Morrow, 1991), p. 71.

80. These variables are directly drawn from Portes and Rimbaut, *Immigrant America*, see especially pp. 57–92.

81. See In-Jin Joon, *On My Own*, p. 55.

82. Pyong Gap Min, *Caught in the Middle* (Berkeley: University of California Press, 1996), esp. pp. 49–50.

83. Ibid., p. 55.

84. For example, Leon Festinger, *A Theory of Cognitive Dissonance* (Stanford, CA: Stanford University Press, 1957).

85. Suzanne Oboler, *Ethnic Labels, Latino Lives* (Minneapolis: University of Minnesota Press, 1995), pp. 156–157.

86. Ibid., p. 127.

87. Susan Keefe and Amado Padilla, *Chicano Ethnicity* (Albuquerque: University of New Mexico Press, 1987), p. 109.

88. Ibid., especially chapter 8; see, too, Martha Bernal and George P. Knight, eds., *Ethnic Identities: Formation and Transmission among Hispanics and Other Minorities* (Albany: State University of New York Press, 1989).

89. For example, Waters, *Ethnic Options*, pp. 55–56.

90. Randolph S. Bourne, "Transnational America," in *War and the Intellectuals* (New York: Harper, 1964), pp. 113–114.

91. Ibid., p. 114.

92. See the interview with Stuart Hall in Onyekachi Wambu, *Empire Windrush* (London: Victor Gollancz, 1998), p. 87.

93. Bourne, "Transnational America," pp. 115–116.

7

Social Class and Social Conflict

RURAL AMERICA

Every conference needs a theme. That of the Housing Assistance Council (HAC) was perfect: A Place for Everybody. HAC is what those in the economic development business call an "intermediary." It first raises and then redistributes housing dollars otherwise unavailable to self-help groups representing African Americans in the Mississippi Delta, rural female heads of household in Oregon, or the 1.5 million (mostly) Chicanos living in the "concentrated pockets of poverty" called *colonias*.

The sun always shines on the colonias because they exist only along the U.S. Mexican border, in Arizona, New Mexico, California, and Texas. By definition colonias lack decent water and sewage systems. Housing is literally pieced together but, since colonias fall outside the jurisdiction of nearby cities, nothing changes unless groups like HAC ask the rest of us to sit up and take notice. Meanwhile, 1.5 million Americans experience frequent flooding due to the lack of paved streets or more disease due to the use of open cesspools.[1]

HAC held its December 1998 conference at the Omni Shoreham Hotel in Washington, D.C. Coincidentally the Omni applauded its own housing developments by announcing to all who entered the gold-plated lobby a "restoration" of the hotel's most expensive and sumptuous suites. On easels holding antique frames, the hotel highlighted the presidential apartment. Brocaded fabrics in burgundy would adorn couches placed next to mahogany tables accented by superb marquetry. The "sidewall art" (i.e., the room moldings) seemed as thick as a railroad tie, and designers planned to paint its many Greek details with a coat of the best gold leaf.

To an outsider the Omni seemed like a strange place for a national conference on the substandard or absent housing associated with rural poverty. Besides the featured restoration, hotel staff lavishly celebrated the joys of Christmas by placing, in the center of the lobby, a toy train that endlessly circled a small city of candy-etched gingerbread houses. The only thing missing was a statue of Santa Claus, yet the hotel made up for Santa's absence by lining the corridors leading to the conference with a long row of at least twenty "theme" Christmas trees. Each contained an orchestrated set of decorations—toys, candy, balls—and the only bow to rural America appeared in the shape of a cowboy without a horse. Arms pinned back like those of a scarecrow, the smiling cowboy stood in for the angels who blew their horns from the tops of other trees.

One corridor led to the Diplomat Room. It hosted a seminar on "Financing Homeownership" in surroundings that, like the plaster-work on the ceiling, brought into bold relief the distance between the "haves" and the "have-nots," between those with two or more homes and those with none. Omni service staff (some Chicano) had precisely positioned roughly one hundred metal chairs—all painted a garish gold—on a regal red rug and lit up the room with a crystal chandelier big enough for the largest mansion.

Seminar participants focused on finding funds for rural Americans. In the heartland, a significant mass of people confronted persistent poverty, today exacerbated by the rising rush of "city folk" eager to transform farmland into buffalo ranches for the superrich or Forest Glens for the upper middle class. On some rustic roads in Maryland part-time residents driving Mercedes now lobby locals to preserve for posterity ten-foot-wide roads that are dangerous to farmers driving sixteen-foot-wide harvesting combines.[2] Meanwhile, in Freiburg, Maine, old-timers disparagingly call the newcomers "flatlanders." It's said in a tone of disdain, especially when the monied class drives away from the local general store in a $40,000 sport utility vehicle.

Lunch brought Secretary of Agriculture Daniel Glickman to the podium. As listeners tried to make sense of his speech, I tried to make sense of the situation. This was *not* the banquet I had in mind. So much luxury in the face of so much poverty seemed to perversely reconfirm a point made by a variety of economists. On urban thoroughfares and country roads the rich are leaving the poor in the dust. In 1965 the typical corporate CEO earned about twenty times the salary of the average production worker. The ratio for 1989 tripled to 56 and by 1997 "relative CEO pay had more than doubled again to 116 times the pay of the average worker."[3]

In the conference hallways HAC received criticism for the choice of venue. Yet, for all the pomp and polish, HAC did get the secretary of agriculture to the banquet and, in doing so, it used a luxury hotel in the nation's capital to make a powerful point about rural and urban poverty. They are linked in the most varied ways, to each other and to race, ethnicity, and especially undocumented migration.

Community activists came to Washington because it is the urban seat of U.S. political and economic power. On the stump Republican and Democratic politicians champion the family farm, but glance at a chart of federal funding for rural self-help projects and it looks nearly as deflated as the "flatlanders" invading Freiburg, Maine.[4] As only urban poverty gets attention, one reason organizers chose the Omni Shoreham was its close proximity to mass transit. For a small fee, activists use the superb Metro system to lobby Congress and corporate supporters to obtain the funds needed for paved roads and safe housing.

A sometimes-neglected link between rural and urban America is the motivation of many community activists. *They come to the city to stop the city from coming to them.* Call it urban sprawl or the more fashionable "exurbia," but either way the nationwide reality is increasingly difficult conditions in rural America as well-off newcomers in search of "breathing room" raise both the cost of rural living and the level of "class conflict."

On Wadmalaw Island in Charleston, South Carolina, farmers now use rising realty values as collateral for the loans that support their threatened farms. Apparently, you save some land by subdividing the rest of it into small waterfront lots or other high-density developments. However, what's good for a farmer in trouble is not good for other members of the community. Rural town meetings thus turn into "furious" battles about city seepage when, as farmer John Walpole lectured his neighbors, "We have a lot of wonderful people who in their zeal to preserve the land, are blind to reality."[5]

Reality also appears when, a few blocks from the Omni, visitors encounter the extraordinary residential segregation of African Americans, linked to deteriorated housing, unemployment, poor schools, and crime.[6] As for muckrakers in 1910, it is still the shame of the cities but this is the nation's capital where, each evening, the District of Columbia empties out into rich Virginia farmland and pricey Maryland suburbs. Walk the streets near the refurbished waterfront on a Saturday in December and you encounter a ghost town that needs a sign: closed for the weekend.

It's a very vicious cycle. Whether in Hartford, Chicago, Lansing, or Washington, D.C., deteriorating cities produce the crime and school problems that move those with money to move out. Continuing migration produces pressure on rural America that is often exacerbated when, instead of a national effort to create self-sustaining urban economies, one city after another desperately shoots craps with the future. For example, despite failure in Atlantic City, Detroit also wagered on gambling casinos. In Hartford, politicians extol the virtues of laissez faire as they simultaneously plan to invest over a half billion dollars of public money to build a sports stadium for the New England Patriots football team. Service jobs will be created, but only when, according to the Connecticut government's guarantee, wealthy citizens drive in from rural Hebron or Columbia to sit in boxes that cost as much as $100,000 a season.

We are all Americans, joined at the hip by the perfectly paved highways that easily connect rural and urban America. Forget this and we lose a spiritual tie, not only to the land, but also to one another. Equally important, even the most heavily guarded apartment building or gated suburban development cannot protect us from the ripple effects of both urban and rural poverty.

Recall the militias and the explosive conjunctions between farm and city, unemployment and stress, bankruptcy and race. While 20 percent to 25 percent of our people—roughly 60 million Americans—live in rural locations, they account for close to 40 percent of those labeled poor. Stereotypes center on men and women yoked to the soil, but "nearly sixty percent of the net income now realized by farm families comes from off-farm jobs." To have any chance of making ends meet husbands and wives work in the restaurant or maintenance trades. They clean motel rooms instead of barns and they struggle to survive and (at times) to control their anger. In both Colorado and Iowa, serious studies document significant increases in spousal and child abuse.[7]

Joel Dyer, editor of the *Boulder Weekly*, argues that weekend visitors from the city miss the spiritual significance of "non-metropolitan" America's economic woes. People love the land. With a respect for ancestors associated with China or Japan, rural Americans consistently root their images of self and world in soil that was tilled by their grandparents and will (they hope) be tilled by their children. Urbanites may move at the drop of a hat, but farmers continually display a religious attachment to place that, instead of being anachronistic, is as central to their existence as rural poverty.[8]

By definition, farmers who lose their land also lose the axis of their personal and family life. Desperation is especially evident at foreclosure sales, the best place for militia recruiters to fill out the ranks. Responsibility is continually assigned to the "Zionist Occupied Government" (ZOG) but, not satisfied with linking poverty to a specific ethnic group, militias also tie it to race and religion. In its most extreme forms the White Identity Movement argues that only white Christians are the true Israelites of the Old Testament. White Americans are God's chosen people, destined to separately inhabit a huge nation, the United States of America. Impediments to this dream include Jewish bankers and "sub-humans" with origins in Africa. Take care of these human obstacles and you clear not a field, but a pathway to the Promised Land.[9]

However ugly and dangerous, this ideology of cause (Jewish bankers, the federal government, African Americans, Adam and Eve) and effect (foreclosure and poverty) explains an economic outcome in terms of race, ethnicity, and the word of God. In that sense it reverses the academic debates that perpetually seek to explain the residential and occupational dilemmas of African Americans in terms of social-class variables.[10] All too often it is only one or the other, when, in real life, class, ethnicity, race, and religion are inextricably intertwined.

This chapter focuses on class; to get to the cultural banquet people need the wherewithal to pay for the meal. But, isolating one variable need not blind us to the dangerous ethnic and "racial" consequences of rural poverty and farm foreclosures. People search for an explanation, and, in a society as poisonously divided as ours, they surrender to the appeals of hate. Malcolm X's chickens once again come home to roost, but instead of the barnyard, they appear in Oklahoma City, an urban target for the explosive consequences of rural problems and rural poverty.

In truth, it's two sides of the same coin: Militia groups seek to destroy the federal government while at the Omni Shoreham other segments of rural America seek Washington's assistance. Either way, "non-metropolitan" problems find their way to the nation's capital, a potential source of great assistance if we root urban and rural economic strategies in one of the great, enduring strengths of U.S. culture, community-based self-help groups.

The Local Initiatives Support Corporation (LISC) is the largest "intermediary" in the nation. Since its founding in 1980, LISC has successfully raised and redistributed so much money to especially urban localities that foreign governments have asked LISC to repeat its organizational successes in Poland or Russia. On a number of occasions LISC staff have tried to help, only to conclude reluctantly that the United States is virtually unique. Only America seems to produce the community groups that can literally and efficiently organize people at the grassroots level.[11]

This ability is, like wheat and corn, one of America's home-grown products. The intermediary, itself steeped in the ideology of self-help, unites local activists from the remotest parts of rural America, who come to Washington to pressure Congress and make a face-to-face case to banks and corporations. So far few people are heeding their urgent call. But, rooted in a federally financed program of urban and rural economic development, community-based self-help groups offer an all-American means to define ourselves by what unquestionably unites us: poverty and wretched housing in urban *and* rural America.

TRUST AND THE WEALTH OF A NATION

During the Civil War Southern soldiers from Alabama often refused to obey officers who came from North Carolina. Political loyalties and an accompanying sense of trust never extended beyond Alabama's or Georgia's borders. In organizing a military effort, Confederate commanders quickly discovered that their region's focus on states' rights produced an army that fought, not only the North, but itself as well. At war's end, with Lee's troops desperately in need of clothing and shoes, North Carolina officials refused to hand over thousands of uniforms reserved for only one military force: North Carolina's.

What does this have to do with economic development in rural and urban America? A great deal. In *Trust: The Social Virtues and the Creation of Prosperity*, Francis Fukuyama discusses trust "as the expectation that arises within a community of regular, honest and cooperative behavior, based on commonly shared norms, on the part of other members of the community."[12] The trouble for the Confederacy was that despite all-important military and economic goals—preserving slavery and defeating the Union forces—state borders often defined the limits of social trust. This persistently impeded military efficiency and, from Fukuyama's perspective, it also established significant roadblocks to economic success.

Whether in the budding national economy of the nineteenth century or in today's global economy, trust creates social capital, a natural resource every bit as valuable as oil, gold, or significant levels of higher education. Defined here as a cultural capability that exists when people from different geographic regions, ethnic groups, religions, and social classes use trust as a means to work together in a profitable and cooperative manner, social capital creates an independent and powerful *basis* for economic activity. In its best forms social capital works, side by side, with motives as diverse as self or national interest; and it can even significantly reduce the "transaction costs" of everyday economic activity.[13]

Think not of the Confederate army, but of the army of lawyers and auditors who today stand guard over the smallest and largest business transaction. In the United States distrust is so all-pervasive that Fukuyama points to a hidden tax of U.S. economic life. It's the salaries we pay to lawyers, auditors, and the support staff of "paper pushers" who cross the t's and dot the i's of the contracts and documentation needed in "low-trust" societies. To any rational person $800 for a toilet seat seems absurd, but not to military procurement, where distrust is so low that mountains of paperwork are mandatory because "contractors will try to cheat taxpayers if at all possible."[14]

Another example. At our state university officials assume that faculty will or may cheat when they travel. Thus, the travel office staff must require all faculty to produce zero-balance receipts; if they forget to do so or return incorrect paperwork, travel staff must ask faculty to get the proper paperwork or their forms will not be processed. Given faculty arrogance and egos, this produces, on an everyday basis, stressful "incidents" for all concerned and an inefficient expenditure of both travel staff and faculty time.

Fukuyama's point is crucial: Rooted in trust, social capital is the oil that allows people to cooperate without friction and without the administrative costs that eat up profits, profits that could be invested in enterprises creating self-sustaining urban and rural economies.

A positive example of social trust is the family enterprises so characteristic of the Korean community discussed in chapter 6. Families profitably work together without the need for contracts, and trust is the glue that allows parents to leave children at the cash register. However, if family marks the limits of social trust, a business cannot expand in an indefinite manner. As families are only so large, Fukuyama reasonably argues that the reliance on family is a key variable in understanding the historical limits of, for example, Chinese business enterprises.[15]

Given the fierce competitive nature of the global economy, the United States needs all the social capital it can muster. But, instead of family or state, the biggest American barriers to the creation of increased social capital are the racial and ethnic identities that consistently engender not only mistrust, but also, as with the militias, fierce hatreds.

In New England one insurance company after another tries to insure cooperation by paying "big bucks" for consultants who offer top management both sensitivity and diversity training. This additional tax on the cost of doing business is necessary because the workplace now includes a variety of newcomers—women, African Americans, Indians, Koreans, Japanese, and Puerto Ricans. The shared norms that produce trust and its profitable by-product, social capital, are in short supply. So management tries to create them, as a way to avoid increased social conflict in the office and as a way to compete in the global marketplace—a cross-cultural economy if ever there was one.[16]

Three conclusions are in order. First, let's stop thinking like Karl Marx. The economy is not the base and the rest of society the superstructure of human life. Anywhere on earth, economic life in general and capitalism in particular are partially shaped by cultural beliefs and values. To use a Marxian phrase, the relationship is dialectical; one factor acts back upon the other, producing a welter of self-help organizations in one society and a genuine reliance on the central government in another.[17]

Second, because ethnic and "racial" issues have economic consequences, eliminating our poisonous differences can be enormously profitable for all Americans. Demolish the ethnic and color barriers that divide us and you create a world in which, instead of paying passed-along "taxes" to get along, we continuously create the social capital that—free of charge!—helps produce jobs, profits, and "A Place for Everybody."

Finally, let's play to our cultural strengths. Community-based self-help groups already provide a sound basis for producing economic and social changes. Arm those groups with substantially increased levels of social capital and they have the chance to significantly and peacefully reduce the income differences that, like ethnicity, race, and immigration, divide us from one end of the continent to the other.

NATURE AND LOGIC OF CAPITALISM[18]

Beliefs matter. Internalized as assumptions taken for granted, they make social life possible—in interactions as mundane as standing on a line and as important as the shaping of economic policies. However, using inherited cultural assumptions, even the most intelligent people may see not the world that is there, but the world brought into focus by their preconceived beliefs.

Say, for example, that free markets are a fiction, an illusion as dangerous as the mental meanderings of the White Identity Movement. This could be true,[19] but as with our use of the concept of race, we refuse to let reality interfere with our perceptions of social life. Instead, the mental anchors of economic thinking remain buried in thick cement pillars.

This section aims to challenge some of the root assumptions of everyday economic thought. My argument is this: Poor people have a much better chance to come to the cultural banquet if new economic policies are grounded in a serious rethinking of our most basic assumptions about the nature and logic of capitalism.

Start with the supposed crux of the capitalist system: the right of owners to use their private property in any way they see fit. Robert Heilbroner forcefully argues "that such a dangerous social right has never existed."[20] From the local zoning regulations that guide use of any person's home to the national regulations that specify the precise nature of food-packaging labels, government authorities have always claimed—and been granted—more or less public authority over the use of any private property.

Battles often center on a debate about rights versus obligations.[21] In a city section zoned residential the owner of any home presumably has some obligations to his or her neighbors. Certain businesses are forbidden or tightly restricted because the rights of people take precedence over the rights of property owners. Similarly, a factory owner accepts—however reluctantly—restrictions on the right to pollute the rest of us into an early grave. In the real world laws may or may not be enforced, but the unchallenged acceptance of obligations to the larger society is basic to any laws that, for at least a century, have regulated U.S. banks, corporations, and (later in the century) radio and television networks.[22]

Heilbroner argues that by focusing so much attention on the alleged rights of property owners, we actually miss "the critical aspect of money or capital goods as private property." That is the owner's right to *withhold* funds or factories from use if owners deem it necessary or profitable. It is the right to withhold "that enables the capitalist to dominate the sphere of trade and production to which his or her authority extends, as other legal rights enable military officers or priests or political figures to dominate the spheres in which their authority extends."[23]

Dominate is a strong word, which aptly captures the essential power of American capitalists. They dominate, with such power that rural Americans must come to the Omni Shoreham to plead with Congress for the investment funds withheld by corporations or banks in search of more profitable investments.

Meanwhile, the acceptance of the right to withhold is so great that even though property owners nakedly assert their power, many Americans quietly accept their fate. Call it the Deindustrialization of America or the Downsizing of America,[24] either way, capitalists padlock factory and office doors while the suddenly unemployed presumably accept the supposed exigencies of the American capitalist system. Indeed, however angry or distraught, even upper-level executives quietly walk off to "transition classes" while comparatively few demand laws like those that exist in German capitalism. There, any company that lays off workers "must come up with a social plan to protect workers' needs as the company downsizes."[25]

Americans could enact comparable laws, especially if similarly exposed African, Latin, Asian, and European Americans worked together. For example, activists could root their economic demands not in a revolutionary challenge to the right to withhold capital from use, but in a revolutionary debate (for the United States) about the obligations of capital and government to the rest of the society. Again using German capitalism as an example, as early as 1951 the German government enacted laws "that gave unions as well as owners and management a voice in how major companies operate." They did this because they "temper the profit motive with a strong dose of social responsibility"; they accept that, as Germans, "workers have a legitimate interest in how business operates."[26]

Mention ideas like this to American capitalists and, along with many U.S. politicians, they cite two of the most damaging fictions in U.S. economic life. The first is the belief in free markets. The second is the supposed need for a "hands-off the economy" approach by, especially, the federal government.[27]

This is easily provable nonsense. Consider, for example, the Caribbean Basin Initiative of President Ronald Reagan. Instituted in 1982, the central government economic strategies of a laissez faire president soon put a quarter of a million people in the Caribbean out of work, as those policies simultaneously and dramatically increased legal and illegal immigration from Haiti and the Dominican Republic to the United States.[28]

Fighting a war in Central America, President Reagan wanted to help allies throughout the Caribbean. He and his staff used an economic plan devised in Washington to stimulate economies from Jamaica to Costa Rica. Traditionally walled off from U.S. markets, Caribbean nations would now find open access to U.S. ports and stores. However, Congressmen investigating the proposal noted that since 86 percent of Caribbean products already entered the U.S. market on a duty-free basis, did the Reagan administration plan to free up markets—such as sugar and textiles—now closely regulated by the federal government?

Assistant Secretary of State Thomas Enders hoped so. But American sugar and textile interests needed to have their interests "secured." They came first. As one hand used the federal government to stimulate Caribbean economies, the other used the federal government to disprove the notion of free markets. Under pressure from U.S. producers in Hawaii and Louisiana, President Reagan imposed, in 1982, country quotas on the amount of sugar that could be imported to the United States. Dominican officials immediately alerted Congress to the impact of these free market controls. Sugar provided close to 35 percent of all that nation's foreign exchange receipts. Close U.S. doors to most of the island's sugar, and you would move people off the land and into Florida or New York.[29]

By 1988 the consequences of sugar quotas produced such havoc in the Caribbean that David Rockefeller warned Congress to take immediate action; it must "address the appalling effects of current U.S. policy on these countries we are supposed to be helping."[30]

Haitian boat people and half a million Dominicans in New York did not come without a big push from President Reagan. He and his colleagues made a horrible policy blunder. The even bigger problem is this: A man who spent his life celebrating free markets closed our doors to Caribbean sugar and, in the process, he repeated history by imitating a distant predecessor, President Franklin Roosevelt. It was, after all, Roosevelt who first instituted country sugar quotas in 1934. (They remained in force until 1974.)[31]

From Roosevelt to Reagan, where was the free market? And where was the absence of government involvement in the economy? Indeed, the largest of President Reagan's contradictions was that, in the name of laissez faire and free enterprise, he used one federal economic program—sugar quotas—to successfully undermine another federal economic program, the Caribbean Basin Initiative.

The confusion was real and continues because, as in the 1980s, today's economic debates too often forget that markets for goods and services are controlled not only by the federal government but also by corporations. *Trusts and cartels are, instead of an aberration, a predictable and inherent part of the capitalist economic landscape.*

For at least the last century one manufacturing corporation after another encounters the same problem: overproduction. You cannot make a fair profit, much less a huge one, if the market contains an oversupply of (say) light bulbs. As early as 1896, General Electric and Westinghouse closely monitored the number of bulbs available to American consumers. It made no sense for businesses of equal size to "duke it out" in the marketplace—they could both lose—so they controlled the number of bulbs available by parceling out first the United States and then, as the century wore on, the world. Meanwhile, as essential members of the cartel, suppliers like Corning Glass signed a deal limiting their sales of materials to other potential manufacturers of light bulbs.[32]

This was normal. It is normal. By definition one capitalist is always "inescapably exposed to the efforts of others to gain as much as possible of the public's purchasing power."[33] Because competition, instead of being healthy, can be ruinous, a sharp capitalist often unites with his or her colleagues to place a secure fence around the limits of competition. Thus, Westinghouse paid a penalty fee to General Electric if it sold more light bulbs than its allotted share of the market. As we move into the twenty-first century, high tech giants like Microsoft imitate their predecessors. Control the marketplace if you can because it limits your inescapable exposure to the profit-making efforts of others, such as Intel, Netscape, and IBM.

If governments and businesses control markets, urban and rural citizens certainly have the same right. The issue, after all, is not whether free markets exist but who controls those markets and in whose ultimate interest.

Enter the government yet again. "However harsh the domination of capital my be, it always operates at a remove and with a degree of voluntary submission."[34] In feudalism the lord of the manor combined political, economic, and military power. Refuse to work or to tender the mandated portion of your produce and the lord could literally beat you into submission.

Capitalism is a subtler system. By definition federal, state, and local governments regulate property rights while workers, instead of being beaten into submission, do have the right to enter and leave jobs at will. This is unquestionably a wonderful "emancipation"[35] from the harsher rigors of a system like feudalism, but capitalists, operating through governments (albeit indirectly), still watch out for their economic interests by using tools like money to control the political and regulatory process.

Walk through the Capital in Washington, D.C., or the one in Hartford, Connecticut, and you spot the same thing: well-paid lobbyists trying to influence the political process for economic gain. Sugar interests have been doing this for more than a hundred years and, as capitalists, they would be crazy to do anything else. Meanwhile, the nation's economic debates are still wedded to notions of no government involvement or interference in the free market process.

Those seeking change need to think like capitalists. Grasp the Wall Street bull by its horns and absolutely refuse to discuss policy in terms of fictions like laissez faire and free markets. Capitalists certainly have rights, but in a world in which 300 multinational corporations control roughly 25 percent of the world's productive assets,[36] capitalists also have—or must be made politically to accept—significantly increased obligations to the rest of us. For example, a different computation of giant multinationals notes that "during the last generation the world's 500 largest multinational corporations have grown sevenfold in sales yet the worldwide employment of these firms has remained virtually flat since the early 1970's." Meanwhile, these same corporations help shape a debate that champions free markets yet neglects to mention that more than 40 percent of U.S. exports and 50 percent of its imports are "goods that travel not in the open marketplace, but through intrafirm channels."[37]

As companies trade with themselves, the rest of us are still taught to believe that, however wide the gap between rich and poor, the system ultimately benefits everyone. This too is a cultural inheritance with deep roots in our European and English past. Philosophers like John Locke faced a presumably impossible conundrum: How justify the unlimited acquisition that impoverishes others and uses goods, such as second and third homes, that could be used by others? Locke solved the riddle "by dwelling on the capacity of acquisitiveness" to increase everyone's wealth.[38] Two hundred years later we call this the trickle-down theory of capitalism but, somehow, the 1.5 million Americans living on the colonias still live in very arid conditions.

Get people to the cultural banquet by first reevaluating the conventional economic wisdom and then organizing African, European, Asian, Latin, and Native Americans around a question that has the potential to unify the most diverse and distant social groups. What are capitalism's obligations to the rest of us and, especially, to our urban and rural poor?

Answers to this question could include, as in German capitalism, laws that require any firm employing more than 2,000 people to allocate an equal number of seats on their boards of directors to employees and shareholders. Or, as in Japan, we could decide that instead of shareholders, employees are the number one stakeholders in any business enterprise. Finally we could decide that if capitalists exercise their right to withhold investment funds, federal and state governments will, as William Julius Wilson suggests in *When Work Disappears*, provide work through a variety of "public-investment infrastructure maintenance roads."[39]

Here, specific answers are less important than a reframing of the public debate. Free markets do not exist. Whether at the federal, state, or local level, governments are inextricably involved in economic policymaking. Trickle-down capitalism is hard to accept in an America where, just from 1989 to 1997, the share of all wealth held by the top 1 percent of households grew from 37.4 percent to 39.1 percent. Meanwhile the share of all wealth held by the middle fifth of the population dropped from 4.8 percent to 4.4 percent.[40]

Finally, the defining power of any capitalist is his or her right to withhold capital from use if they see fit.

At recent economic development conferences in Ponce and San Juan, Puerto Rico, I met representatives from "Made in America" shoe- and bluejean-producing companies. Their jobs included combing the Caribbean for new manufacturing sites. When they found one, the U.S. firms invested as little as possible. Instead, they used a group of waiting Asian and local investors who, under headquarters supervision, built the factory and trained workers according to the American companies' specifications.[41]

Trading on its name and distribution outlets, the prime manufacturer reduced its exposure by "sourcing out" the actual fabrication work to others. Subcontractors earned a good profit from precise, short-term contracts and reduced their own exposure by demanding or receiving substantial inducements from local governments for the cost of the site, the construction of the facility, and the training of the workers. Eventually large numbers of (especially) young women got jobs, but in the global economy, capitalists with so little exposure moved on to other locations when and if it suited their international strategies. As one executive after another assured me, "Our strategies are global." The era of national thinking was as anachronistic as the world of Norman Rockwell and the down-home loyalties he so lovingly depicted.

Obligations to workers and their rural and urban communities never exist in a historical vacuum. Capitalism is shaped by culture and by the specific economic conditions that exist at a point in time. Thus, any analysis of obligations must consider the "Wild West" world now labeled the global economy.

PUNCTUATED EQUILIBRIUM

"Punctuated equilibrium" is tough to say but easier to understand. Sometimes, in the course of animal and human history, change occurs so rapidly that evolution takes a quantum leap. Natural selection, which normally works on the margins, suddenly alters the core of the system.[42]

With animals, the best example of punctuated equilibrium is the dinosaurs. Here one day, gone the next, the dinosaurs died at the mercy of a massive cloud of sulfuric dust. It destroyed their environment so abruptly that even these giants of nature offered no viable defense. Forces they could never control erased them.

People are different. We have brains and we can use them to react, not to a cloud of sulfuric dust, but to a series of economic changes that are quickly and decisively transforming the core of the world's economic system. Indeed, while no one knows exactly what the future holds, we can, with the Japanese, think of change and crisis as opportunities. Now is the time to analyze key elements of the emerging system in relation to the potential obligations of capitalists and governments to the blue-, white-, and pink-collar workers who, whether in Panama or Pittsburgh, can lose their jobs as quickly as the dinosaurs lost their environment.

By definition capitalists are always exposed to the profitmaking efforts of others. However, one crucial difference today—and in the twenty-first century—is that threats to profits can come from anywhere, even when the national government "protects" workers. In Japan the government-owned and-managed postal service charges roughly eighty cents to mail a letter, compared to thirty-three cents in the United States. Direct marketers in Japan discovered that they saved money by mailing catalogs from Los Angeles instead of Tokyo. Over time many Japanese printing and layout jobs also traveled to the United States. When the Japanese government forbid the bulk mailing of direct-marketing materials into Japan by Japanese companies, firms responded by turning to the Internet. They "file transferred" their direct mail to Hong Kong and the United States and then individually mailed them to Japanese consumers.[43]

Score one for a few U.S. workers, who, like their Japanese counterparts, nevertheless remain as exposed as ever. Under anything but Yuletide conditions, Christmas and other U.S. toys are now overwhelmingly manufactured in China, which also clothes Americans by stamping out enormous quantities of our under- and outerwear. Incidentally, to keep jobs in China, government officials issued in April of 1997 a dangerous challenge. Threaten our growth and, if only 1 percent of the Chinese people migrated in search of work, East Asia would have 12 million new job seekers on its soil.[44]

The global economy is indeed interconnected, by the extraordinary mobility of capital, people, and ideas[45] and by the technological *equality* that now characterizes so much of the industrialized world. Texas Instruments now designs its most sophisticated computer chips in India. Motorola established design centers in both China and India while an aviation monopoly once enjoyed by U.S. manufacturers now makes way for the European consortium called Airebus and, waiting in the wings, the Japanese and (eventually) Chinese engineers who also want a piece of the aviation action. Thus, in a message that gave new meaning to global mobility, the Connecticut "based" United Technologies Corporation recently announced that it might move its world headquarters to the Far East for at least three months of each year.[46]

William Greider emphasizes the "manic logic of global capitalism." With so many competitors producing goods and services of equal quality, corporate strategists modernized as the only way to remain competitive. This increased their productive capacity, which increased their—and their modernizing competitors'—need for more sales. Meanwhile, as each produces more than ever before, the stockpile of unsold production grows. For American and European "manufacturers" the Chinese produce 1 million men's shirts every day. Unfortunately, no one really needs these shirts, since Chinese warehouses already contain more than 1.5 *billion* men's shirts.[47]

Overproduction is the manic side of this competitive equation. But, for U.S. and other workers, the runaway roll of the snowball affects jobs when they lose their livelihoods to both technology *and* capital flight. After all, if a manufacturer refuses to modernize, he or she loses orders to competitors outsourcing their work to a distant, low-wage competitor. But, if he or she does modernize, "some jobs are eliminated and even the survivors remain vulnerable."[48]

Empathetic analysts can of course understand the position of the capitalist. But to argue that those same capitalists owe no significant obligations to white-, blue-, and pink-collar workers is to give the fox free reign in the hen house. Following the bottom line logic of (especially) American capitalism, managers should follow profits wherever the road leads, with workers making do with lower-paying service jobs that often reduce both income and self-esteem.[49]

As with the self-help groups who came to Washington, government is the political court of last resort. Asserting American interests, federal and state governments need to be an essential part of any panethnic debate about the obligations of capital to labor and of the government to everyone.

To those who understandably complain about the limits of national sovereignty in a world without borders recall the regulatory and economic power of quasi-governmental organizations like the World Bank and the International Monetary Fund. With sacks of U.S. dollars they underline the perpetual involvement of government agencies in world economic development, and just as important, the positive and negative effects of IMF policies produce ripple effects throughout the world. When, as in Asia, the IMF allegedly derailed economies, the lower value of Far Eastern currencies had an immediate impact on workers in the United States. By one estimate, 100,000 U.S. workers could lose their jobs to Far Eastern goods that were, overnight, cheaper than ever.[50]

A final point revolves around the obligations of the government, economic, and educational institutions to prepare Americans for the global economy. For example, the banquet mindscape suggested in this book is a form of social capital that already helps world-class corporations produce more profits and (hopefully) better-paying jobs. As an American engineer born in Israel recently noted, when he attends business meetings in Europe executives often speak in English, but the transition to German, French or Spanish is "seamless." One language follows another as people profitably jump into and out of other cultures.[51]

This could be the worst future of all: an America in which the rich smilingly cross more cultures than ever before while the rest of us deal firsthand with the consequences of the militia movement and its camouflaged soldiers flying a flag labeled "the White Identity Movement."

ETHNIC NICHES, AFRICAN AMERICANS, AND CHICANOS

My maternal grandmother died when she was 88. Arriving in 1900 she only spoke Spanish. Leaving in 1971 she only spoke Spanish. She lived, worked, and died surrounded by a small community of people from Northern Spain. Like a moat around a castle, the ethnic enclave kept outsiders at bay while my grandmother and her friends felt comfortable only inside the businesses, churches, and clubs frequented by those who knew the passwords: Spanish from Spain.

In Preston, Oregon, immigrants from Sweden settled the town. As late as 1939 the Baptist church conducted its services in Swedish, and, if you wanted a job at the Swedish-owned mill, this local joke contained more than a grain of truth: "They said if you were Swedish, you had a chance of getting a job at the mill. And if you were Swedish Baptist, you had the job."[52]

Walk through New York's Chinatown, and you miss as much as you see. Unless you spoke Chinese and people expressed a willingness to open up to strangers, how could a visitor know that "it is common to meet Chinatown residents who, having lived in the United States for twenty-five years, are not able to communicate in simple English." Like my grandmother, Chinese people still live, work, and die within the ethnic enclave because "from the moment of their arrival" newcomers "rely on their relatives or friends to get them jobs and teach them how to work." Because it's cheaper, easier, and avoids issues of legal or undocumented status, employers prefer to let reliable workers train newcomers. One person recommends another, the newcomer now owes a favor, and the enclave perpetuates itself because it's not only who you know that counts, it's who you are.[53]

Ethnic enclaves and ethnic employment niches are a historical constant. Their existence predates that of the Republic. Despite theories that suggest their demise, contemporary ethnic enclaves are not only stronger than ever, their existence creates new and serious problems for African Americans. At the very end of the twentieth century, "the ethnic division of labor stands as the central division of labor" in cities like New York, Houston, Miami, and Los Angeles. Equally important, "niche creation by African Americans and immigrants has evolved into a mutually exclusive carving up of the pie."[54]

Conventional wisdom suggests that unskilled immigrants should not be finding jobs. This is postindustrial America,[55] an economy that produces work for the well-educated and unemployment lines for those without skills or the education required to obtain those skills.

Reality loves to deride both common sense and social theory. Thus, as late as the 1990s 44 percent of all jobs in New York went to people with twelve or fewer years of schooling. Theory says this should not be so, but as those working in hotels, garment shops, and restaurants can testify, in many postindustrial cities "the tendency toward skill deepening has slowed since 1960."[56]

Unskilled immigrants take those new service and manufacturing jobs. It could be, as in Chinatown, what amounts to a postindustrial form of sweat-shop serfdom.[57] Or, as with West Indians in New York's health care sector, the service jobs are monopolized by those who speak—very well—the King's English. Whatever the specific ethnic niche, the end result is a serious con-striction of opportunities for a large but unspecified number of poorly ed-ucated African Americans. Those with an educational or family leg up do have their own ethnic niche in municipal jobs in cities like Detroit, Hartford, or Newark. But, given more than 20 million immigrants since 1965, poorly educated African Americans today find new, powerful ethnic barriers to the entry-level jobs that, if not proliferating, are still providing employment for millions of recent and older unskilled immigrants.[58]

Trying to precisely determine the class and prejudice parts of this un-employment equation is indeed a difficult task. History suggests avoiding the arrogance that produces generalizations for the nation. Specific cities and the exact ethnic mixes they contain will produce different conse-quences for African Americans. For example, in Los Angeles deindustriali-zation compounded the consequences of immigration and the ethnic niches they produce. In New York, as African Americans never held many manufacturing jobs, the consequences of the new ethnic niches are a more central part of any explanation for the unemployment problems of African Americans.[59]

Prejudice is also part of any explanation. Race still trumps ethnicity in all too many cases because, as one African-American construction worker stressed, "When the white workers are in the room, it's fuckin' guinea this, stinking kike that, polack this. When I come into the room, they're all white."[60] Moreover, discussing Korean communities in both New York and Los Angeles, Pyong Gap Min indicates that "many Korean immi-grants have a sense of superiority over Blacks." A variety of factors ac-count for this sense of superiority—such as Korean culture, negative experiences in their stores—but prejudice is nevertheless an inextricable part of any explanation for the severe unemployment problems of un-skilled urban African Americans.[61]

We need not seek mathematical certainty about the exact role of all the involved variables. The consequence is our concern. Immigration since 1965 has created ethnic niches that close the doors on the entry-level jobs most needed by unskilled African Americans. Thus, since Washington policymak-ers are responsible for immigration and its admittedly unintended conse-quences, it would seem that they bear a special responsibility for creating the public works jobs that may, in many cities, be the only doors open to unskilled African Americans.

At the end of 1998 the Census Bureau reports 268 million Americans. Over 29 million are Latino (up from 23 million in 1990) and over 60 percent of all Latinos trace their roots to Mexico. This population still lacks most of the tools needed for social mobility. Less than 25 percent of Mexican immigrants possess a high school diploma. Into the third generation they are still three times less likely than other immigrant children to live in a home where the family head boasts a college diploma.[62] Thus, a recent study of the children of today's immigrants cites this unique historical fact. "At the turn of the century no single group could have altered the generalization that most immigrants were much more likely than natives to start out near the bottom."[63]

Mexicans are different. So many start out at the very bottom in urban and rural America that they alone skew the generalizations about immigrants that are so often made. For example, fully 35 percent of all pharmacists in the Los Angeles area are foreign born; the figure for dentists is 25 percent, and for engineers, computer specialists, and physicians the figure is 20 percent.[64] Excluding Mexicans, the foreign born are more likely to have reached college than the native born. They are not the downtrodden immigrants of historical legend, and they do not require the assistance that must be offered to Mexican Americans.

Given the hundred-year history outlined in chapter 2, that assistance should be offered as "back pay" compensation for what different generations of national policy makers labeled "a form of economic slavery." Those who eschew compensatory arguments rooted in the past should consider the future in terms of self-interest and fear.

Eighteen million fully integrated Mexican Americans offer the potential for an enormous increase in the nation's social capital and the wealth of everyone. We could therefore act like good capitalists and recognize that to succeed in a global economy of technological equals, America needs all the social capital it can muster.

An alternative is a different type of muster, a million man and woman march of determined Chicanos. Concentrated in states like California, Texas, and Illinois, Mexicans have the potential to alter the political balance in states that are crucial to any president's election. We can help each other as Americans or, faced with a deaf ear from public and private resources, Chicanos could act like Zapatistas and move off the colonias for a powerful assault, not on the Omni Shoreham but on the Capitol dome.

THE COLORS OF CHANGE

A great juggler is a joy to watch. Especially for those of us who lack coordination, the ability somehow to keep plates or balls in the air produces an open sense of envy and admiration. Sometimes, the juggler even manages to add additional objects to the mix, all the while talking to the audience of both children and adults.

To deal effectively with the issues raised in this and other chapters, activists need to juggle a series of interconnected variables: ethnicity, race, immigration, capitalism, and the global economy, among others. Take our eyes off one of the "plates" and we risk the sound of failure.

Consider President Lyndon Johnson's war on poverty. One of its main goals included the *ability* of people to work. Training programs therefore focused on increasing personal education and marketable skills, yet neglected implementation of the individual's *right* to work. Throughout the nation, the federal government relied on traditional labor organizations to actually implement the war on poverty. One consequence was continuing discrimination against African Americans who found barriers to jobs as high as ever.[65]

Racism remains an elemental part of American life. At the Census Bureau and on the street, the black/white dichotomy continues to define us by what divides us. Meanwhile, powerful politicians like Representative Joseph Barr (R., Georgia) speak at organizations like the Council of Conservative Citizens. In June of 1997, Barr received a welcome from individuals who argue that the "the white race faces the danger of extinction." Thus, Mark Cerr, head of the National Capital branch of the CCC, indicates, "I would separate the races by having non-Europeans sent back to the Third World. The United States was founded by my people, the British people, not by Asians or Indians or Negroes, and we are going to take it back."[66]

Extremists? Of course. But the group nevertheless received endorsements from Senate Majority Leader Trent Lott (R., Miss.) and North Carolina's Governor, Kirk Fordice.[67]

Forget race and any assault on poverty will once again fail. But, focus too much or singular attention on African Americans (or Chicanos) and those seeking significant change risk a self-defeating struggle over who is the most victimized and exploited group in the country. At the Omni Shoreham the Housing Assistance Corporation also sold copies of a volume entitled *The Poorest of the Poor: Female Headed Households in Non-Metro America.* On the cover is a photo of a mother and her two children. None is African, Latin, Native, or Asian American. Yet the woman looks as exhausted as anyone who appears in photos depicting the human devastation of the Great Depression.

Like the great juggler, the trick is to keep all the balls in the air. When economic themes are the issue, zero in on what unites too many Americans: poverty, vulnerability to the global economy, and a decided need to precisely define the obligations of capital to each and every American.

The best-case scenario is this: All ethnic groups cooperate to achieve their economic goals and, as a wonderful by-product of their collaborative efforts,

"We go a long way toward easing prejudice and helping people to see through each other's eyes."[68]

One factor acts back upon the other. It's a dialectic as powerful as any envisioned by Karl Marx.

NOTES

1. Housing Assistance Council, *The Border Colonias Region: Challenges and Innovative Approaches to Effective Community Development* (Washington, DC: Housing Assistance Council, 1998), esp. pp. 1–5.

2. Susan DeFord, "Saving the Country's Rural Byways," *Washington Post*, December 3, 1998, p. M01.

3. Economic Policy Institute, *The State of Working America* (Washington, 1998), p. 10. See the Executive Summary, downloaded from ⟨www.epinet.org⟩; see, too, Lester Thurow, *The Future of Capitalism* (New York: Morrow, 1996), especially chapter 2.

4. For example, Housing Assistance Council, "A Brief and Selective Historical Outline of Rural Mutual Self-Help Housing in the United States" (Washington, DC: Housing Assistance Council, 1998).

5. Motoko Rich, "Development Limits Sow Charleston Farmers' Fury," *Wall Street Journal*, Southeast Journal, December 2, 1998, p. SE1.

6. For example, Douglas Massey and Nancy A. Denton, *American Apartheid* (Cambridge: Harvard University Press, 1993).

7. Joel Dyer, *Harvest of Rage* (Boulder: Westview Press, 1997), p. 17.

8. Ibid., especially chapters 1–3.

9. Ibid., especially chapter 5; see, too, Morris Dees, with James Corcoran, *Gathering Storm: America's Militia Threat* (New York: Harper, 1997); also Jess Walter, *Every Knee Shall Bow* (New York: Harper, 1995).

10. For example, William Julius Wilson, *The Declining Significance of Race* (Chicago: University of Chicago Press, 1978); and *The Truly Disadvantaged* (Chicago: University of Chicago Press, 1987).

11. Based on interviews with LISC personnel.

12. Francis Fukuyama, *Trust: The Social Virtues and the Creation of Poverty* (New York: Free Press, 1995), p. 26.

13. Ibid., p. 27.

14. Ibid., p. 28; on costs, see, for example, Lester Thurow, *The Zero-Sum Solution* (New York: Simon and Schuster, 1985).

15. Fuyuyama, *Trust*, especially Part 2, "Low Trust Societies and the Paradox of Family Values."

16. This is based on my personal experiences, plus interviews with insurance executives.

17. For example, Charles Hampden-Turner and Alfons Trompenaars, *The Seven Cultures of Capitalism* (New York: Doubleday, 1993); Michel Albert, *Capitalism vs. Capitalism* (New York: Four Wall Eight Windows Books, 1993); Hedrick Smith, *Rethinking America* (New York: Random House, 1995); Thomas Friedman, *The Lexus and the Olive Tree* (New York: Farrar, Strauss and Giroux, 1999).

18. Robert Heilbroner, *The Nature and Logic of Capitalism* (New York: W. W. Norton, 1985).

19. For example, Robert Kuttner, *Everything for Sale: The Virtues and Limits of Markets* (New York: Knopf, 1997); also George Soros, *The Crisis of Global Capitalism* (New York: Public Affairs, 1998).

20. Heilbroner, *Nature and Logic*, p. 38.

21. R. H. Tawney, *The Acquisitive Society* (New York: Harcourt Brace, 1920).

22. For example, Harold Faulkner, *The Decline of Laissez Faire* (New York: Rinehart, 1951).

23. Heilbroner, *Nature and Logic*, p. 38.

24. Barry Bluestone, *The Deindustrialization of America* (New York: Basic Books, 1982); New York Times, *The Downsizing of America* (New York: Times Books, 1996).

25. Smith, *Rethinking America*, p. 211.

26. Ibid.

27. On the essential role of governments in Far Eastern economies, see Peter Berger, *The Capitalist Revolution* (New York: Basic Books, 1986).

28. Ronald Fernandez, *Cruising the Caribbean: U.S. Influence and Intervention in the Twentieth Century* (Monroe, ME: Common Courage Press, 1994).

29. Ibid., pp. 400–401.

30. Ibid., p. 391.

31. For a solid history, see John E. Dalton, *Sugar: A Case Study in Government Control* (New York: Macmillan, 1937).

32. George W. Stocking and Myron W. Watkins, *Cartels in Action: Case Studies in International Business* (New York: Twentieth Century Fund, 1946). The electric light bulb cartel is discussed in detail in chapter 8.

33. Heilbroner, *Nature and Logic*, p. 57.

34. Ibid., p. 40.

35. Ibid.

36. Richard J. Barnet and John Cavanagh, *Global Dreams: Imperial Corporations and the New World Order* (New York: Simon and Schuster, 1994), p. 15; see, too, Lester Thurow, *Building Wealth: The New Rules for Individuals, Companies and Nations in a Knowledge-Based Economy* (New York: Harper Collins, 1999).

37. William Greider, *One World, Ready or Not: The Manic Logic of Global Capitalism* (New York: Simon and Schuster, 1997), pp. 21–22.

38. Heilbroner, *Nature and Logic*, pp. 112–113.

39. Lester Thurow, *Head to Head: The Coming Economic Battle between Japan, Europe and America* (New York: Morrow, 1992), p. 33; also Albert, *Capitalism*, p. 112; William Julius Wilson, *When Work Disappears* (New York: Vintage, 1996), pp. 226–227.

40. Economic Policy Institute, *The State of Working America* (Washington, 1998), ⟨http://www.epinet.org⟩, p. 12. This is from the executive summary of a larger volume.

41. These conferences—held in 1996 and 1997—were sponsored by the New Waves in the Caribbean Foundation, a consortium of five universities and a number of local and global corporations. At the time, I was president of this nonprofit foundation.

42. Thurow, *Future of Capitalism*, p. 7.

43. Kenichi Ohmae, *The End of the Nation State: The Rise of Regional Economies* (New York: Free Press, 1995), pp. 134–135; see, too, Andrew Grove, *Only the Paranoid Survive* (New York: Doubleday, 1999); Bill Gates, *Business @ the Speed of Thought: Using a Digital Nervous System* (New York: Warner Books, 1999).

44. *Migration News* 4, no. 9 (September 1997): 21.

45. Rosabeth Moss Kantor, *World Class: Thriving Locally in the Global Economy* (New York: Simon and Schuster, 1995), pp. 42–43.

46. Kenichi Ohmae, *Triad Power: The Coming Shape of Global Competition* (New York: Free Press, 1985); Thurow, *Future of Capitalism*, p. 59; on aviation see Greider, *One World*, pp. 124–134.

47. Ibid, Greider, pp. 72, 45–47; on the shirts, see *Migration News* 4, no. 9 (Sept. 1997): p. 20.

48. Greider, *One World*, p. 72–74.

49. On the orientation of U.S. capitalists, see Thurow, *Head to Head*, esp. chapter 2; also Robert Reich, *The Work of Nations: Preparing Ourselves for 21st Century Capitalism* (New York: Knopf, 1991).

50. For example, Jeffrey Sachs, "The IMF and the Asian Flu," *American Prospect*, no. 37 (March/April 1998): 16–21.

51. Based on a discussion with an engineer who lives in Simsbury, Connecticut but, for much of the year, travels throughout the world designing and building machine tools.

52. Jack Hopkins, "Pastoral Rural Communities Hear Footsteps of Growth," *Seattle Post Intelligencer*, December 5, 1998, p. C1.

53. Peter Kwong, *Forbidden Workers* (New York: New Press, 1997), pp. 116–117.

54. Roger Waldinger, *Still the Promised City?: African Americans and New Immigrants in Postindustrial New York* (Cambridge: Harvard University Press, 1996).

55. For example, Daniel Bell, *The Coming of Post-Industrial Society* (New York: Basic Books, 1976); also Bell's *The Cultural Contradictions of Capitalism* (New York: Basic Books, 1978).

56. Waldinger, *Still the Promised City?*, p. 13; see, too, Roger Waldinger and Mehdl Bozorgmehr, eds., *Ethnic Los Angeles* (New York: Russell Sage Foundation, 1996); also, for cities like Houston and Miami, see Roberto Suro, *Strangers Among Us: How Latino Immigration Is Transforming America* (New York: Knopf, 1998). See, too, for an overview of the nation, Sanford Ungar, *Fresh Blood: The New American Immigrants* (Urbana: University of Illinois Press, 1998).

57. Kwong, *Forbidden Workers*.

58. Waldinger, *Still the Promised City?*, esp. pp. 140–147.

59. David M. Grant, Melvin L. Oliver, and Angela D. James, "African Americans: Social and Economic Bifurcation," in Waldinger and Bozorgmehr, *Ethnic Los Angeles*, pp. 379–411, esp. pp. 388–389; on the number of manufacturing jobs held by African Americans, see Waldinger, *Still the Promised City?*, p. 14.

60. Ibid., Waldinger, p. 30.

61. Pyong Gap Min, *Caught in the Middle: Korean Communities in New York and Los Angeles* (Berkeley: University of California Press, 1996), esp. pp. 119–127.

62. Suro, *Strangers Among Us*, p. 14; for the census numbers, see *Rural Migration News* 4, no. 4 (October 1998): 1–2.

63. Joel Perlmann and Roger Waldinger, "Are the Children of Today's Immigrants Making it?" *Public Interest* (summer 1998): 73–96, esp. 81.

64. Ibid., p. 79.

65. Jill Quadagno, *The Color of Welfare* (New York: Oxford University Press, 1995), especially chapter 3.

66. Thomas Edsall, "Barr Rejects Racial Views of Groups He Visited," *Washington Post*, December 12, 1998, p. A4.

67. Ibid.

68. Ellis Cose, *Color Blind: Seeing Beyond Race in a Race Obsessed World* (New York: Harper Collins, 1997).

PART THREE

WHERE DO WE GO FROM HERE?

8

Compare and Contrast: Great Britain, Israel, India, and the United States

"Whatever the requests of the minorities be, if they are not absolutely fantastic then that request should be met to the maximum extent; because if there is a fear, real or imagined it is better in the larger interests . . . to assuage that fear and to look at it from the point of view of minority psychology."

—*Constitutional Assembly of India*, May 26, 1949[1]

ANCESTRAL ROOTS

I thought I was home. Driving through the English countryside the signs posted names that read like a New England roadmap. Gloucester, Worcester, Windsor, Hebron: I saw these words every day, yet rarely made the conscious connection between the Old World and the new, between the British Isles and New London or New Britain, Connecticut.

First appearances suggested I was anyplace but home. In the posh London section of Kensington harmony reigned despite a breathtaking display of Balzac's human comedy. Everyday pedestrians included leather-jacketed "punk rockers" weighted down by their earrings and spoke bracelets, well-dressed executives in bowler hats, many Caribbean/English couples, and an abundance of Muslim women. Most covered themselves in traditional clothing, but right in front of an Iranian bank, one woman wore a dark plastic face mask that resembled the headgear worn by a "rec" room poker dealer. Attached to the protruding peak was a mask that covered both nose and cheeks. To an opinionated outsider the silk scarves seemed sensible, the switch to plastic a glaring accommodation to a world fueled by oil and its by-products.

Driving to Brixton, the heart of London's Caribbean community, the neighborhoods changed but nothing as dramatic as the distance between Harlem and Park Avenue, Watts and Beverly Hills. Brixton seemed like a solid working-class district until you read the local newspapers. Then, just as with the signs marked Windsor, you could be in any of America's major cities. To the surprise of no one who lived in London, the delightful differences of Kensington's streets masked hair-trigger animosities highlighted by this headline in the July 31, 1998, number of *The Caribbean Times:* "Will the Force Ever Be with Us?"[2]

The force was the British "bobbies" and this was the painfully hard question posed to Brixton's "coloured" residents: "Should black people join the police force?" Official statistics showed that of 28,000 officers in London, only 850 boasted "black or Asian" ancestry. That translated into 3 percent of the police force; despite vigorous recruitment efforts, in 1997 officials "managed to persuade just 62 non-whites out of 1200 new recruits to join up."[3]

Lee Jasper, head of England's National Black Caucus, told readers, "Our message is simple: Do not do it. Why should we urge our young people to enter an institution where they will be destroyed by their experience?" Jasper argued that for all the talk of change, the bobbie on the beat did just that to the "black" residents of London. Over time Caribbean officers either internalized the "racism" of their colleagues or the abuse of their own kind. Either way, the London police force "offers the most hostile working environment for black people in the whole of London, which is why I say, no, no, and no again to recruitment."[4]

Readers disagreed. In a section devoted to the opinions of local residents, most said that blacks ought to join the force. Ronadi, a shop supervisor, argued, "If there are more black people in the police then the police's views will become less racist and our community will feel less intimidated." Oona King, a member of the local government, told her constituents, "Despite the entirely valid fears that black people have, it is important for them to join the police. But the onus is on the police to seriously take on the racists in their ranks and to set in place a strategy to re-educate existing officers."[5]

Whatever their vote on the police force, "everybody" agreed that Britain had a problem with its "coloured" population. In London, Edinburgh, and Cardiff the word *colored* covered Indians and West Indians, Pakistanis, and (depending on the informant) Arabs. English people utterly monopolized the word white, Chinese residents were "chinkies," and, as the Times told it, whites used "Paki" in the same way an American racist used "nigger."

An August 13, 1998, story discussed the successful lawsuit of Gurpreet Singh Mundy, a Pakistani chauffeur who sued the owner of a firm famous for designing clothes worn by Diana, Princess of Wales. Allegedly, a company executive told Gurpreet to use a van "parked outside the Paki shop" and the chauffeur not only sued his employer, he reached a healthy out-of-court settlement for "racial discrimination."[6]

Sensitivities reached such a pitch that "mums" in Manchester angrily made this demand of school principals: Get rid of the "Golliwogs." This is a toy with a hundred-year history in white English life. The doll typically has huge white eyes on a dark black face, with a mountainous head of electrified hair. It makes America's "Buckwheat" look normal. When school officials refused to remove the doll, parents removed their kids from the Raynor Independent School. To Sue Duffy the Golliwog symbolized "black oppression" and "I am not having my child brought up in a racist environment."[7]

Britain does resemble the United States. The surprising thing is that, using the racial situation in the United States as a negative role model, Britain dramatically changed its immigration laws in the same year, 1965, that the United States reversed its "evil" national origins legislation. However, instead of opening its doors to the world, Britain slammed them shut on the "coloured" members of its Commonwealth. The new sign said "whites only," and if his government colleagues berated the deliberately outspoken Enoch Powell in public, they nevertheless produced policies that echoed the fears of this proudly British, Conservative member of Parliament.

As Powell put it to anyone who would listen: "All about me I hear it, as you do. In your town, in mine, in Wolverhampton, in Smethwick, in Birmingham, people see with their own eyes what they dread, the transformation during their own lifetime or, if they are already old, during their children's, of towns, cities and areas that they know into alien territory."[8]

As in Washington in 1924, the "locust" (see chapter 1) had arrived, and the British meant to kill the bug before it ruined their sense of homogeneity. Today the 1999 results are in and it is clear that, both morally and practically, the British failed. They closed the doors and still got animosities every bit as serious as our own.

What happened? What can we learn from the British experience?

ROYAL HYPOCRITES

Shortly before he resigned in 1955, Prime Minister Winston Churchill received a memo from the chief whip of the Commonwealth Affairs Committee. The confidential communication asked a pointed question: "Why should mainly loyal and hard-working Jamaicans be discriminated against when ten times that quantity of disloyal Southern Irish [some of them Sein Feiners] come and go as they please?"[9]

The question had a simple answer: Jamaicans were black, Irish were white. Incredibly, a civilization that colonized the world permitted few members of the Empire to visit, much less to live in the United Kingdom. As late as 1939 fewer than 7,000 "coloured" people lived in the British Isles. That number equaled a small fraction of 1 percent of the population. Indeed, shortly before Churchill received that memo in 1955, fully half of the English people had—this late in their colonial history—never met a black person.[10]

The idea was to live off the British Empire, not absorb its consequences. To avoid competition for Lancashire looms, colonists brusquely chopped off the thumbs of entire communities of Indian weavers, but never invited the incapacitated subjects to live in the mother country.[11]

Problems developed after World War II. On the one hand, England needed a workforce to rebuild the nation and manufacture its future. Colonies like Jamaica or Barbados offered a plentiful pool of labor, but to keep as many blacks as possible at bay, England eagerly and earnestly recruited white people from throughout Europe. Poles, in the United Kingdom to escape Hitler, remained in England after the war and, when they expressed concern about their relatives, England happily admitted more than 30,000 Poles in the late 1940s. Italians followed in the Polish wake, accompanied by Latvians, Lithuanians, and Estonians once imprisoned in German "displaced persons" camps. Code-named "Westward Ho!" British recruiters combed the camps for anyone white enough to pass muster.[12]

Despite these recruitment efforts, many West Indians nevertheless imitated the roughly 700,000 Irish already living in Great Britain. The Irish came and went as they pleased, yet the British Nationality Act of 1948 argued that Jamaicans and their kind also owned "free" access to the motherland. In a deliberate and well-advertised effort to retain what was left of the British Empire (after all, almost 50 percent of British overseas trade occurred within the Empire/Commonwealth),[13] government officials idealized a symbolic sense of community. As if in a loving family, all British possessions belonged to the Commonwealth. Thus, all "Citizens of the United Kingdom and the Colonies" theoretically enjoyed equal access to England because preserving the right of free entry cemented one of the few remaining links to the once mighty British Empire.[14]

Theory dangerously collided with reality in June of 1948. Sailing on a British troopship, the SS *Windrush*, no fewer than 400 Jamaicans arrived to take advantage of opportunities never available at home. For more than 200 years British colonists forced Jamaicans to produce what they never consumed and consume what they never produced. Postwar Jamaica therefore offered few opportunities for an ambitious person. In an effort to reverse the flow of funds, Jamaicans hoped to find in Britain what they could never find at home: money for self-sustaining economic development.[15]

Officials instantly recognized their predicament. Offer free access and people took you at your word. As Americans openly discriminated against Greeks, Italians, Chinese, and Jamaicans (in 1952), British officials said one thing and did another. In public ministers said that all Commonwealth citizens were created equal. In private both Labor and Conservative govern-ments used tactics as nasty as those of the characters in a Dickens novel.

In Africa people crossed borders with a British Travel Certificate, con-firming that the holder was a British subject. When Africans realized they now had access to the motherland British officials reacted by "laundering" the documents. If the person was black, officials omitted any reference to British citizenship. Then, when the African arrived in a port city like Cardiff, he could be returned as an alien even though port officials "knew perfectly well" that they had just deported one of their own.[16]

All over the Commonwealth officials in London applied the screws to colonial governments. Thus, instead of discriminating at the point of entry, colonial governors used a variety of tactics to stop immigration at its source. In the Indian subcontinent officials only accepted passport applications from whites. In the West Indies "governors were asked to tamper with shipping lists and schedules to place workers at the back of the queue; to cordon off ports to prevent *passport holding* stowaways from boarding ships and to delay the issue of passports to migrants" (emphasis added).[17]

Nothing worked. When the United States closed its doors to the West Indies in 1952 (see chapter 1), the pressure on Britain seemed greater than ever. In reality, even in 1955 no more than 37,400 people migrated to Britain from "the tropical Empire/Commonwealth."[18] However, the potential both-ered successive British governments to such an extent that they commis-sioned studies aimed at documenting the corrosive effects of tropical migration. From housing to employment, officials looked for something that would arouse public opinion to the supposed threat at hand. No evidence appeared, and even a stab at blaming West Indians for prostitution offered no hope. Instead, the government discovered but never published this find-ing: A British pimp was far more likely to come from Malta than the West Indies.[19]

In private officials resolved to do something drastic, even make laws that put an end to Commonwealth migration. Still, well into the 1950s no gov-ernment had the nerve to openly endorse racism. Each looked for an inge-nious way to whitewash the facts, and each contended with a variety of dramatically conflicting interests. For example, while officials in London wanted to stop migration, officials in the colonies reminded their distant colleagues that "ill judged policy decisions" could easily produce a final rup-ture between Britain "and her black colonies." For the Colonial Office the only policy that made sense was one of "caution, tact, restraint and a policy of doing nothing."[20]

While the government searched for a prejudice-free way to discriminate, Nigerian Wole Soyinka, later a Nobel Prize winner in literature, searched—in the mid 1950s—for an apartment in Leeds. He found a likely prospect but, given the tenor of English life, Soyinka decided to call first. After he

told the landlord, "I am African," she responded with "How dark? . . . are
you dark? Or very light?" Both angered and amused, Soyinka first tried "like
plain or milk chocolate?" and he then artfully invented a new color: "West
African sepia." The landlord got the point. And so did he. As in the United
States, no blacks allowed.[21]

By 1958 everyday prejudice helped create two new English hobbies: "nigger hunting" and "nigger baiting."[22] Riots lasting ten days (August 23 to
September 2, 1958) erupted in Nottingham and the Notting Hill section of
London. Described by the press as "hooliganism," the government first saw
the riots as public pressure that meshed with its own unstated desire for
immigration restriction. But, not wanting to base public policy on the will
of "hooligans," ministers delayed legislative action because of public perceptions—and because the contradictions of Commonwealth once again made
an appearance.[23]

Pressure on West Indian and South Asian governments to keep their people at home produced a decided unwillingness to take responsibility for obviously unpopular actions. As islanders migrated in search of work, leaders
like Michael Manley (in Jamaica) and Eric Williams (in Trinidad) responded
to pressure by consistently producing some of their own. For example, using
a threat that moved U.S. as well as British leaders, Eric Williams privately
told Prime Minister Harold Macmillan that England had three likely alternatives in the Caribbean. The mother country could maintain open doors,
provide the economic aid that would compensate for immigration restrictions, or face the possibility of "a social revolution and a Castro like situation" in British waters.[24]

Britain first chose to engage in a prolonged debate about restrictions. One
result of legislative delay included the largest influx of "coloured" immigrants
in English history. From India and Jamaica, Nigeria and Pakistan, Commonwealth citizens flocked to London and Cardiff in a huge effort to "beat
the ban." Thus, in June of 1960, the "coloured" population totaled approximately 250,000, one in two hundred of Great Britain's people. By June of
1962, the "coloured" population reached half a million. "It had taken three
hundred years for the Asian and black population to reach ten thousand, a
further fifteen years to reach a quarter of a million, and only two more years
to achieve half a million."[25]

A variety of factors account for Britain's willingness to finally embrace
immigration restrictions. These include everything from economic problems
to the massive yet largely unanticipated influx of beat-the-banners; from
serious political pressure at the local level to the sense of "White Supremacy"
that, like the Queen, remained a British constant.[26]

Ultimately Parliament adopted a measure "that was a triumph of invention
inspired by prejudice."[27] The legislation never mentioned color. Instead it
established three categories of an indefinite number of labor vouchers. Category A included "applications by employers in this country" who had a

specific job for a specific Commonwealth citizen. Category B included immigrants who, lacking a job, nevertheless possessed desired skills, such as nurses, teachers, and doctors. Category C included "all others." No one country could receive more than a quarter of the changing number of Category C vouchers, and in all instances veterans received a special preference.[28]

The 1962 legislation also included this precedent-setting stipulation. The vouchers applied only to the Commonwealth and its governments. If you were born in the United Kingdom (e.g., you were Irish) or you held a passport issued by the British government, you were 100 percent English, that is, you "belonged" to the United Kingdom. Meanwhile, those in the Caribbean and the rest of the Commonwealth now enjoyed a form of unincorporated citizenship. If vouchers existed, Jamaicans and Indians could come, but since the whole purpose of Category C was to exclude the "coloured," the number of vouchers was at first limited. When even that didn't work, in September of 1964 the British government stopped issuing Category C, that is, "coloured" vouchers.[29] That effectively closed Britain's doors as tightly as those of the United States in 1924; not satisfied with this effort, the Labor government of Harold Wilson introduced, in 1965, the legislation that struggled to make Britain a "zero immigration" nation.[30]

Ironies abound. In contemplating restrictions, ministers used the United States as a negative role model; no one wanted "new Harlems."[31] Meanwhile, in the same months that the United States laudably struggled to break free of prejudices whose deepest roots lay in England, Parliament—under a Labor Party that once fought restrictions—reaffirmed those same prejudices. It instantly erased *all* Category C vouchers. In an effort to stop the family pyramiding that had profoundly bothered the U.S. Congress in 1924, the British Parliament in 1965 cited its "review of the present practice of admitting freely children aged 16 and under 18 who are coming to join one or both parents." In practice these children were "young immigrant workers" masquerading as members of their own and the British family. Effective immediately the adolescents would stay home, although Parliament did agree to look at "hardship" applications.[32]

Like the law passed by Congress in 1965, the British legislation also set the tone for the following decades. Britain first sealed itself off from the Commonwealth and then, in 1971, refined its restrictive legislation by replacing the terms *alien* and *British subject* with "the essentially race-defined categories of 'patrial' and 'non-patrial.' "[33] Patrials, subject to no restrictions, included anyone born or naturalized in the United Kingdom or anyone with a parent or grandparent born in the United Kingdom. Since England contained less than 10,000 "coloured" people in 1939, this new distinction followed in the crafty footsteps of its 1965 predecessor. Once again no one mentioned color; Parliament simply created the objective categories that have consistently imposed even tighter restrictions on only "coloured" people. Thus, when too many husbands joined wives living in the United Kingdom, Parliament offered this change in 1980. It only allowed the husbands of "patrials" to join their spouses. Since the vast majority of Commonwealth women are not patrial, Great Britain managed to seal yet another tiny crack in doors that, like those at London police stations in 1998, are clearly marked "whites only."[34]

RECONSIDERED ROOTS

This overview of British policy suggests four "pointers" for the United States. The first is to refrain from unexamined endorsements of our ancestral roots. Thus, "an Irishman might be described as a lazy, ragged, dirty Celt when he landed in New York, but if his children settled in California they might well be praised as part of the vanguard of the energetic Anglo-Saxon people poised for the plunge into Asia."[35]

In creating U.S. culture, the first Americans managed to establish a culture that still energetically applauds our British roots while too often forgetting that England is also the deepest source of the black/white dichotomy that poisons American life. For all their attempts to turn us into a nation of victims and victimizers, multicultural activists are nevertheless on the mark when they argue for a thoroughly revised judgment of our English heritage in particular and our European roots in general.

The second "lesson" is well-deserved praise for presidents Kennedy and Johnson. Documents at both their libraries indicate that idealism was a principal motive behind their efforts to transform U.S. immigration laws in 1965. When a journalist like Peter Brimelow argues, in *Alien Nation*, that "the American nation has always had a specific ethnic core and the core has been white,"[36] he is advocating immigration restrictions that, as Robert Kennedy rightly indicated, "contradict our basic national philosophy and basic values."

We opened our doors in the same year the English slammed them shut. Thus, to reject the English example is to once again champion the common sense that produced the Declaration of Independence.

A third point is this: Thirty-three years of arguably the tightest restrictions in Europe did little to improve "race" relations in Great Britain. Both our societies confront two basic choices. We can attack color prejudices at their foundation stone, that is, the false concept of race. Or we can endlessly whittle away at beliefs that still dichotomize the English-speaking world into whites and the "coloured" after effects of five hundred years of colonialism.

A final point is the unintended consequences of immigration policies. In 1960–1961 British ministers failed to foresee the burst of immigration that followed their announcement of possible restrictions. In 1965, U.S. policymakers remained blind to the consequences of the changes they advocated. Too often (e.g., as with refugees), changes in policy are discussed in the backrooms of Congress and not on the front pages of the nation's newspapers. By definition, we will never avoid all unintended consequences. But, in widely and openly debating policy, we can at least achieve a consensus that makes it easier to work though the surprisingly unexpected consequences of our policies. For example, the profound impact of the Cuba lobby in Washington and the wealthy Cuban "refugees" who, after thirty-five years in Puerto Rico, are now among the staunchest advocates of making the island the next "shining star" in the American flag.

ISRAEL AND THE LAW OF RETURN

It's a huge difference. In the United States the foreign-born population today totals more than 9 percent of the American people; our highest percentage of foreign born equaled roughly 14 percent of the nation in 1910. In Israel the latest figure (for 1996) is 39 percent of the population foreign born, and that number is itself a significant "improvement." In 1980 the foreign born totaled 44 percent, and in 1960 fully 63 percent of all Israelis possessed birth certificates from other countries.[37]

Like the United States, Israel is a nation of immigrants; but instead of leaving for a New World, an *oleh* (an immigrant) to Israel participates in a "return" loaded with religious and cultural symbolism. In Biblical times religious law required that Jewish people "go up" to Jerusalem four times a year. As a forceful way to unite past and present, even secular Israelis now discuss immigration in relation to the number of "aliyahs." The word denotes a culturally applauded "going up," and the numbers refer to the different waves of immigration that created what is today Israel. For example, in Israeli eyes the initial "aliyah" dated from 1882 to 1903; and the latest includes the roughly 700,000 Russian immigrants to Israel since 1989.[38]

Incidentally, if a Jewish person leaves Israel for, say the United States, he or she is a *yored*, a word that denotes a significant "going down."

In another sharp contrast to the United States Israel created a Ministry of Immigrant Absorption. This central government organization assumes responsibility (some would say too much responsibility) for the economic, occupational, social, and cultural integration of immigrants during their *first three years* in Israel. For example, in a manner that might startle Amerasian refugees to the United States, Israel provides an "absorption basket." This includes rent for the first twelve months, assistance with housing expenses, living expenses while the person is learning to speak Hebrew, the cost of the children's education, and the purchase of basic furnishings—everything from a bed and mattress to plates and silverware.[39]

As much as 20 percent of the first year's allotment is "dispensed at the airport"; however surprising to American observers, this level of government involvement is actually *less* than in the past. Over fifty years Israel has tried to learn from its mistakes and especially from government efforts to transform one million African and Asian Jewish immigrants who arrived in the 1950s. Ironically, people who desperately desired to "go up" remain, after half a century in Israel, concentrated at the geographical and prestige periphery of Israeli political, economic, and cultural life.[40]

A New Nation

The Law of Return represents a significant spiritual commitment. Under this legislation (passed on July 5, 1950) "every Jew" has the right to come to Israel as an immigrant. Unless the person endangers the public health or the nation's security, he or she cannot be refused the right to immigrate to Israel. Understandably Israeli leaders hope that those who return have skills that help the nation; yet, as long as the person is proven to be Jewish, the skilled and unskilled are both welcomed as members of the nation of Israel.

In 1950 this permanent spiritual commitment received firm support for its own sake and for the sake of Israel's national security and military power. Prime Minister David Ben-Gurion lectured his colleagues, "We might have captured the West Bank, the Golan, the entire Galilee, but those conquests would not have reinforced our security as much as immigration. Doubling and tripling the number of immigrants gives us more and more strength." For example, immigrants in the periphery produced a human barrier to Arab armies as they simultaneously settled "conquered territories." As settlement represented the "real conquest," Israeli leaders combed the world for newcomers.[41]

Bribes opened doors. In fact, given Israel's desire and the all-pervasiveness of anti-Semitism, gifts and secret bank accounts often seemed the only way to produce a welcome level of cooperation. In Bulgaria "every person who left" had a price on his or her head. The Hungarians demanded $80 a body, or $2 million for 25,000 people. In Morocco Israeli officials opened Swiss bank accounts for Arab cabinet ministers, while in Yemen the Sultans preferred cash. Sometimes, as in Switzerland, Egyptian Jews received permission to land because Swissair pressured politically neutral officials to look at the company's bottom line. After all, the Egyptian Jews flew from Cairo to Switzerland and then on to Israel.[42]

Immigrants came so quickly that, if the United States tried a similar effort, it would need to admit no fewer than 30 million immigrants a year to equal the efforts of Israel. In 1948 the Jewish population totaled 717,000; five years later the new nation contained as many newcomers (724,000 from 1948 to 1953) as original settlers. Housing, feeding, educating, and "absorbing" the immigrants became such a gigantic task that officials later called the process "a mad operation, at a mad time." Realistically officials wanted to reduce the number of immigrants, but like the United States with its belief in human equality, Israeli leaders felt hemmed in by the Law of Return and partisan politics. Nobody sought a reputation as the person who recommended keeping Jewish people from "going up" to Jerusalem.[43]

Most of the immigrants came from North Africa and Asia. Only 2 percent boasted a higher education. Overwhelmingly these Jewish immigrants lacked skills, literacy, and any resources. Because "they arrived destitute," they depended on the central government for everything from health care to food, from education to their place of residence in the Promised Land.[44]

Ben-Gurion and his colleagues had a plan. Since they needed to create a nation, "the main goal of the development program was population dispersion and prevention of over concentration in the major cities in Israel." Where the United States dispersed Indochinese immigrants to avoid overloading the welcoming capacity of the American people, the Israelis scattered the African and Asian immigrants as a means to national security and social development. For example, the new nation needed profitable farms in the periphery and, throughout the rest of the country, "development towns" that would advantageously balance the distribution of industrial and other economic opportunities.[45]

Like public housing in the United States and Great Britain, the development towns boasted the architectural distinction of a bag of toy building blocks. However, given the extraordinarily high level of immigration, prefabricated homes nevertheless marked a significant achievement for policymakers. For 1 million children, women, and men, they meant a huge advance over the tent cities that sheltered—housed is too positive a word—the earliest postwar immigrants.

Many of the "development towns" maintained such a striking degree of ethnic homogeneity that roughly 90 percent of the inhabitants traced their origins to Africa or Asia. In apartments measuring 36 to 50 square meters these Jews lived and learned (e.g., Hebrew) in facilities bought and maintained by an extremely generous welfare state. Jobs supposedly followed the construction of homes, and while they waited for industrialization to take off, citizens received a "resocialization" that is still rippling through Israel and its people.[46]

The Hebrew words are *mizug galuyot*, denoting a mixing of the exiles that was every bit as forceful as the Americanization movement led by the "charge!" approach of Theodore Roosevelt.[47] On the one hand, some national leaders self-identified first as Israelis and second as Jewish. They refused to permit the cultivation of a "hyphenated Israeli" and "they discarded ancient Jewish cultures . . . without compunction, for they believed they were making the only relevant history; the State of Israel meant more to them than the preservation of Jewish culture abroad."[48] In its extreme form, this arrogance moved representatives of the Zionist State to declare that "in Israel there is no need for sidelocks." Immigrants from Yemen, Tripoli, or Morocco saw their sidelocks forcibly removed, or horrified parents watched their children cut off their sidelocks with a piece of broken glass or other sharp objects, in an effort to conform.[49]

Arrogance had a partner: A belief in the "primitive" nature of the African and Asian immigrants. Powerful Ashkenazi (or European) Jews often described *all* the newcomers as *Avak Adam*, "human debris." While Bulgarian and Hungarian Jews also got lumped into this polluted pool, special beliefs guided the attitude of Israeli leaders toward the North African Jews. As one writer noted as early as April 1949, "A serious and threatening question is posed by the immigration from North Africa . . . here is a people whose primitiveness reaches the highest peak. Their educational level borders on absolute ignorance. Still more serious is their inability to absorb anything intellectual. How many obstacles have to be overcome in educating the Africans."[50]

Discussing those obstacles, sociologist S. N. Eisenstadt classified immigrants (in 1952) in relation to "attitudes of crucial importance," that is, "the extent to which the immigrant expects and is prepared to change his behavior and undertake the performance of new roles."[51] In this analysis success meant a person who willingly surrendered their culture of origin and adapted to the beliefs, values, and aspirations of the European founders of Israel and Zionism. Eurocentrism ruled in the Mid-East in the mid-1950s, but even those immigrants who tried to conform often encountered severe disappointments. Arrogance and prejudice never permitted their entrance into mainstream society, and as if underlining their irrelevance, the state dispersed African and Asian immigrants into the periphery of the nation where, despite bold plans, economic development proceeded at a much slower pace than in the more industrialized and industrializing sections of the society.

The result, as of 1999, is a dual system of social stratification. Jewish citizens trace their roots to Europe and America or to Africa and Asia. Numerically each group contains roughly the same number of people, but "European-Americans hold the higher positions in all dimensions of social stratification, including income, occupation, political power, standard of living and place of residence."[52]

In explaining this disparity Israeli critics cite the arrogance and prejudices of the Ashkenazi majority. But, as a lesson for the Jewish immigrants to come, critics also note that Israel's first leaders "*ignored culture as an adaptive mechanism*" (emphasis added). From what clothes to wear to their place of residence, the state gave people no say in their own lives; it simultaneously asked them to relinquish ties to their cultures of origin and, in the process, forgot that "part of a culture's adaptiveness lies in its conservatism." It acts "as a filter accepting, rejecting, and modifying new influences in a way that necessary change can be incorporated into the ongoing cultural system."[53]

In general the first African and Asian immigrants lost any chance to adapt in a conservative fashion. European radicals ruled the absorption process of Israel's first million immigrants. However, in an effort that deservedly captured the attention of the world's media, Israel first rescued and then welcomed many thousands of Ethiopian Jews in the 1980s. For critics the new immigrants posed a simple question: Had the nation learned anything from the mistakes that still divided one-half of Israel's Jewish population from the other.

OPERATION MOSES

They go by many names. In Ethiopia neighbors called them *Falashas*; this pejorative label denoted a group of strangers, people with no land or meaningful ties to their place of birth. As a positive form of identification the people called themselves *Beta Israel*. This phrase underscored a startling claim; these Ethiopians believed they represented the only surviving Jewish people on earth. As if imprisoned for centuries, the Beta Israel lingered in the Diaspora, waiting for their return to the Holy Land.[54]

Today the appropriate form of self-identification is "the Jews of Ethiopia." More than 30,000 African people saw their dreams come true yet, thanks to the best of intentions, that dream often turned into a nightmare of Biblical proportions.

Start with the Israelis. Reception centers contained more volunteers than they could absorb. In a marvelous manifestation of their identification with other Jews, Israelis gladly worked twelve- and fourteen-hour days to welcome their African brethren. Bypassing skin color, level of economic development and geography, many Israelis immediately trumped all other labels with a cultural generalization—Jewish—that enabled them to use an ethnicity in the most exemplary manner: One human being happily embraced another.[55]

Problems arose for a variety of controllable and uncontrollable reasons. The Ethiopian exodus took a huge physical and spiritual toll on the immigrants; some call it the Ethiopians' "own unique Holocaust."[56] After crossing the Sudan, thousands of men, women, and children arrived exhausted and even quite ill; in many instances, the Ethiopians also experienced severe guilt because they had survived the journey that, in the Sudan, killed husbands, wives, fathers, mothers, sons, and daughters.

Another uncontrollable variable revolved around the Ethiopians' lack of contact with the Talmudic tradition. Secreted in a remote part of a remote land, the "last Jews" developed customs that instantly clashed with those prevailing in the Promised Land. For example, ritual baths assume serious significance in historical and contemporary Israeli life. But the Ethiopian Jews linked bathhouses to Christianity. They did not want to be baptized.[57]

Cultural conflict is inevitable in any immigrant experience. Alternatives for the welcoming society include allowing the original culture to be an adaptive mechanism, or, as in Israel, the agents of absorption can often disregard even the most sacred customs. Thus, Ethiopians found themselves forced to wear skullcaps, and the women, whose customs mandated isolation during menstruation, received instruction that "we don't do things like that here." The bleeding women then hid themselves in closets—for days at a time—rather than risk "polluting" the rest of the family.

The harshest blow of all came from the rabbis who questioned the authenticity of the Ethiopians' claim to being Jewish. Orthodox rabbis demanded that the newcomers convert—with a ritual washing, no less!—and the reaction of the Ethiopians ranged from astonishment to anger. As one young man noted, "They can't tell me that I'm not Jewish and that I have to convert . . . what are we if not Jews? It is especially difficult for older people like my parents who all their lives dreamed of coming to Israel and now are suddenly forced to convert."[58]

Forced conversion underlines the tension between religious and secular Jewish people. In 1999 orthodox rabbis assume part of the authority given in 1950 to atheistic, Eastern European Jewish socialists. The Ethiopians got caught in the middle of a cultural war, yet, as if repeating the worst examples of their religious and secular kin, absorption authorities even replaced—for nonreligious reasons—the immigrants' first and last names.

Ethiopian Jews lack surnames. Men are called by their own names and the names of their fathers. Women, on the other hand, never change names when they marry but instead use their father's names. Thus, family members have different names. Permissible at home, this was impossible in their new home. Israeli absorption authorities needed one name for their records so they decided—without asking the Ethiopians—that all families would adopt the name of the grandfather on the father's side. When Ethiopian first names proved hard to pronounce in Hebrew, absorption officials acted like the uniformed welcoming agents at New York's Ellis Island. Newcomers got new names. Whether using their first or last appellation, many Ethiopians no longer knew who they were. In the extreme they rejected their new names with such vehemence that they refused to use them, even when they needed to do so for required medical services.[59]

Critics argue that the naming process reflects a deeper problem with the process of Ethiopian absorption. As in the 1950s, officials demanded that newcomers relinquish their culture of origin and surrender self and family to the authorities. One social worker who focused on children noted that "because the parents didn't know Hebrew, the authorities labored under the false impression that they could be disregarded."[60] Thus, if a child missed school, officials consulted with anyone but the parents. In a terrible dilemma for all concerned, "the Jewish Agency made a policy decision to encourage all Ethiopian children in the 11–18 age group to enter boarding schools." This guaranteed everything from a loss of parental authority to cultural clashes that shook the home, but "the alternative was to be faced with a generation of immigrants unable to cope with the demands of twentieth century society."[61]

In the United States the adjustment problems of the Hmong come immediately to mind. Whatever the personal and cultural pain experienced by the Ethiopian children and their parents, these children received at least some compensation in the form of a decent education, linked to a minimum of one year's language training in a noteworthy Israeli institution, the *ulpan*. At government expense the ulpan (or Hebrew-language school)[62] provides all students with the language skills required for "success" in Israeli society. It is a marked contrast to the free-for-all atmosphere that prevails in the United States; despite the cultural "training" that also occurs in the ulpans, these language schools freely offer a skill that helps immigrants with everything from social mobility to the perils of everyday social interaction.

As in the 1950s, balance is once again the watchword—but not for many absorption officials. As one noted, "Severing them (the children) led to a total break with traditional values . . . they seemed to be in a state of moral limbo. They no longer relied on their elders, the family, the customs and taboos regulating relations with the opposite sex. . . . There are no easy shortcuts in the process of internalizing a new culture and values system."[63]

But there are alternatives. Using original culture as an adaptive mechanism, it is possible to thoroughly respect the past. Thinking in terms of a banquet rather than a melting pot, it is even possible to support immigrants who use their culture as a more or less long bridge to a world continuously created by the oldest and newest inhabitants of Israel or, for that matter, the United States.

SEVEN HUNDRED THOUSAND RUSSIANS

Even in 1950 immigrants to Israel mixed spiritual and practical motives in the most diverse fashion[64]; yet so many shared a passionate desire to create a new society that political and religious idealism rightly stand out in any overview of the period and its people.

The "FSUs" (people from the former Soviet Union) are different. While more than 700,000 Soviet Jews have appeared at Israel's doorstep since 1990, their overall motivation appears to be anything but idealistic. As Zvi Gitelman notes, the flood of FSUs "consists mostly of people who have been fleeing what they see as a dangerous or hopeless situation in their native land. Since Israel is the only nation that will take them in, that is where they go."[65]

While they also go to the United States, the limited number of refugees permitted by Washington means that Israel—especially given the idealism of the Law of Return—bears the human brunt of the heralded fall of the "evil empire." Even in 1998 more than 50,000 FSUs continued to arrive, with consequences that include widespread resentment and a new, Russian-centered political party.

FSUs represent an incredible brain drain for Russia. Fully 35 percent of the new immigrants to Israel boast academic and scientific credentials. As only 9 percent of Israelis possess this level of education, in five short years the nation witnessed a doubling of its engineering corps and a 70 percent increase in the number of physicians. The 22,000 Soviet teachers "make up almost a quarter of the number of Israeli teachers."[66]

This "panic migration"[67] occurred in a period when absorption officials reassessed the melting-pot approach to newcomers. If only because of perceived problems with the Ethiopian experience, officials now foster a "free market" approach to immigration. Called "direct absorption" by the ministry, the idea is to link the government's substantial language and financial support to the wishes and desires of the new immigrants. Thus, at the very time that Israel is receiving its first—huge—influx of relatively uncommitted immigrants, absorption officials are pursuing policies that, in sharp contrast to the treatment of African and Asian Jews, allow the Russians "to decide for themselves, based on their own personal considerations, how they wish to be absorbed."[68]

One response is to vote with their feet. Given the option of nicer apartments in the peripheral regions that still house so many of the African and Asian immigrants, Russians are either renting the new homes—the "fence sitters"—or moving into crowded quarters in the metropolitan areas. In any event, despite government attempts to disperse the immigrants, the right to choose means that, as of 1998, "the immigration wave has hardly changed the (residential) pattern at all ... the immigrants of the 1990's prefer the metropolitan areas, just as immigrants to Western countries do."[69]

The FSUs also share many of the prejudices harbored by their Ashkenazi predecessors. Gitelman, for example, recently asked a series of "thermometer" questions. What groups made Russian blood pressure rise? The answer, right after Arabs, was Moroccan and Ethiopian Jews. Suggested explanations include cultural beliefs brought to Israel (i.e., "a general wariness of dark people"), which are exacerbated by "prejudices quickly picked up from (some) Ashkenazi Jews."[70]

Meanwhile the introduction of so many well-educated Russians produces, as with African Americans in the United States, fears of even further displacement by African Jews, by Asian Jews and by the roughly 100,000 "noncitizen" Arabs who also live and work at the very margins of Israeli society.[71] Called in Israel the "hewers of wood and the drawers of water," the Arabs add another element to an already explosive cultural, religious, economic, and political situation. Indeed, because their lack of economic development far surpasses that of the African Jews, Arabs with skills and a higher education risk losing their few positions to Russians as their less-educated kin live lives that some Israeli academics compare to those of the Chicanos toiling in the American Southwest.[72]

Israel's immigration future is as uncertain as the status of the Arabs. Hopefully the marvelous sense of humanity displayed toward the Ethiopians will eventually prevail. No matter what happens, this is the greatest paradox of all: In a period when the nation of Israel desperately needs a sense of unity, its absorption officials endorse a "free market" approach to the integration of more than 600,000 relatively uncommitted Jewish people.

Israel may or may not help itself. But it can help the United States.

THE UNITED STATES AND ISRAEL

One constant of the Israeli experience is the central role of the central government. Even when a so-called free market approach takes hold, the Israeli government still provides *substantial* social, financial, and educational support for at least three years. Moreover, with the ulpans (the language training schools) the government tries to ensure a degree of integration that allows all citizens a chance to communicate more effectively and easily across cultural lines. The goal is not "Hebrew Only"; instead, the ulpans underline a sensible, instrumental objective: Freely give immigrants a chance to learn the language, and you increase the likelihood of "success" for all concerned.

Especially with the Ethiopians the Israeli government assumed a degree of cultural and economic control that often undermined any sense of personal responsibility. As in the United States, the central government often failed to coordinate its "dispersal" of immigrants with the local governments. Thus, some Israeli municipalities understandably complained that they paid for commitments made without their consent by myopic government bureaucrats.[73]

However valid, specific complaints need not obscure the substantial benefits of well-designed and implemented federal immigration programs. The ulpans alone suggest the need for a revaluation of U.S. policies. To those who champion a free market approach, history recommends an analysis of the Cuban American experience. The one success story cited by "everyone," the Cubans received far more central government support than virtually any other immigrant group in U.S. history.

A second "lesson" of the Israeli experience is the failure of the melting-pot approach to newcomers. As in the United States, the Israelis tried to fit African and Asian immigrants into an existing Ashkenazi (European) mold. Prejudice and a policy of geographical dispersal assured that the newcomers could never fit in, but even without the arrogance of the Ashkenazi majority, to forget that culture is an adaptive mechanism is to exacerbate always serious problems of cultural and personal adaptation to a new society. For example, by serving as cultural and language interpreters, immigrant children often help their parents adapt to the host society. However understandable the desire to educate the Ethiopian youngsters, an "absorption plan" that provided education while living at home offered conservative assistance to the Ethiopians and to the Israeli social workers, who (in 1997) still stressed the crucial need for "indigenous paraprofessionals." Train somebody—train anybody!—because, especially without the children, the cultural gap between migrant and host is wider than ever.[74]

Societies accepting as many immigrants as Israel and the United States need to reconsider the melting-pot approach. In a world focused on globalization the melting pot is at best an anachronism. Moreover, by arrogantly questioning the validity of the immigrant's culture, pressure to assimilate often generates more support for cultures of origin than would otherwise exist. In *Asian Panethnicity*, Yen Le Espiritu stresses that keeping serious social distance from U.S. culture is closely linked to the ethnic categories imposed by the host society. Joining forces as Asian, Korean, Japanese, Chinese, Indian, and Filipino Americans accentuates the very cultural origins the melting-pot ideology seeks to dissolve.[75]

Finally, if a metaphor like the banquet ultimately guided our integration efforts, fitting into a mold would never be a national goal. Instead we would seek a society that is continuously recreated by all who come to the banquet table. We would, in short, eagerly "perpetuate the paradox that our American cultural tradition lies in the future."[76]

A final point is the laudable role of idealism in both Israeli and U.S. society. Whether it is the Law of Return or the belief that all people are created equal, both societies root their immigration policies in ideals that touch the society's soul. Assuming a continued adherence to political, ethnic, and religious ideals it is impossible for either society to close the doors to newcomers with dramatic cultural differences. However, in the United States, commitment to the ideals of equality has also generated, besides controversy about immigration, a heated and often ugly debate about "preferential policies" for those who lack an inherited head start.[77]

It's a battle about affirmative action, a battle that began in India long before it ever reached U.S. shores.

DEBATES OF A DEVELOPED NATION

The United States is roughly four centuries old; it is a developed nation. India owns a history that stretches over several millenia; it is an underdeveloped nation. By the standards of ordinary logic the distinction is "ridiculous," yet it nevertheless serves as a staple of everyday discourse. Western political analysts spot a society rooted in tradition, religion, and a relative lack of technology and immediately a nation as remarkable as India receives this instant exhortation: It's "backward" enough to be developed by the World Bank and partially ruled by the International Monetary Fund.[78]

For a different perspective on human development consider the 1949 debates of the Constituent Assembly of India. Delegates writing a constitution wrestled with a immense problem; how could they create a nation with any sense of unity when roughly 65 million Indians—then 15 percent of the total population—still experienced the cruelest forms of ideological and institutional prejudice as a perverse birthright.

One group of these Untouchables—the Parayans of Kerala—gave English a memorable word: *pariah*.[79] Synonyms include *derelict* and *social outcast*, but none of these words gives a real sense of life as an Untouchable in mid-twentieth-century India.

Brahmins considered groups like the Parayans so contemptible that they bathed again if the mere shadow of an Untouchable crossed their path. In one southern region, tradition demanded that Untouchables walk while carrying a mental tape ruler. Why? Because at all times they needed to keep 33 feet away from the lowest castes, 66 feet from the "middling" castes, and a full 99 feet from Brahmins. By some rules Untouchables needed to shout a warning before they entered a street, thereby giving "decent" people a chance to run for cover. As a way of assuring no change, Untouchables never entered a classroom. Instead, they sat outside in the dirt near the door or, if the school contained a verandah, Untouchables might receive permission to learn what they could from squatting on the porch.[80]

Delegates to the Constituent Assembly discussed the Untouchables (also called the Scheduled Castes and Tribes) as "minority groups." All agreed they deserved special consideration because the fledgling Indian nation could easily crash land unless political leaders devised a way "to bind the minorities with *hoops of steel* to the cause of national integration and progress" (emphasis added).[81]

Simple self-interest demanded that minorities receive special consideration. But the developmental significance—the human beauty—of the Indian debates is the moral basis of political action. Pandit Thakur Das Bhargava called special provisions for Untouchables the "soul of the Constitution." Write specific preferences into our basic body of law because they "place upon the entire nation the obligation of seeing that all the disabilities and difficulties of the Depressed Classes (i.e., the Untouchables) are removed . . . in a sense this is an oath taken by the House, an oath to see that within the coming years we will provide all the facilities which can be provided by the nation *for expiating our past sins. . . .* If any community continues in backwardness, socially, culturally or educationally, then it should not be a question of ten years or fifteen years but up to the time they are brought up to normal standards, facilities should be given and continued for them"[82] (emphasis added).

Shri Jawaharal Nehru, soon to be prime minister, echoed these sentiments when he also spoke in favor of constitutional support for minorities. Indeed, five years before the U.S. Supreme Court banned racial segregation in public schools, Nehru stressed that "this historic turn in our destiny" meant that the nation "discarded something that was evil" in exchange "for a path which we consider fundamentally good for every part of the nation."[83]

That path included provisions that made—and make—India unique. Articles 330 and 332 of the Indian Constitution reserve as many as 22.5 percent of legislative seats for the Untouchables in both the national and the state assemblies. All Indians can vote in these legislative elections but, as an idealistic commitment to actually represent all social groups, the Scheduled Castes and Tribes are guaranteed a democratically meaningful number of representatives (85 out of 545 members of Parliament) in the debates, compromises, and maneuvering that decide public policies.[84]

Nehru understood the controversial nature of these provisions. But, convinced of their morality, Nehru also spotlighted his and his colleague's potential immorality. "Because in our heart of hearts we *were not sure about ourselves* nor about our own people when all these reservations were removed," the constitutional delegates decided to create a sense of national unity by legally perpetuating the divisions that so dreadfully divided the Indian people (emphasis added).[85]

One after another, Indian delegates consciously grasped a simple fact: They were trying to square the circle. In an ideal world creating national unity via mandated preferences made no democratic sense; thus, Article 15 of the Indian Constitution announced, "The State shall not discriminate against any citizen on grounds only of religion, race, caste, sex, place of birth or any of them."

But, given thousands of years of God-endorsed prejudice, the real world ridiculed democratic ideals. Delegates knew that more than 15 percent of the Indian people continued to encounter the basest forms of religious, educational, and economic discrimination. The Indian constitution legalized a thoroughly comprehensive form of affirmative action nearly twenty years before the United States adopted a much weaker initiative.

Theoretically the preferences lasted ten years. After a decade of special treatment, the Scheduled Castes and Tribes would erase their historical handicaps and a united India could then march into a future where all groups began life at the same starting point.

However, as soon as the process of change began, one Brahmin angrily disputed the new constitution. In a 1951 case with striking similarities to the Bakke challenge of U.S. law in 1978,[86] a young Indian argued that a special admissions provision for Scheduled Castes and Tribes into a professional school violated the Indian constitution's guarantee of no discrimination based on religion, race, caste, and gender. When the Indian Supreme Court sided with the Brahmin, the quick result was the very first amendment to India's constitution: "Nothing prevented the State from making any special provision for the advancement of any socially and educationally backward classes of citizens."

As this of course included the Untouchables, the Indian Supreme Court soon indicated that reservations (i.e., quotas) represented a conspicuous exception to equal treatment under law for all citizens. With this mandated anomaly one analyst writes that "the Indian Constitution and the Court forestalled the tension that prevails in other Constitutions [e.g., the United States]."[87] De jure, that is certainly the case. De facto, this argument assumes a consensus about the need for "expiating past sins"; however, since many Indians still thought of the Untouchables as both contemptible and inherently inferior, enforcing the law guaranteed a cultural clash inextricably linked to the most significant religious issues.

Equally important, the court never got specific. It let politicians translate constitutional provisions into actual numbers (i.e., the specific quotas and ratios) and, in a related dilemma that plagues India to this day, the court never defined the composition of the "other backward classes."[88] The Indian constitution is clear: The state could do whatever was necessary to help the socially and educationally backward classes. But who, *exactly*, deserved the label backward? The Court passed the buck to politicians who, to their everlasting credit, actually tried to specify the millions of Indians who deserved "protective discrimination."[89]

Political leaders provided that protection because, as the 1953 *Report of the Backward Classes Commission* reveals, "We have to recognize the painful fact that all the efforts of the social reformers belonging to the upper classes [e.g., then Prime Minister Nehru] have been more than counter-balanced by the blind-selfishness and traditional self justification of the upper classes . . . there is an unsympathetic uniformity in the attitude of the majority of the upper classes, from which the backward classes have to suffer."[90]

Turning to the actual criteria they would use, officials experienced no problems with Scheduled Castes and Tribes: "It is *untouchability* for Scheduled Castes and *the segregated life, the habitat in jungles or hills and their unique culture that are* the main criteria for Scheduled tribes" (emphasis in original).[91] The trouble came when legislators turned to the Other Backward Classes who, in their extreme form, represented the "really dumb masses."[92] Characteristics suggested included women, residents of rural areas, landless laborers, the illiterate, a lack of self-esteem rooted in caste divisions, and those having a belief in magic, superstition, and fate.[93]

With so many variables involved, Indian leaders never reached a consensus about the definition of "other backward classes." For example, while many agreed that women received grossly unequal treatment, women never formed a separate community. If you included women, a huge mass "of the country's millions could be counted as coming within the category of backward." While this was overkill for some legislators, it nevertheless represented a logical extension of the word *backward*—especially if you also included illiterate, landless, and living in a rural area.[94]

In the published report one dissent followed another, and added to the arguments about specifics was a fear as widespread in mid-1950s India as it is in contemporary America. Speaking for the Ministry of Home Affairs, G. P. Pant noted that "the tone and temper" of the commission's report highlighted "the dangers of separatism inherent in this kind of approach." He fully agreed that "it cannot be denied that the caste system is the greatest hindrance in the way of our progress towards an egalitarian society." History hung over India like a mass of thunderclouds waiting to unleash their fiery bolts of lighting. But, "the recognition of the specified castes as backward may serve to maintain and even perpetuate the existing distinctions on the basis of caste."[95]

Remember that this questioning never included the Scheduled Castes and Tribes. For them, Indian leaders had already agreed "to use the thorn to remove a thorn"; in essence, only caste-based preferences for untouchability and segregated living could compensate for the consequences of upper-caste prejudices. But, when it came to another 28 percent of the population, the consensus collapsed. Legislators submitted their report, and Congress quietly let it die a slow death. In fact, it was not until 1961 that the central government issued this suggestion: "While the State Governments have the decision to choose their own criteria for defining backwardness, in the view of the government of India it would be better to apply economic tests than to go by castes."[96]

Meanwhile, the reservations for Scheduled Castes and Tribes included the following aspects of public life. Besides the seats reserved in the legislatures, at both the federal and state level roughly 22 percent of all public employment posts theoretically went to the specified minorities. Originally this only included recruitment, but over time even promotions came under the quota system. This mandate also produced Supreme Court challenges that Indian justices resolved by stipulating "that total reservations shall be less than 50% of the positions filled."[97]

In reality the number of minorities who actually worked in public employment rarely approached (or approaches) the number of reserved positions. Moreover, as you moved up the ladder of power and prestige, the Scheduled Castes and Tribes approached (at the end of the twentieth century) 5 percent of the senior positions in government and less than 1 percent of the Army's Officer Corps.[98]

As in the United States, the fact of any reservations or preferences raised the ugly specter of inefficiency. Indians therefore battled about a supposed absence of merit as they simultaneously called minorities "sons-in-law" of the government and "government Brahmins." Minorities countered by arguing that if Brahmins or sons-in-law got jobs because of caste or family preferences, where was the merit in the old system? It preferred only its own kind. The critics of quotas could sweep their praise of meritocracy into the same dustbins that held the evil caste system and its degrading consequences.

Because those consequences lasted much longer than many people expected, the Indian government established a myriad of additional programs for the Scheduled Castes and Tribes. These include an "elaborate and complex" reservation of seats in professional colleges, after high scholarships, and grants-in-aid to dormitories and reservation of dormitory facilities. Additional programs provide relaxation of the maximum age at which a person enters civil service and an institutionalized system of remedial work offering extra assistance "at all stages of school education." Finally, in order to increase the number of minorities who pass civil service exams, the government created schools that "extensively" train minority candidates for their upcoming employment tests.

In the United States such programs generate great concern; figures as prominent as Supreme Court Justice Clarence Thomas worry about the deleterious effect of preferences on self-image. Allegedly recipients will assume that preferences exist only because European Americans are inherently superior to African Americans.[99]

Indians see things so differently that "there is a clamor for inclusion in the backward class list"[100]; recent counts include no less than 3,753 backward castes, with no end in sight for the number of subdivisions that can or will be made. Presumably Indians understand that to embrace the notion of inferiority is to accept the "wisdom" of the caste system that, despite fifty years of preferences, still confines Untouchables to the dirtiest and most humiliating jobs in Indian life.[101]

Whatever the variables involved, the clamor for reservations finally produced another commission (established in 1978) to definitively determine the nature and extent of the "other backward classes." Criticized for everything from methodology to membership (five of the six committee members came from the "backward" classes), the Mandal Commission nevertheless recommended a 29 percent increase in the number of reserved positions. That meant backward quotas exceeding 50 percent of not only government positions but also all public projects—at the federal and state level and in all nationalized banks.[102]

One after another, Indian governments forgot the Mandal Commission's report. Then, in 1990, Prime Minister V. P. Singh announced that his government meant to implement the presumably dead Mandal recommendations—at once, and without consulting the Parliament or engaging in a public debate.

Students instantly protested. They threw stones, deflated bus tires, and blocked roads. Following Gandhi, others engaged in hunger strikes, and when even that tactic produced no change, Rajiv Goswani did something drastic: He burned himself alive on September 19, 1990. Goswani lived, but a month after his self-immolation no less than 150 other students had followed his suicidal example. "Reservation mania," for and against, gripped the nation. The Singh government quickly lost power; after a challenge to the Supreme Court, Indian justices once again tried to make legal sense of a caste order that, after many millennia of existence, resolutely resisted both the spirit and the letter of Indian law.[103]

Justices accepted the legitimacy of reserving positions on the basis of caste. Indeed, as Americans moved to eliminate their weak (in comparison to India) preferences based on race, Indian jurists reaffirmed their idealistic commitment to the principles established by the 1949 Constituent Assembly. Given the depth and extent of caste discrimination, a majority of the justices still saw no way—fifty years into the process!—to avoid using a caste thorn to remove a caste thorn.[104]

But, in yet another similarity to the U.S. process, justices conditioned their support for the Mandal recommendations on the ineligibility for preferences of the "creamy layer" of Indian life. The accurate criticism relates to (for example) the children of those who benefited from the initial preferences established in the 1950. Indian justices argued that to extend reservations into the second or third generation was unconscionable, unnecessary, and self-limiting. Fifty years of history with reservations showed "that of the 130 million members of the Scheduled Castes and Tribes, sixteen percent are urban dwellers *taking the lion's share of reservations*" (emphasis added).[105] To extend reservations to those most in need, justices eliminated the preferences for those already assisted by the state. Arguably, the creamy layer might also experience the "rage of a privileged class," but in comparison to the millions of Untouchables still afraid of their own shadow, the creamy layer no longer needed protective discrimination.

As of early 1999 Indian society is still torn apart by its efforts to "atone" for the past. One totally unintended benefit for the United States is the immigration of an elite that perceives diminished opportunities at home. However, despite emigration, public turmoil, and the insidious use of caste as a politician's means to power, India's remarkable commitment to profound social change offers the United States a number of valuable lessons and suggestions.

The first lesson is the reason for reservations and other mandated opportunities. Call it affirmative action. Call it protective discrimination. Either way these programs *"represent action in the face of what history hands us"* (emphasis added).[106] They exist to counteract the evils of brick walls like racism, and they are predicated on the realization that, whether in India or the United States, millions of people experience systems of oppression far beyond the disadvantages associated with "only" class barriers to mobility.[107] Well-intentioned people can honestly argue about the extent and basis of any particular program (e.g., what's a backward person?), yet it is to be hoped that those same people never mistake the forest for the trees. Protective discrimination is action in the face of a cultural inheritance that includes impermeable barriers to a wide variety of educational, political, and employment opportunities.

A second lesson is the inherent limitation of even the most pervasive form of protective discrimination. Reserving seats in the legislature or in public employment certainly provides democratic representation for formerly excluded sectors of the population. But, fifty years into the process, India still cannot find candidates to take advantage of the many openings that exist. Thus, whether challenging a caste system in India or in the United States, protective discrimination is still only one tool to help people overcome the huge head starts obtained by those who inherited educational, religious, racial, and social privileges. Change will occur more quickly if we seriously challenge inherited cultural beliefs and practices; in the meantime, it is pernicious to focus only on merit when in rural India or the "colonias" of New Mexico and Arizona, men and women live lives very similar to those of their parents and grandparents.

A third lesson is the extraordinary difficulty of defining who requires assistance. For example, as with the creamy layer in India, I too would exclude privileged Latinos, African Americans, and Asians from any affirmative action programs. I would also limit the assistance now offered to privileged Africans and West Indians. But, there must be agreement about the meaning of privilege and, even more important, a national consensus about those actually in need of protective discrimination. The turmoil that engulfed India in the early 1990s was inextricably linked to the lack of consensus about who was and who was not a member of the "backward" classes.

A final point is the use of caste (or ethnicity) to eliminate the consequences of caste privileges and discrimination. The Indian experience suggests that this is both unavoidable and just. As Justice John Paul Stevens noted, "There is no moral or constitutional equivalence between a policy that is designed to perpetuate a caste system and one that seeks to eradicate racial subordination."[108]

If our goal is to define ourselves by what unites us, programs like affirmative action perpetuate what divides us. The dilemma is real, and it must be resolved if we are ever to achieve a sense of unity as admirable as that displayed by the Israelis when they first welcomed their Ethiopian kin.

NOTES

1. *Constituent Assembly of India*, vol. 8, *Report of the Advisory Committee on Minorities*, May 26, 1949, p. 10, as downloaded from ⟨www.alfa.nic.in/debates/vol8⟩.

2. *Caribbean Times*, July 31, 1998, pp. 2–3.

3. Ibid., p. 3.

4. Ibid.

5. Ibid.

6. *The London Times*, August 13, 1998, p. 6.

7. *The Voice: Britain's Best Black Newspaper*, August, 10, 1998, p. 3. I bought this newspaper in Wales; it is, however, sold throughout the United Kingdom. On the Golliwogs and Britain, see Jan Nederveen Pieterse, *White on Black* (New Haven: Yale University Press, 1995), especially chapter 10.

8. Enoch Powell, in Onyekachi Wambu, *Empire Windrush* (London: Victor

Gollancz, 1998), p. 139; see, too, Douglas Schoen, *Enoch Powell and the Powellites* (New York: St. Martins, 1977).

9. B. Carter, C. Harris, and S. Joshi, "The 1951–55 Conservative Government and the Racialization of Black Migration," *Immigrants and Minorities* 4, no. 3 (1987): 343; the article appears on pp. 335–347.

10. Ian R. G. Spencer, *British Immigration Policy Since 1939* (London: Routledge, 1997), p. 3. Many of my other sources were derived from this lucid overview of British immigration policy.

11. Shashi Thadoor, *India: From Midnight to the Millennium* (New York: Harper, 1997), p. 14.

12. Colin Holmes, *John Bull's Island: Immigration and British Society, 1871–1971* (London: Houndsmill, 1987), esp. chapter 5, pp. 211–214.

13. Spencer, *British Immigration Policy*, p. 66.

14. N. Deakin, "The British Nationality Act of 1948," *Race* 11, no. 1 (1969): 77–83; the quote is from p. 82.

15. For example, Ronald Fernandez, *Cruising the Caribbean* (Monroe, ME: Common Courage Press, 1994).

16. Carter et al. "Racialization of Black Migration," p. 336.

17. Spencer, *British Immigration Policy*, pp. 23–31; Carter et al., "Racialization of Black Migration," p. 336.

18. Spencer, *British Immigration Policy*, p. 90; see, too, Paul B. Rich, *Race and Empire in British Politics* (Cambridge: Cambridge University Press, 1986); also Zig Layton-Henry, "Britain: The Would-be Zero Immigration Country," in Wayne Cornelius, Philip L. Martin, and James F. Hollifield, *Controlling Immigration: A Global Perspective* (Stanford, CA: Stanford University Press, 1994), pp. 273–300.

19. Spencer, *British Immigration Policy*, p. 111.

20. For example, F. Cass, "Coping with Colonial Migration, the Cold War and Colonial Policy," *Immigrants and Minorities* 6, no. 3 (1987): 305–334, esp. p. 316.

21. Wole Soyinka, telephone conversation, in Wambu, *Empire Windrush*, pp. 105–106.

22. Holmes, *John Bull's Island*, p. 259.

23. Nicholas Deakin, "The Politics of the Commonwealth Immigration Bill," *Political Quarterly* 39 (1968): 24–45, esp. pp. 40–41.

24. Spencer, *British Immigration Policy*, esp. pp. 120–121.

25. Ibid., pp. 118–119; see, too, Bob Carter, Marci Green, and Rick Halpern, "Immigration Policy and the Racialization of Migrant Labor: The Construction of National Identities in the USA and Britain," *Ethnic and Racial Studies* 19, no. 1 (January 1996): 135–157.

26. Holmes, *John Bull's Island*, pp. 260–263.

27. Spencer, *British Immigration Policy*, p. 116.

28. See the report, *Immigration from the Commonwealth*, presented to Parliament by the Prime Minister by Command of Her Majesty, August 1965, London, p. 3.

29. Ibid., p. 6.

30. See Layton-Henry, "Zero-Immigration Country."

31. See Carter et al., "Racialization of Black Migration," p. 341.

32. *Immigration from the Commonwealth*, p. 7.

33. Spencer, *British Immigration Policy*, p. 143.

34. See Heather Booth, *The Migration Process in Britain and West Germany* (London: Avebury, 1992), p. 21.

35. Reginald Horsman, *Race and Manifest Destiny: The Origins of American Racial Anglo-Saxonism* (Cambridge: Harvard University Press, 1981), p. 4.

36. Peter Brimelow, *Alien Nation* (New York: Random House, 1995).

37. Israeli Population Statistics, see ⟨www.us-israel.org/jsource/SocietyandCulture/demographics.html⟩.

38. Jewish Student Online Research Center, <www.us-israel.org/jsource>

39. See Ministry of Immigrant Absorption, ⟨www.israel.mfa.gov.ilgov/immabsor.html⟩; This is from p. 2 of a document entitled "Ministry of Immigrant Absorption."

40. For example, Jeff Halper, "The Absorption of Ethiopian Immigrants: A Return to the Fifties," in Michael Ashkenazi and Alex Weingrod, eds., *Ethiopian Jews and Israel* (New Brunswick: Transaction Books, 1987), pp. 112–139.

41. Tom Segev, *1949: The First Israelis* (New York: Macmillan, 1996), p. 97; see, too, Gabriel Lipshitz, *Country on the Move: Migration to and Within Israel, 1948–1995* (Dordrecht: Kluwer Academic Publishers, 1998), esp. pp. 43–44.

42. Segev, 1949, pp. 100–108.

43. For the number of immigrants, see Lipshitz, *Country on the Move*, p. 43; for the mad comment and the unwillingness to say no to immigrants, see Segev, *1949*, pp. 105, 139.

44. Lipshitz, *Country on the Move*, p. 42–44; also Halper, "Absorption of Ethiopian Immigrants."

45. Ibid., Lipshitz, pp. 44–46.

46. See, for example, S. N. Eisenstadt, "The Process of Absorption of New Immigrants in Israel," Human Relations 5 (1952): 223–245; also S. N. Eisenstadt, *The Absorption of Immigrants* (London: Routledge, 1954).

47. Halper, "Absorption of Ethiopian Immigrants," p. 114.

48. Segev, *1949*, p. 118.

49. Ibid., pp. 225, 227.

50. Quoted in Halper, "Absorption of Ethiopian Immigrants," p. 116; the writer was Arye Gelblum; the article appeared in the respected paper *Ha'aretz* on April 22, 1949.

51. Eisenstadt, "Process of Absorption," p. 226.

52. Ismael Abu Said and Richard E. Isralowitz, "Social Cohesion and Intergroup Conflict in the Negev: Jewish and Arab Attitudes toward the Absorption of Russian Immigrants," in Ivan Light and Richard E. Isralowitz, eds., *Immigrant Entrepreneurs and Immigrant Absorption in the United States and Israel* (Aldershot: Ashgate, 1997), p. 96.

53. Halper, "Absorption of Ethiopian Immigrants," pp. 119–120.

54. Nurit Banai, *Ethiopian Absorption: The Hidden Challenge* (Israel: United Jewish Appeal, 1988), p. 1; also Ruben Schindler and David Ribner, *The Trauma of Transition: The Psycho-Social Cost of Ethiopian Immigration to Israel* (Aldershot: Avebury, 1997), pp. 1–3.

55. Banai, *Ethiopian Absorption*, especially chapter 1.

56. Schindler and Ribner, *Trauma of Transition*, p. 3.

57. Ibid., p. 37.

58. Halper, "Absorption of Ethiopian Immigrants," pp. 126–131; also Banai, *Ethiopian Absorption*, p. 102.

59. Banai, *Ethiopian Absorption*, p. 15.

60. Ibid., p. 66.

61. Schindler and Ribner, *Trauma of Transition*, p. 54.

62. See, for example, Tamar Horowitz, "The Absorption of Immigrants in Israel in the 1990's: Policy Parameters and Impacts." Professor Horowitz is a Senior Lecturer at Ben-Gurion University. The web address for this article is ⟨www.newschool.edu/icmec/horowpap.htm⟩.

63. Banai, *Ethiopian Absorption*, p. 89.

64. Segev, *1949*, pp. 113–115.

65. Zvi Gitelman, *Immigration and Identity: The Resettlement of Soviet Immigrants on Israeli Politics and Society* (Ann Arbor: The Susan and David Wilstein Institute of Jewish Policy Studies, 1995), p. 14.

66. Ibid., p. 12.

67. Ibid., p. 13; also Lipshitz, *Country on the Move*, especially chapters 4 and 5.

68. Lipshitz, *Country on the Move*, p. 89.

69. Ibid., p. 98.

70. Gitelman, *Immigration and Identity*, pp. 39–40.

71. Abu Said and Isralowitz, "Social Cohesion."

72. Moshe Semyonov and Noah Lewin-Epstein, *Hewers of Wood and Drawers of Water: Noncitizen Arabs in the Israeli Labor Market* (Ithaca: ILR Press, 1987), pp. 14–15.

73. Banai, *Ethiopian Absorption*, p. 36.

74. See Schindler and Ribner, *Trauma of Transition*, p. 87; the insight about the children is Brenda Harrison's.

75. Yen Le Espiritu, *Asian Panethnicity* (Philadelphia: Temple University Press, 1992), p. 10.

76. Randolph Bourne, "Transnational America," *War and the Intellectuals* (New York: Harper, 1964).

77. Thomas Sowell, *Preferential Policies: An International Perspective* (New York: William Morrow, 1992).

78. Robert Nisbet, *The Present Age* (New York: Harper and Row, 1988), p. 72.

79. Shashi Thadoor, *India: From Midnight to the Millennium* (New York: Harper, 1997), pp. 103–104.

80. Harold Isaacs, *India's Ex-Untouchables* (New York: John Day, 1964), pp. 27–28, 75.

81. *Constituent Assembly of India*, May 26, 1949, p. 10.

82. Ibid., pp. 8–9.

83. Ibid., pp. 11–12.

84. Thadoor, *India*, p. 107.

85. Ibid., p. 12.

86. See, for example, McGeorge Bundy, "The Issue Before the Court: Who Gets Ahead in America," *Atlantic Monthly*, November 1997.

87. Krishna K. Tummula, *Public Administration in India* (Singapore: Times Academic Press, 1994), p. 225.

88. Ibid.; see, too, Krishna Tummula, "Reservations In Indian Public Service,"

in Krishna Tummula, ed., *Equity in Public Employment Across Nations* (Lanham: University Press of America, 1989), pp. 49–77.

89. Gopal Singh and Hari Lal Sharma, *Reservation Politics in India* (New Delhi: Deep and Deep Publications, 1995), p. 10.

90. Government of India, *Report of the Backward Classes Commission*, vol. 1 (New Delhi: Government of India Press, 1956), pp. ii, iii; see, too, e.g., vol. 3, p. 58.

91. Ibid., vol. 3, p. 22.

92. Ibid., p. 41.

93. Government of India, *Report of the Backward Classes Commission*, vol. 1, pp. xiv–xv.

94. G. B. Pant, Ministry of Home Affairs, *Memorandum on the Report of the Backward Classes Commission* (New Delhi: Government of India Press, 1956), p. 2.

95. Ibid., p. 3.

96. Singh and Sharma, *Reservation Politics*, p. 31.

97. Tummula, *Public Administration*, p. 227.

98. Ibid., pp. 228–229; see, too, Anirudh Prasad, *Reservational Justice to Other Backward Classes* (New Delhi: Deep and Deep Publications, 1997), esp. pp. 268–271.

99. Charles Lawrence and Mari J. Matsuda, *We Won't Go Back: Making the Case for Affirmative Action* (Boston: Houghton Mifflin, 1997), p. 124.

100. Tummula, *Public Administration*, p. 248.

101. See, for example, Barry Bearak, "Caste, Hate and Murder Outlast Indian Reforms," *New York Times*, September 19, 1998, p. A3.

102. Tummula, *Public Administration*, pp. 236–237.

103. Singh and Sharma, *Reservation Politics*, pp. 65–77; also Tummula, *Public Administration*, pp. 237–243.

104. Ibid., Singh and Sharma, pp. 101–115; also Prasad, *Reservational Justice*, pp. 267–293.

105. Tummula, *Public Administration*, p. 247.

106. Lawrence and Matsuda, *We Won't Go Back*, p. 7.

107. See Stephen Steinberg, *Turning Back: The Retreat from Racial Justice in American Thought and Policy* (Boston: Beacon Books, 1995), p. 133.

108. Ellis Cose, *Color Blind* (New York: HarperCollins, 1997), p. 102.

9

The Twenty-first Century

LEZA

The myth is African, from the Kaonde of Zambia, a nation that contains significant remains of the earliest human beings. Leza, the tribe's supreme deity summoned a honey bird to his chambers. God gave the bird three calabashes, all tightly closed at each end. Secreted in two of the calabashes was a supply of seed. Flying off, the honey bird tried to remember the word of God: Give the first human beings the calabashes with seeds, but until Leza himself appears on earth, never touch the third calabash. That was God's work.

The honey bird refused to contain his curiosity. He opened the calabashes on the way to earth and, with a fury every bit as destructive as experienced by Pandora, out popped death, sickness, and all the other maladies that characterize human life.

Angry yet compassionate, God tried to help the honey bird "recapture" the harsh consequences of curiosity and disobedience. Nothing worked. Death was out of the box, "and so it was that people had to build huts and shelters for their protection."[1]

While huts and houses certainly help, the strongest protection devised by people is much harder to touch. It is culture, a set of beliefs, values, and practices that provide people with structures that offer a firm foundation for every facet of human life.[2]

People, and only people, create culture. It is a stupendous ability, always pregnant with the potential to give birth to any set of beliefs we please. But, however paradoxically, our cultural creations too often come back to haunt us. They "protect" us from life's mysteries by teaching hate, and in the process, cultures often open a cache of woes every bit as harmful as the calabash provided by Leza.

In Rwanda the Christian myth of Ham remains a "template" for social interaction and genocide. Brought to Rwanda by the Englishman John Speke, the myth argues "that the Africans who best resembled the tribes of Europe were inherently endowed with mastery." Tutsis ruled because, as anyone with eyes could see, they resembled the lords of the universe: European explorers and the settlers who followed in their wake.[3]

When the League of Nations turned Rwanda over to the Belgians, they used the myth of Ham to accord special privileges to the Tutsi minority. When a group of Hutu intellectuals laid a basis for independence in 1957, they published a tract that, instead of rejecting their cultural inheritance, embraced it. Thus, if Tutsis were invaders with roots in Europe, the new Rwandan state should be "by rights a nation of the Hutu majority," the only Rwandans who deserved to rule an African nation.[4]

As in Rwanda, U.S. culture also contains beliefs that provide divine sanction for the ugliest behavior. The militia-led white identity movement comes immediately to mind. No quick and easy solution to our cultural problems exists. Right now, like an out-of-control boomerang, U.S. culture haunts us as much as it protects us.

The one saving grace is that we are in charge. Only people make culture. If the task seems like a labor fit for Sisyphus, the difference is this: God condemned Sisyphus to failure. Nothing stops us. In fact, in a culture that so lovingly applauds self-help, only we deserve blame if we fail to get the rock over the hill created by a cultural inheritance filled with divisions as enduring as those in Rwanda.

OUR INHERITANCE

It was a page-one story. On December 29, 1998, the *New York Times* told readers that "A Racial Divide Widens on Network TV." White people watch the all-white *Friends*, black people watch the all-black *Steve Harvey Show*, and the "segregation" of programming is so intense that African-American shows are now increasingly bundled together on one night. Concerned executives worry that "by doing segregated blocks" the networks might widen the already large racial divide; however, unless black writers "broaden the appeal of their shows" (i.e., add more white characters), blacks get one night of the week, whites the rest.[5]

Rwandans divide on the basis of tribe. We do it on the basis of race. The irrelevance of "racial others" is so great that this *New York Times* story literally discusses Latinos and Asians in a *parenthesis*. They also "complain," but when placed beside the dichotomy that definitively divides the nation, the concerns of 29 million Latinos and roughly 10 million Asians are a demonstrable afterthought. As of December 29, 1998, Latinos and especially Asians remain Americans without a color.

Unless challenged at the level of everyday generalizations, culture endures, one generation after another, one century after another. We can continue to argue that America is colorblind as we simultaneously "segregate the blocks" of TV time. Or, we can agree to make society impossible until and unless we teach children the truth: The concept of race is scientific nonsense. Its enduring existence as a core cultural construct is no reason to tolerate—for even one more second—its dichotomous division of the American people.

TV can help. As it offers access to virtually every home in America, a president who wanted a place in U.S. history as important as Abraham Lincoln's could address the nation with a proclamation that instantly begins to emancipate us from the fiction of race. He or she could provide the evidence that begins, in every classroom in the nation, a debate about the concept of race.

Meanwhile, the rest of us could argue that seeing is believing. Make society impossible by taking every reasonable opportunity to challenge use of the words black and white. Call African Americans what they are—an ethnic group—and begin to use that label when all ethnic groups meet at the cultural banquet table.

This will indefinitely unsettle the nation, producing profound challenges to our deepest beliefs, our summary self-images, and our behavior in the countless situations now inextricably interconnected by the black/white dichotomy.

The reward is an America in which we *begin* to unite by first recognizing and then celebrating our joint and lifelong membership in the only race that actually exists, the human race. Along with Italians, Irish, Japanese, Mexicans, Cubans, Chinese, and Polish, African Americans would be an ethnic group with a specific set of social and historical experiences. Like any ethnicity, African Americans would be discussed in relation to their experiences, their cultural creations, and the public policies (e.g., affirmative action) those experiences or creations might require.

Under all circumstances all ethnic groups would recognize physical differences for what they are, diverse manifestations of our underlying and indissoluble unity. In this manner our children would inherit a world free from two of the biggest barriers to "changing colors": the concept of race and the dichotomy that divides us into blacks, whites, and those in parentheses.

Because race continually subsumes all other variables, eliminating it from our cultural vocabulary is the essential first step toward a comprehensive national consensus about ethnicity and immigration. Another task is to confront a cultural inheritance that still includes the "melting pot" as the approved or dominant disposition toward ethnic differences.

This metaphor implies the welcome addition of new ingredients to an existing mixture. However, as with the national origins legislation of 1924, some ethnic ingredients (i.e., Asians) were instantly discarded, others reduced to a "pinch" because they promised too much spice (e.g., Italians and Greeks) in the white American pot. In practice melting meant rapid assimilation; as Randolph Bourne emphasized, the metaphor looked backward, to a culture that already owned the best recipes for every facet of human life.[6]

The melting-pot metaphor also creates tremendous and unnecessary social, economic, and political conflicts. Whether in the United States or Israel (see chapter 8) those already in the pot disparage the newcomers who, unless they are masochists, refuse to embrace a culture that arrogantly assures them of their own inferiority, lack of development, or ignorance. One result—in both Israel and the United States—is the creation of ethnic communities that, instead of melting, adamantly proclaim the beauties of the old culture as they simultaneously resent the representatives of the new. Or, as with Chicanos confronting farmers like those discussed in chapter 2, the immigrants create a political ideology that justifies their militant opposition to the "Anglos."

As a way of affirming its own ideals, the United States unintentionally opened its doors to the world in 1965. This forever changed the ethnic composition of the United States; more than 20 million immigrants arrived, and at the rate of almost a million people a year, they are still coming. The result is that a metaphor already problematic in 1915 seems absurd in a nation that, just to make the new mix even more problematic, now welcomes 50,000 "diversity" immigrants (and their relatives to come) each and every year (see chapter 1).

Think, too, of the other differences between yesterday and today. By closing off immigration in 1924 we created one of our contemporary poles: people to whom ethnicity is irrelevant or insignificant. By reaffirming our most basic values in 1965 we created the other pole: more than 20 million newcomers and the endless chain of relatives who indefinitely sustain the new immigrant's culture of origin. Thus, while many millions of third-, fourth-, and fifth-generation Americans now affirm their *multiethnic* backgrounds, except for symbolic identifications, ethnicity means little in terms of everyday salience and summary self-image. Meanwhile, cities like Miami and Houston highlight their thriving ethnic communities, corporations prepare their "comers" to effectively interact across the cultures of the global economy, and universities sponsor both programs and courses that profoundly question the "Eurocentric" roots of U.S. culture.

If there was ever a time for what Randolph Bourne called the "effective integration" of the American people, this is it. The beauty of the banquet metaphor is that it promises that integration in ways that mesh with a variety of all-American values and beliefs.

Start with politics. To receive an engraved invitation to the cultural banquet, all participants would first agree to accept democracy, the Bill of Rights, and the U.S. Constitution as the indispensable basis for political and social life. This allegiance must be paramount.[7] While we can endlessly debate the meaning and significance of different cultures, it is impossible to do so without the public freedoms—speech, assembly, worship, press—that, for all our faults, are nevertheless an elemental and eminently laudable fact of U.S. life. From this perspective a respect for democratic politics is the sacrosanct *means* to discuss our disposition toward the cultures that now exist in the United States of America.

The political commitment is paramount. Then, using the banquet metaphor, we indefinitely resolve the traditional problem of the "one and the many"[8] cultures by selecting neither. In essence we collectively and enthusiastically agree to step up to a variety of unfamiliar "dishes" because the ethnic strands are here and we definitely need to decide "What shall we do with our America?"

In answer to that question we would act like pioneers who peacefully settle virgin tracts of land or like our distant and recent ancestors who came to the United States to build and create new lives. *We agree to live between past and future,*[9] because that is the only world that is there and because, instead of a problem, we appreciate our contemporary situation for what it is—an unprecedented opportunity for all Americans.

Start with a privilege. At the "best" U.S. universities students get a chance to study abroad (typically) in their junior years. Experiencing other cultures is perceived to be an essential part of any higher education because actually "touching" the lives of others often shapes mind and character in the most positive ways. Living elsewhere we are "forced" to be empathetic, to replace a selfish or ethnocentric perspective with the eyes and ears of others. We see what they think, we enlarge our own body of knowledge, and, as a final gift, direct experience with other cultures often produces a fresh, creative, and even profitable perspective on life in Peoria, Illinois, or Austin, Texas. One generation after another, students who receive the privilege of studying abroad report a "a significant leg up" in their personal and professional lives.

Is this the logic of those who resist the eager exploration of cultural differences: What's good for the best and brightest is not good for the rest of us? Let Harvard and Yale graduates experience other cultures, and we will regard their "broadening" experiences as an impressive part of their personal and professional resumes. But, let's make sure that we don't take advantage of the opportunities that, like real acres of diamonds, are readily available in our own backyards.

Empathetic exploration does not mean a suspension of judgment or, even worse, repudiating all standards by arguing that all cultures are equally good. How, after all, can all cultures be equally good if we have just repudiated all standards of judgment?[10]

Taking a seat at the banquet is based on a disposition, a willingness to learn about others on their own terms. It is empathy married to an "active engagement" in experiencing and respecting the cultural beliefs, values, and practices of others.[11] Thus, if I accept an invitation to the home of Shashi

Singh (see the preface), I could try to understand the meaning of multiple gods in her and her family's life. I need not become a Hindu, nor need I accept Shiva or Ganesh as essential or even incidental elements of my religious life. But, I could enlarge my own cultural vocabulary and also achieve a delightful sense of unity—with different kinds of Americans—by showing respect, interest and empathy for the cultural creations of others.

Remember, nobody said I had to accept the invitation to the Singh home. As at any banquet, I need not eat everything at the table, and I need not decide that ethnicity is an all-important aspect of my summary self-image. But the disposition to recognize and respect the other continually provides the mind and character benefits of "study abroad." And it is also, along with the abolition of race, a wonderful way to achieve a sense of national unity. Instead of informing newcomers that American culture is better than any other—you have to melt into the pot!—we endorse an active engagement that welcomes everyone. In addition, we make judgments not on the basis of culturally inherited prejudices, but on the basis of empathy, respect, first-hand information, interaction, and interest.[12]

Active engagement is a two-way street. By definition newcomers accept democracy and the Constitution, ideally because they perceive and cherish the rights and freedoms of this system of government. Beyond that, the banquet metaphor implies that newcomers will also show a willingness to learn about Americans on our own terms. Give us the same chance we give you, respect the right of someone to choose no ethnicity or many, and understand that despite the accepted recognition of group boundaries, the future must also contain the right and ability of people to cross cultural boundaries if they choose to do so. Intermarriage is a given, a welter of new multiethnic Americans the certain promise of the active engagement required by those who attend the banquet.

That is our future. It is an open road because active engagement in other cultures assures social change, as does any serious challenge to the concept of race and the metaphor of the melting pot. Thus, however paradoxically, our American cultural tradition lies in the social world we jointly create in the twenty-first century.[13]

In accepting this challenge, we need not have, nor could we have, an exact blueprint for the future. Given our cultural realities, that blueprint is being created from a wide variety of richly different sources, all fed by a political commitment to the free expression of ideas and beliefs. We will indeed live between past and future. Nevertheless, we can pledge allegiance to an ideal that, like the sky, provides a solid backdrop for our joint efforts.

An American is someone with a spiritual goal welded to the commitment of a pioneer. The commitment contains two promises, one to build, one to destroy. We promise to eliminate those parts of our cultural inheritance that, for no good reason, profoundly divide us. We agree to jointly recreate American culture by—when it comes to ethnicity—actively participating in the banquet that is a vital part of our *new* cultural inheritance.

The spiritual goal is a nationwide sense of community, founded in a bedrock allegiance to democracy, the U.S. Constitution, and a twenty-first-century reaffirmation of the Declaration of Independence.

All people are born equal, none deserve to inherit either poverty or a culture poisonously divided into whites, blacks, and 40 million others.

Class issues must be an essential part of this American work in progress.[14] From a moral point of view the poor have every right to be at the banquet. From a practical point of view, the global economy presents so many challenges and vulnerabilities that it offers a multitude of self-interested reasons for diverse groups to pool their efforts. Ideally, as exposed Americans debate, delineate, and legislate the cultural obligations of capital, rural and urban, new and old Americans peacefully reach the same revolutionary conclusion: There is only one race, the human race.

It is a labor fit, not for Sisyphus, but for women and men who thankfully accept an undeniable fact of social life: People and only people make culture. We are in charge. Especially when we pick up the ball and run with it.

POLICY ISSUES

One primary aim of this book is to help make society impossible, to challenge the beliefs that so profoundly divide us. However, the evidence amassed in the preceding chapters suggests overarching guidelines for immigration and other public policies. My "general direction" proposals focus on three issues: The role of the federal government, affirmative action, and undocumented labor migration.

Role of the Federal Government

The federal government is the undisputed axis around which immigration policies revolve. It could provide a strategy to guide the nation. Unfortunately, as with "diversity" immigrants, legal and undocumented labor migration, and the enormous, institutionalized increase in the number of refugees, (see chapters 1, 2, and 3), Washington too often responds to political pressures while leaving the states and localities to deal with the financial, educational, and "absorption" consequences of migration.

The plight of too many Amerasians[15] symbolizes our laissez faire approach to loudly proclaimed moral obligations. Washington's goal is to make adolescents exposed to severe prejudices—youngsters with few or no language and employment skills—self-sufficient in the shortest period of time. When self-sufficiency is not achieved, state and local governments are left holding the bag, while invited immigrants deal with the animosity understandably expressed by their "new neighbors."

Fight politics with more politics. Make presidents, senators, and congresspeople pay for "the death of common sense."[16] Do not invite people whom the federal government is not willing to financially, educationally, and culturally support. It is a horrible dilemma if the group is as exposed as Amer-asians, but experience suggests that the "solution" is at least as bad as the problem. At the very least Congress needs to examine closely the arguments made by members of the "refugee industry." As the evidence in both Israel and the United States argues, many former residents of the Soviet Union are fleeing, not for their lives, but for any port in a financial storm.

Equally important, before any additional changes to immigration policies occur, reconsider the proper role of the federal government in a variety of areas—personal adjustment, language skills, and employment, especially of African Americans in cities affected by immigration and the ethnic niches that immigration creates.

For all its mistakes, the central role of Israel's central government suggests a model for the United States. Israel argues that newcomers need to learn Hebrew to function effectively in Israeli society. The *ulpans* (the language training institutes) are heavily subsidized by the central government, and the state provides this mandated assistance for instrumental as much as idealistic reasons. How, even with skills, can newcomers contribute effectively if they lack the ability to communicate in Israel's principal language?

Our "free market" approach in the United States proposes that newcomers can learn for themselves. Often they do. But, like my grandmother, many immigrants also live here for seventy years with no ability to communicate in English and no desire to participate in the political or cultural process.

Besides ulpans, the federal government needs to significantly increase its degree of educational and employment training. In the best of all worlds this assistance would be linked to substantial planning and financial packages for states and localities seriously impacted by immigration and the ethnic niches that systematically deny opportunities to less-skilled African and other Americans. Working with the states and local governments should cut down significantly on the resentments generated. To those who suggest that this is not feasible or workable, my response is that they should analyze the Cuban experience.

Under Presidents Kennedy, Johnson, Nixon, Ford, and Carter, the federal government provided the same assistance suggested in the preceding para-graph. It worked. It's our biggest success story. Thus, one lesson suggested by the Cuban experience is to give groups with far less education and busi-ness experience, at least as much—if not substantially more—assistance from the federal government.

No one strategy will work. Each immigrant group is different, and the situation of African Americans in urban areas differs from that in rural areas. But, that is no excuse to disregard the central role of the central government, in classroom theory and in Cuban practice.

Affirmative Action

Like many other universities, ours reserves special facilities and staff for student athletes. These include nicely furnished, secluded study areas meant only for the players. Full-time personnel regularly monitor the players' classroom progress. Those personnel call faculty if a player is "in trouble." They provide assistance with the preparation of course work, assistance with the preparation of the complicated paperwork necessary for financial aid, and hot meals if players miss dinners scheduled for regular students. Finally, those personnel will also turn a blind eye and a deaf ear to academic credentials if the prospect can play ball.

Athletes receive these preferences *as a group*; it is a long-institutionalized form of what the Indians (see chapter 8) might call protective discrimination, yet this very affirmative action on behalf of athletes is somehow acceptable to many if not most Americans.

Significant institutionalized preferences also exist for a variety of other groups, among them veterans and university legacies. Despite their weaker academic credentials, Harvard, Yale, and Princeton regularly reserve roughly 10 percent of student slots for legacies. The figure at Notre Dame exceeds 20 percent, yet, as with athletes, it is uncommon to hear complaints that a rejected student lost his or her seat to a legacy whose parents possess a fat checkbook. It is also uncommon to hear legacy students discuss the sense of inferiority acquired as a result of their preferential admission to the university.[17]

These examples of long-institutionalized preferences for individuals as members of a group suggest that the debate about affirmative action often occurs in a mental and moral vacuum. The obvious contradiction (e.g., preferences for athletes but none for minorities) is ignored and so too the chasm between the supposed reliance on merit and the way the world actually works. In theory people get jobs because they have the requisite skills or credentials. In practice, who you know is often far more important than what you know. In my thirty years of university experience, institutions regularly spend enormous amounts of time supposedly searching for the best candidate when, in truth, they often know who will be hired before the search process actually begins. Minorities are included in the final pool as a way of "covering your behind."

Even when the search is "clean," a variety of subjective factors perpetually assume importance. A word often heard in university corridors is "fit"; does the job applicant's personality and style "fit" into the atmosphere desired by those making the faculty or administrative selection? If not, merit makes way for a bad fit, and the individual is rejected, along with his or her otherwise excellent qualifications.

My request is that we root any debate about the need for affirmative action in the world that is actually there. Among others, group preferences for athletes, legacies, and veterans are built into the fabric of U.S. life. *The issue is not whether preferences will exist but whom those preferences will favor and with what goals and values in mind, e.g., perpetuating institutionalized inequalities or reducing them.*

Equally important, the debate about merit not only discusses a world that has never existed, it ignores a more significant point: "There are plausible ways to distribute goods and opportunities other than relying on merit."[18] U.S. citizenship is presumably one of the greatest opportunities we can bestow. Yet this opportunity is awarded on a first come, first served basis. In 1997 roughly 300,000 people were legally admitted to the United States on the basis of *family preferences*. Diversity visas (especially for the Irish) underline another way that opportunities are distributed by relying not on merit, but on a preference for "old blood" immigrants.

Finally, we can never ignore the persistance of prejudice. For example, in January 1999 the Department of Agriculture announced settlement of a suit brought by thousands of African-American farmers. They had charged that the department discriminated against them by denying loans and other subsidies; farmers with the best evidence got the most money, but the fact of discrimination was not denied.[19]

As long as systematic discrimination exists, affirmative action is one tool that must be employed. Following the idealistic example set by India, any nation that seeks to represent its citizens must make room for those men, women, and children denied access because of prejudice or the institutionalized absence of educational and other opportunities. To those who eschew reasoning based on justice, consider simple self-interest. As does India, the United States also needs to place "hoops of steel" around groups that understandably feel little commitment to the nation and its worthy ideals.

Whatever we do, let us at least substitute honesty and the real world for hypocrisy and contradiction. Otherwise we bestow preferences on athletes, legacies, and immigrants as we deny them to African-American farmers who, throughout the 1990s, encountered institutionalized discrimination from the federal representatives of political and economic power.

Undocumented Migrants

Chapter 2 argues that four generations of powerful American political and economic leaders avidly desired Mexican and other undocumented migrants. These workers were and are pulled to the United States as much as they are pushed out of Mexico and the Caribbean. Equally important, after so many years the human networks act as an independent variable propelling migrants to come to the United States. Finally, as Senator Aiken of Vermont suggested to his colleagues in 1951, more undocumented migrants work outside agriculture than in it. From restaurants to meatpacking, undocumented labor is a fixture of American life.

In response U.S. policymakers produced what Douglas Massey correctly calls an "inept, self-contradictory and self-destructive policy." More border patrol agents moved more undocumented migrants to forever remain in the United States. From Los Angeles to Maine, the nation boasts "an underground economy" that has driven down wages for natives as well as immigrants. Meanwhile, the barring of immigrants from U.S. benefits spurred a massive move toward greater naturalization, with the likelihood of substantially increased migration from the relatives of those who were "forced" to naturalize.[20]

Massey offers a solution, as sensible for the Caribbean as it is for labor from Mexico and Central America. For example, because of the increased border patrols, immigrants now pay $500 or more to a coyote who smuggles them across the border. Charge labor migrants $300 for a visa, and pool that money in accounts designed to keep the immigrants at home. Also add U.S. Social Security deductions to that pool and then "establish a binational agency for economic development that would make matching grants to Mexican [and I would add Caribbean] communities for the construction or improvement of local infrastructure." The money could also be used for the development of self-sustaining economies, which, in the long run, is the only sure way to stop labor migration at its source.[21]

Another suggestion is to help migrants find ways to pool the remittances they send home to wives, husbands, and other relatives. Get these funds into developmental banks and you create another way to help our neighbors as we help ourselves.

A final suggestion echoes one made by Senator Paul Douglas in the 1950s. Take agents off border patrol, send them to the urban and rural work sites where undocumented migrants are employed, and "vigorously enforce the tax, labor, environmental and occupational health and safety laws of the United States."[22]

These suggestions offer a way to seriously undermine, over time, the push/pull/network dynamic that has fueled undocumented migration for more than eighty years. What is lacking is the political will and the grassroots organizations that, perceiving a golden opportunity to join forces across ethnic and class lines, convince Americans to work together. Indeed, using Massey's suggestions, those groups could lessen the need for Mexicans or Dominicans to migrate as they simultaneously increased the likelihood of higher wages and better working conditions in the United States.

CREATIVE CROSSROADS OF THE WORLD

St. Lucia is a small Caribbean island, roughly 12 by 20 miles in length and width. Its total population slightly exceeds 100,000, and it lacks many of the educational and economic advantages that generally facilitate cultural creativity. Yet St. Lucia somehow produces world-class artists, among them

Nobel Prize–winning poet Derek Walcott. Nearby Trinidad nurtured novelist V. S. Naipaul, while Jamaica gave the world artists as different as the singer Bob Marley and the classically inspired dancer/author Rex Nettleford.

One explanation for so much creativity is the coincidental conjunction of so many cultures. The Caribbean is the Crossroads of the Americas because African, European, Asian, Indian, and native sources produce inhabitants who perpetually need to switch cultural codes, moving from British to American to Jamaican culture in the course of an afternoon.

People see things differently because the mix of cultures makes it harder for Caribbean citizens to accept the one set of generalizations that normally make societies possible, predictable, and at times boring. Especially in the arts, fresh and ingenious insights are an inherent, institutionalized part of Caribbean life.[23]

European colonialism produced the Caribbean's creative conjunction of cultures. In the United States our latest injection of fresh cultural sources initially occurred because presidents Kennedy and Johnson genuinely sought to bring our national ideals into line with reality. Neither president meant to invite the world, but the result in the year 2000 is this: The United States of America could easily be the creative Crossroads of the World. Through a self-help union of wills we have the potential to take advantage of a spectacular conjunction of world cultures and deliberately produce unprecedented examples of artistic, educational, business, scientific, and cultural creativity.

It is a new-millennium ambition, an America in which our inherited banquet of cultures produces the creativity required for self-sustaining prosperity and the elimination of the cultural barriers that now deeply divide 270 million people, all Americans.

NOTES

1. Arthur Cotterell, *A Dictionary of World Mythology* (New York: Oxford University Press, 1986).

2. Peter Berger and Thomas Luckmann, *The Social Construction of Reality* (New York: Doubleday, 1966).

3. Philip Gourevitch, *We Wish to Inform You That Tomorrow We Will Be Killed with Our Families* (New York: Farrar, Strauss and Giroux, 1998), chapter 4, especially pp. 47–58; see, too, Sven Lindqvist, *Exterminate All the Brutes (New York: New Press, 1996).*

4. Ibid., Gourevitch, p. 58.

5. James Sterngold, "Racial Divide Widens on Network TV," *New York Times*, December 29, 1998, pp. 1, A12.

6. For an overview, see Milton Gordon, *Assimilation in American Life* (New York: Oxford University Press, 1964).

7. T. Alexander Aleinkoff, "A Multicultural Nationalism," *American Prospect*, no. 36 (January/February 1998): 80–86.

8. David Hollinger, *Postethnic America* (New York: Basic Books, 1995), p. 162.

9. Ibid.

10. Amy Gutman, ed., *Multiculturalism* (Princeton, NJ: Princeton University Press, 1994), p. 78. This comment is from Susan Wolf.

11. Aleinkoff, "Multicultural Nationalism."

12. Ibid., p. 84.

13. Randolph Bourne, "Trans-National America," in *War and the Intellectuals*, edited by Carl Resek (New York: Harper, 1964), p. 115.

14. Nathan Glazer, *We Are All Multiculturalists Now* (Cambridge: Harvard University Press, 1997), p. 16.

15. Vietnamese Amerasian Resettlement: Education, Employment and Family Outcomes, *General Accounting Office* (Letter report 03/31/94, GAO?Pemd-94–15), Washington, DC, 1994.

16. Philip K. Howard, *The Death of Common Sense* (New York: Random House, 1994).

17. For example, Charles Lawrence III and Mari Matsuda, *We Won't Go Back: Making the Case for Affirmative Action* (Boston: Houghton Mifflin, 1997); Dana Takagi, *The Retreat from Race* (New Brunswick, NJ: Rutgers, 1992); Farai Chideya, *Don't Believe the Hype* (New York: Penguin, 1995), p. 83, for the Notre Dame statistic.

18. Lawrence and Matsuda, *We Won't Go Back*, p. 104.

19. David Firestone, "Agriculture Department to Settle Lawsuit by Black Farmers," *New York Times*, January 5, 1999, pp. A1 and A14.

20. Douglas Massey, "March of Folly: U.S. Immigration Policy after NAFTA," *American Prospect*, no. 37 (March-April 1998): 22–33.

21. Ibid., pp. 31–33.

22. Ibid., p. 32.

23. For example, Rex Nettleford, *Inward Stretch, Outward Reach* (London: Macmillan, 1993).

Bibliography

Alba, Richard. *Ethnic Identity*. New Haven: Yale University Press, 1990.

Ancheta, Angelo N. *Race, Rights and the Asian American Experience*. New Brunswick: Rutgers University Press, 1998.

Bass, Thomas. *Vietnamerica*. New York: Soho, 1996.

Bourne, Randolph. "Trans-National America." In *War and the Intellectuals*, edited by Carl Resek. New York: Harper and Row, 1964.

Brimelow, Peter. *Alien Nation*. New York: Random House, 1995.

Calavita, Kitty. *Inside the State*. New York: Routledge, 1992.

Castles, Stephen, and Mark Miller. *The Age of Migration*. New York: Guilford Press, 1993.

Chan, Sucheng. *Asian Americans*. New York: Twayne, 1991.

Cose, Ellis. *The Rage of a Privileged Class*. New York: Harper, 1993.

Daniels, Roger. *Asian America*. Seattle: University of Washington Press, 1998.

Davis, F. James. *Who Is Black?* University Park: Pennsylvania State University Press, 1993.

Diamond, Jared. *Guns, Germs and Steel*. New York: W.W. Norton, 1998.

Dyer, Joel. *Harvest of Rage*. New York: Westview, 1997.

Dyer, Richard. *White*. London: Routledge, 1997.

Friedman, Thomas. *The Lexus and the Olive Tree*. New York: Farrar, Strauss and Giroux, 1999.

Fukuyama, Francis. *Trust*. New York: Free Press, 1995.

Funderberg, Lise. *Black, White, Other*. New York: Morrow, 1994.

Glazer, Nathan. *We Are All Multiculturalists Now*. Cambridge: Harvard University Press, 1998.

Gould, Stephen Jay. *The Mismeasure of Man*. New York: Norton, 1996.

Gourevitch, Philip. *We Wish to Inform You That Tomorrow We Will Be Killed with Our Families*. New York: Farrar, Straus and Giroux, 1998.

Greider, William. *One World, Ready Or Not*. New York: Simon and Schuster, 1997.

Higham, John. *Strangers in the Land*. New York: Atheneum, 1971.

Hollinger, David. *Postethnic America*. New York: Basic Books, 1995.

Kallen, Horace. *Cultural Pluralism and the American Idea*. Philadelphia: University of Pennsylvania Press, 1956.

Lawrence, Charles R., and Mari Matsuda. *We Won't Go Back*. Boston: Houghton Mifflin, 1997.

Lerner, Michael, and Cornel West. *Jews and Blacks*. New York: Plume, 1996.

Lindovist, Sven. *Exterminate All the Beasts*. New York: New Press, 1996.

Massey, Douglas S., and Nancy Denton. *American Apartheid*. Cambridge: Harvard University Press, 1993.

Nettleford, Rex. *Inward Stretch, Outward Reach*. London: Macmillan, 1993.

Ohmae, Kenichi. *The End of the Nation State*. New York: Free Press, 1995.

Pieterse, Jan. *White on Black*. New Haven: Yale University Press, 1992.

Portes, Alejandro, and Ruben G. Rumbaut. *Immigrant America*. Berkeley: University of California Press, 1996.

Segev, Tom. *1949: The First Israelis*. London: Collier Macmillan, 1995.

Shorris, Earl. *Latinos*. New York: Avon, 1992.

Soros, George. *The Crisis of Global Capitalism*. New York: Public Affairs, 1998.

Sowell, Thomas. *Migrations and Cultures*. New York: Basic Books, 1996.

Spencer, Ian R. G. *British Immigration Policy Since 1939*. London: Routledge, 1997.

Steinberg, Stephen. *The Ethnic Myth*. Boston: Beacon Press, 1998.

Suro, Roberto. *Strangers Among Us*. New York: Knopf, 1998.

Taylor, Charles. *Multiculturalism*. Princeton: Princeton University Press, 1994.

Tharoor, Shashi. *India: From Midnight to the Millennium*. New York: Harper, 1997.

Tummula, Krishna K. *Public Administration in India*. Singapore: Times Academic Press, 1994.

Ungar, Sanford J. *Fresh Blood*. Urbana: University of Illinois Press, 1998.

Waters, Mary. *Ethnic Options*. Berkeley: University of California Press, 1990.

Williams, Gregory Howard. *Life on the Color Line*. New York: Dutton, 1995.

Wilson, William Julius. *When Work Disappears*. New York: Vintage, 1996.

Index

Note: "i" indicates an illustration.

About the Author

RONALD FERNANDEZ is Professor of Sociology at Central Connecticut State University. A widely recognized authority on Caribbean and Hispanic-American issues, his most recent publications include *Puerto Rico Past and Present: An Encyclopedia* with Serafín Mendez Mendez and Gail Cueto (Greenwood Press, 1998) and *The Disenchanted Island: Puerto Rico and the United States in the Twentieth Century* (Praeger, 1996).

DATE DUE

OCT 0 0 2000		
OCT 3 0 2000		
	JUN 1 6 2002	
	NOV 0 9 2004	
AUG 1 6 2001		
MAR 1 3 2001		
MAR 2 8 2003		
		Printed in USA

HIGHSMITH #45230